THE
BLACK
COSMETICS
KINGS

Tony Wade MBE

First Published in 2016 by Hansib Publications Limited
P. O. Box 226, Hertford, SG14 3WY
United Kingdom

info@ hansibpublications.com
www.hansibpublications.com

Copyright © Tony Wade, 2016

ISBN 978-1-910553-67-1 (Paperback)
ISBN 978-1-910553-73-2 (Hardback)

A CIP catalogue record for this book
is available from the British Library

Produced by Hansib Publications

Printed in Great Britain

ACKNOWLEDGEMENTS

My colleagues, Len Dyke and Dudley Dryden, were men of immense vision lending their names to a partnership which in June 1968 became a limited liability with my acquisition of one third of the equity in the business. They were equally magnanimous by their suggestion to me that we rename the company, Dyke, Dryden & Wade, which I declined as completely unnecessary.

As a team, our skills were complementary. We shared a common philosophy, that of putting first the needs of building the business above everything else. Without their vision, hard work and drive, there might not have been this story to tell.

In conclusion, this book would not have been completed without the kind advice and tolerant support of the late Margaret Bishop, to whom I remain indebted for dealing with piles of endless proofreading. Thanks to Maxine McDonnahough, my editor and also to Mrs. Patricia Allen, who came on board at very short notice to complete the typing of my manuscript. Not forgetting my robust young heroes, Lorenzo Henry and Neville Scarlete, who attended the technical matters of graphic design, layout and photography, while Miguel Wilson, my computer wizard, was always on hand to ensure desktop maintenance issues were properly addressed.

Lincoln 'Len' Dyke, born December 18 1926; died July 5 2006
Dudley Dryden, born June 9 1926; died February 2 2002

CONTENTS

ABOUT THE AUTHOR

In the pre-independence decade in the 1950s when West Indians migrated to the United Kingdom to seek jobs, one enterprise, Dyke & Dryden, loomed large on the landscape, creating jobs for the Caribbean Diaspora in the music and hair care industries.

The Cosmetics Kings is a republication of *The Dyke & Dryden Story: How They Made a Million* (Hansib Publications) written by Tony Wade, who joined the company in 1968, guided its success and authored the original book published in 2001.

This success story (a factual account of the purpose-driven pioneers) reveals just how steadfastness and determination to succeed can be a guiding star for a new generation of Caribbean peoples in the Diaspora.

Tony Wade and his partners pioneered the development of the British Black hair care industry in Britain creating thousands jobs. His vision and business savvy influenced the spirit of enterprise in the Diaspora community. This story demonstrates an unswerving belief in self-worth and the community of a people, as they managed the challenges of time. This story clarifies how the dynamism of self-help and self-reliance can remove barriers to progress.

Tony Wade influenced change in many organisations, at the local and national levels, through his commitment to enterprise and community life in Britain. Various roles held are as follows:

In education as one of the governors of the college of North East London; director of Enfield and Haringey Health Authority; founding Director of the North London Training and Enterprise Council: the North London Business Development Agency and as chairman of the Stonebridge Housing Action Trust, where he spearheaded the regeneration of the Stonebridge Estate for its five thousand residents. These are but a few areas of his involvement that speak volumes of his commitment to enterprise and community development.

Earl Jarrett, CD, Hon. LL.D, JP, General Manager Jamaica National Building Society

PREFACE

Reflecting on my gift as someone blessed with the spirit of enterprise, I note that during some of my writing and speaking engagements there has been a call for sharing the success factors that have given rise to my enterprise and leadership qualities which has been evidently obvious.

This perception I ponder could well be pure flattery. In most cases, however, I often try to judge the sincerity on the part of some questioners. The numbers of these persons at times were of such that I have been forced to conclude that so many people cannot be wrong.

A case in point is a letter that really bowled me over. It came from Herb Holman of Holman Financials Services, 351 California Street, San Francisco, C94104. He wrote:

"Thanks so much for sharing this really insightful book, *How They Made a Million*. I was transfixed by it. The period in which I was building my first distribution business parallels the era of growth for Dyke & Dryden. I find it amazing how minority business owners have so many common experiences. Nearly all the things Tony Wade described in his book happened to me too. It was an eye opening experience (the first time around) and to this day, it shapes the way I approach all business ventures."

June 2015 marked 50 years since the founding of our company. This represents a *milestone* in the life and times of Dyke & Dryden Ltd. My colleague and I chose to live in a country where we learned very early that to succeed, we must work hard, be street wise and at the same time, always remembering that the world does not owe us a living. Any personal achievements that we have made are attributable to hard work, many sacrifices and determination. A copy of the thanksgiving service to celebrate the company's success is to be found on the back pages of this book.

Tony Wade MBE

FOREWORD

The Black Cosmetics Kings is a title coined by the press in marking the company's 25th anniversary. This event was held and celebrated on 26th May 1990 in the Oak Ballroom at the Inn on the Park, Hamilton Place, London W1.

The press, in bold print, headlined what was considered an appropriately fitting tribute for the event. There could not be a more appropriate title in that *The Cosmetics Kings* encapsulates the entire story by the many leadership roles the partners played in pioneering black business development in Britain.

The story to begin with, started out merely being armed with an idea (with huge challenges) in an attempt to stake out a toe-hold in sourcing supplies of desperately needed hair and skin-care preparations to meet and satisfy the hunger for a products-starved black community ignored by the hair and skin care industry.

The ultimate answer was to invoke the spirit of pioneers and set about doing something about it. First steps were to research what was needed and set into action the process of producing the product lines needed, branding and producing them for ourselves.

The choice of title was later endorsed by the hair care and beauty industry with a banquet held in the company's honour at City Hall London, on 19 January 2007 titled, "A Tribute to the Pioneers of the Black Hair & Beauty Industry". This book is yet another rare opportunity for the author to show, with sage-like pragmatism, his business leadership and accomplishments.

Wade straddled the industrial enterprise stage as chairman and chief executive like a Colossus from 1968 through to the end of the 20th century. This is an iconic story that could only be articulated by Montserratian-born Tony Wade MBE.

Despite racial prejudice and other forms of institutional discrimination, Wade and his business colleagues—Jamaicans Len Dyke and Dudley Dryden—paved the way for others to access economic opportunities in the beauty care industry and other business sectors. Accordingly, community leaders claimed that the rise of the company impacted the lives of thousands of people across multicultural Britain, thus creating what is often referred to as the "cradle of black enterprise" in Britain.

As with previous works, his current book crystallises the pioneering journey that the company made in dominating the Black hair and skin-care industry for the better part of 40 years and remains a name that lives on in print, radio, television interviews, motivational speaking engagements and in film. Undoubtedly, the three Caribbean-born entrepreneurs left an indelible mark in the history of black enterprise in Europe and Britain especially.

Recognition of the company's services to the community came in many ways and one in particular stands out. A national search was advertised for "The Black Enterprise in Business Awards"— sponsored by the Department of Trade and Industry and the Colourful Radio Network—for a black individual or company who can subscribe to and meet the specific criteria set for the title of the award in 2005.

As it happened, Dyke & Dryden Ltd walked away with the award, for the company was regarded as a powerful example of a working partnership founded on the seeds of trust and respect, complemented by an appreciation of each other's immense indomitable will and talent—not forgetting the broader early vision of sustainability that each toiled relentlessly to accomplish, especially during the formative years of the company's operations in North London.

As a celebrated entrepreneur, industrialist and grown-in-stature author, Tony Wade has commandeered a new and unique terrain in business profiling by blending experiential knowledge, with honed professionalism in crafting an expository narrative on an important segment of Black British economic history that is rarely told even by modern, politically-correct equality and diversity specialists.

Whether a firm is micro, small, medium or large, its contribution is a vital component of economic development. In the main, businesses contribute lastingly to local regeneration and related urban renewal policy and Wade's book only serves to confirm this fact.

Rather than limit his work to the worn cliché of race and discrimination (that tend to proliferate in the literature of people of colour for centuries in Britain), Wade chooses instead to weave a storyline of enterprise, founded on the principles of creativity, opportunity, courage, dedication and an unerring determination that leads to progress. He demonstrates that even in difficult times, human potential and raw talent can fill the vacuum of wealth-creation and self-fulfilment. For those who may perceive disadvantage as a stumbling block to their individual rite of passage, this book is clearly a counter-weight to that aberration or constant irritation.

In effect, as the author of *The Black Cosmetics Kings*, Wade has redefined the concept of economic inclusion and social bargaining in the realm of mainstream economic thinking. At its best, this title encapsulates an essential read for those who are keen on starting any type of commercial activity or social enterprise. Of course, it can be validated as more than a welcome addition to the few books on ethnic commerce in the Western world. Such enriching prose on a delicate but important subject of our time is compelling, to even the uninspired among us.

Interestingly, while this book's dominant theme is premised on the hair and beauty care industry, the author has endeavoured, rather successfully, to assess the dynamics of this popular but highly competitive industry. It was useful to observe how he skilfully analysed the effects of this sector on Britain's artistic creativity and entrepreneurial spirit involving hundreds of firms and millions of consumers, respectively. In so doing, Wade makes a very unique and unapologetic case of genuine economic liberation universally, for people of colour at home in Britain and across the Diaspora.

Dr Christopher A. Johnson
Award-winning author and business management consultant

THE BLACK COSMETICS KINGS

In their footsteps

A tribute to the pioneers and innovators of the Black beauty industry

This inspirational story of the journey of the farsighted trio Len Dyke, Dudley Dryden and Tony Wade, who carved out a niche in the multi-million pound British hair care industry, not only kindled the spirit of enterprise within Britain's new Black business community, but has added value to nation building, by making the Black presence felt within society and have changed the business face of Britain forever for the generations that follow.

The story proves, without doubt, that people, who have chosen to make Britain their new home, can create their own opportunities, level the playing field in all areas of our common human aspirations and together work for a more inclusive society. This goal is of paramount importance and in my view, must remain our ultimate aim if we are to achieve a truly caring and harmonious society. Let us work together and let no one tell you otherwise.

BLACK HAIR AND BEAUTY CULTURE

The creative genius that drives black women's hair fashion, in most cases, is always a wonder to behold! These are styles which sport a distinctive personal taste and quiet dignity, which always acknowledges and proclaim an evident truth. A creative stylist always steal "Hair Show Parades" and along came the Cosmetics Kings as facilitators for the widest possible range of beauty products of choice to satisfy, add colour and accentuate the designs.

The good news of the arrival of the Cosmetics Kings was like music to the ears of our women folk who joyously sang the praises of their pioneering brothers, in a melody that rang out across the towns, villages, hills and dales of the land.

The creative genius of hairdressers is a subject that attracts the attention of men and women alike. A fabulous hair style stirs emotions of envy in other women, causing them to give long gasping sighs if only they, too, could sit in the chair of the hairdresser who created a particular look and hair style that is endearing, turns heads and sets tongues wagging. Without doubt, a glowing healthy head of hair is always a woman's crowning glory.

Having conducted business with a good number of both male and female hairdressers, I have had the privilege and pleasure of discovering some traits common to patrons and stylists alike.

Among the unique attributes of a first-rate professional stylist, is his/her creative genius in producing that intrinsic something that satisfies the vanity of the patron by producing a wholesome fulfilment in a particular style and look, that fits a mood or charms the dreams of her admirer! I am reliably assured that the bond of trust between hairdresser and patron is of such that the most reserved and secretive patron, once in her favourite hairdresser's chair, will often pour out the innermost thoughts and secrets of the heart.

COMPANY ACHIEVEMENTS

"Entrepreneurs extraordinaire" is the accolade associated with the pioneering efforts of the company which, against huge odds, succeeded in building an industry which today employs thousands of people and generates revenues in the region of millions of pounds annually.

Revival of the 'enterprise culture' during the difficult years of the early eighties was an extremely challenging time for businesses. There were major hurdles along the way that had to be overcome in a difficult and often hostile climate. Challenges however were not allowed to thwart the aspirations of the pioneers—they soldiered on in meeting a need and achieved the goal of carving out a business slot for the black community in Britain.

Creativity and perseverance proved to be the keys for unlocking institutional doors to the community. Persistence and a dogged determination to find solutions to every hurdle was the catalyst that drove the business and despite the difficulties of the period, the company succeeded in establishing a solid base and without doubt, it was its indomitable will and endurance of its founders that drove the business forward.

Tony Wade at 10 Downing Street with Prime Minister, Mrs. Margaret Thatcher

In February 1984, a reception held at 10 Downing Street by Prime Minister Mrs Margaret Thatcher to celebrate enterprise in Britain, included Dyke and Dryden Ltd as one of the 37 firms invited to be part of the celebration. This was a giant achievement for the company. It represented another first for the business.

'The pursuit of the pioneers' dream to participate in the economic life of the nation remains the legacy left by the company's directors,' noted Cindy Soso of BIS Publications, a leading British publishing house which focuses on the publication of African and Caribbean books.

INTRODUCTION

It was never my intention to write a second edition of this story. This came about as a result of the prompting by many fans and friends who wanted to learn more about my thoughts on enterprise in the 21st century.

Before responding to the call for my thoughts, perhaps I might recall my views on community entrepreneurship in my twenties. I made no secret of my commitment to the struggle for equal opportunity rights and the need as a community to become actively engaged in everything that was happening around us. This long held belief was a personal passion and I became actively involved with issues that called for improving the lot of our people in a number of ways. The perfect route, I determined, was through membership of pressure groups that worked for equal opportunities central to my thinking. To that end, I was relentless in pursuing any activity that would lead to a more equitable society.

Involvement in community social affairs provided a platform to spread the merits of disciplined hard work. It also created the awareness of self-worth and the principle that discipline in all things must underscore community pride. My belief in this core value prompted me to seize the opportunity to enlarge on my thoughts at a number of community gatherings at which I had been invited to speak.

Discipline in all things, I contended, remains the basis for success in whatever the task and, as such, a much needed area of focus for community development. As a rule, I always remind my audiences of this core belief: dedicated discipline has always been and will remain a simple success formula which, if routinely applied to any task, will always ensure success for any individual or group.

These speeches, I dare say, were received with rousing applause and standing ovations at most of the venues at which I spoke. These conversations were, for me, confidence building moments and served as my leadership initiation within the community. By the audience responses, it was clear there was complete agreement with the views I expressed. The responses overwhelmed me! Shouts of, "Ride on brother; ride on!" echoed across the room at times. The audience loved it! And the community, I guessed, would remain the judge about the leadership role they had imposed on me.

As I reconnect with those first momentous speeches of some five decades ago and recall the community leadership role they conferred on me, I count my blessings and remain anchored in the faith placed in me—which, with all modesty, have led to inspiring others. It is without doubt and indeed a great honour to be asked, a second time around, to speak to others through this second edition of my book.

As it happens, enterprise is a subject close to my heart and anything I can contribute to inculcate our grasp of the subject drawn from my years of personal business experience, there is certainly no need for prodding. I have to say, however, that I am greatly encouraged by the new thrust and interest I find these days within the community on the subject of enterprise. The first lesson I believe we must all decide on is where we want to be in society and to follow through in activating that vision. Secondly, is the importance of our approach and thirdly, by setting standards as the benchmark by which we will arrive at attaining the goals we set.

There were a number of young adults of the '60s, and '70s generations who I met while they were pursuing their education at schools, colleges, and universities at which I was invited to speak and share my experiences. I recall the special warmth in the welcome I received at all the establishments I attended. These conversations became a source of mutual understanding, as if to say "we have been waiting to see and hear from you." At the same time, steps were taken to ensure that my books and the knowledge I had to share were circulated in their respective organizations.

The company had been around for a while and the celebration of its 25th birthday was an appropriate milestone in Black business history in Britain to share. The event brought together community members and well-wishers from all walks of life and disciplines. These guests were people who had helped to foster the spirit of enterprise and supported the growth and progress of the company in many ways: first, in retail trading, secondly as wholesale distributors, thirdly, as manufacturers, fourthly, as exporters and lastly as exhibition service providers.

There were also a range of services, called for by our many customers. Our guests to the event came from all segments of society and many parts of the world, from Africa, Asia, the Caribbean, the British Isles, Europe and the USA.

It was the right moment in time, for the company to say a big thank you to a huge number of people, who in their respective ways, made a solid contribution to the company's progress. The journalists, who attended the event, had a field day by their collective themes on the business and their interviews with many guests. And between them, coined the title for this edition, *The Cosmetics Kings*.

The story, it has been argued, is unique in 20th century Britain. The founding of the company in 1965 impacted the lives of thousands of people across the Black communities in laying the cornerstone of what is often referred to as the birth of black enterprise in Britain. The firm and its achievements became a landmark in black British social history during a time when there was as it were a famine among black ladies for their personal essentials for hair and skincare products. This was a powerful argument and I felt compelled to do something about it. As it turned out, it became a three-way hook up, a need waiting to be filled, a vision and mission which together, created a momentum which became unstoppable.

Among the many questions that might readily be asked, "What gave rise to the emergence of *The Cosmetics Kings*? While the obvious answers to some of the questions are to be found in the previous paragraphs, the unique journalistic gifts and skills in creating images, linking the past and labeling them to events at the time, has to be admired and acknowledged, especially in that they are factual.

During the twentieth century, mass migration from the colonies to fill labour shortages in Britain was at an all-time high both during and after World War 2. At the same time, new residents soon discovered there were many things to which they had been accustomed to in their former homeland were not anywhere to be found in their new place of abode. These included such things as native foods, beauty care products and the tools to take care of their hair and skin.

This situation left the ladies screaming for help as established businesses did not cater for the needs of the many new members in their midst. The answer to deal with these shortages was for the new arrivals themselves to do something about it as seen by the example taken by my company.

This reality opened up opportunities for people to do some things for themselves and here was the beginning of traders coming on stream to fill some of the many gaps that existed in the marketplace. The black music industry was the first to blossom in what was a dull and dreary environment. Music from back home to cheer up the long summer evenings was number one on the list. Dancing partners packed dance halls wherever they could be found and as might be guessed, these were truly exciting times, especially for the young at heart.

The beauty industry was next to explode with hairdressing salons and hairdressing schools popping up in many places to cater for what was an insatiable demand which existed and were waiting to be filled. This is where I came into the picture and somehow became a player in the industry.

The majority of Caribbean people who migrated to the UK and other developed parts of the world did so to improve their life chances—and many have successfully achieved their objectives. Looking back however, many of us have led unproductive lives by not putting in place personal plans as far as careers were concerned.

Yet, the first generation, we need not be too hard on ourselves, remembering that most of us started out from dismally poor backgrounds and settling into a new and in some ways was a frightening environment which took time to settle in. In most cases, it took an average of between ten to fifteen years to arrive at some semblance of adjustment in feeling settled.

Nevertheless, many of us, despite our hardships and sacrifices, can stand tall and take pride in seeing our offspring benefit from those years of struggle. Hopefully, they will show due respect and appreciation and build on the start their parents provided for them.

At this point, I would like to express grateful thanks to the thousands of people for their keen interest shown in the original story. This edition embraces a broader picture and calls for one thing above everything else—doing our level best in this highly competitive global market place. We must do our level best to compete, to win and survive.

I am especially thankful to BIS Publications and Cindy Soso, who were passionate in organizing a number of high profile public speaking engagements that attracted a new generation of aspiring individuals determined to make their presence in Britain felt. The energy these gatherings generated, left me in no doubt that this new generation have set their sights on changing the business face of our society and are set to create a more fair and equitable society through the disciplines of hard work and perseverance to succeed. In truth, there is really no other way.

I am mindful in recalling that it was just over a decade ago, in 2001, that the initial story was released. It is interesting to note that, since that time, there has been a huge settling in process taking place commensurate with black advancement in Britain. It is pleasing to note as I travel around the country, that the story still resonates within the community and continues to inspire.

Revisiting the past and making comparisons with where we are today, it is easy to find that we are clearly a more harmonious society with better opportunities. Indeed, with the passing of time, it is evident that a new generation of scholars, are better educated, are now changing the status quo in all areas of national pursuits (based purely on merit) and doing some of the things their parents could at best, only have dreamt about.

Of major historical importance in this first decade of the twenty-first century, there has been the concern by the Qualifications and Curriculum Authority (QCA) which determined that the time had come for the inclusion of 'black history' as a subject, by the official body who has pronounced explicitly on the need in British educational history, for the formal recognition of the black presence in Britain.

The QCA, the public body sponsored by the Department of Education and Skills, and governed by a board appointed by the Secretary of State for Education and Skills has moved to bridge the glaring gap of disadvantage in society.

Quite clearly, the lesson has been learnt that too little attention was given to black and multi-ethnic aspects of British history. The teaching of black history is often confined to topics around slavery and post-war migration and Black History Month, rather than looking at the subject matter in depth as a whole. The effect, if inadvertent, is to have undervalued the overall contributions of Black and minority ethnic people to Britain's past and to ignore their cultural, scientific and many other achievements.

With the endorsement of the Education Secretary of State now in place, let us all say welcome to *The Oxford Companion to Black British History* edited by David Dabydeen, John Gilmore, Cecily Jones and others who have made this possible. My copy, from which I quote, is a gift from my son, acknowledging his presence and place in the country of his birth.

The *Black Cosmetics Kings* expands on the story of the Dyke & Dryden entrepreneurial talents, presented in an earlier publication entitled *How They made a Million,* and the inspiration this work provided for many among the black community—to forge ahead in establishing their own economic enterprises and moving their families ahead in communities in the British business landscape.

In recognition of the dearth of information which exists and credited to many successful black people in Britain today, this second edition is an opportunity to contribute to the broadening of the knowledge based on the many outstanding people who stand out as beacons for ensuring and building on the future generations of ambitious young black Britons. The section on 'Raising the Stakes in Black Britain' highlights successful members of our community who have made their mark in the areas of business, commerce, politics, community development, academia, literature, music, theatre and other aspects of Arts and are making their presence felt.

The *Black Cosmetics Kings* also placed focus on the role of community leadership which more often than not, comes with distinction. Each of the members of the company's management team assumed leadership roles in the community at different times. I am thankful to have been called upon to lead several initiatives including the North London Business Development Agency (NLBDA) and others in becoming the kind of society we can all be proud of.

Finally, I decided to include a selection of speeches that I had the privilege to present at various forums, all of which were well received and which resulted in many requests for similar appearances. I am particularly pleased to explain that through this medium, some of my experiences were all learning opportunities which I am now able to share with others and hopefully reach a much wider audience.

"What one has not experienced, one will never understand in print."—Isadora Duncan

PART ONE

RAISING THE STAKES IN BLACK BRITAIN

CHAPTER 1

THE PIONEERS AND THEIR DREAMS

Conferment of the title 'The Cosmetics Kings' on the pioneers of the black hair care and beauty industry speaks to decades of service and thousands of man hours in meeting the beauty needs of Black women by the company and its subsidiary, Afro Hair & Beauty Ltd. This track record of service to the community is remarkable by whatever measure of judgment one might care to apply.

It is interesting to note that the Dyke & Dryden beauty care industry experience almost never happened. In fact, that the company emerged at all was quite remarkable. The question of trust where money comes into the picture in sections of the black community has been and still remains in some areas, culturally taboo. This outmoded way of thinking is self-destructive and gets in the way of creating a truly enterprising culture.

This story hopefully has served as a wakeup call for many people regarding the importance of investing in the future. This was especially true for all of the folks who had agreed to give their support of cash to Len Dyke in his early attempt of getting into business in 1965.

His story of creating a record distribution business which would import popular pre-release records from Jamaica to supply the demand for music from back home to supply some of the many sound system dance promoters who catered for the earliest forms of entertainment in a 60s London was welcomed. Len Dyke shared his idea with several friends and some agreed to support him by providing a cash investment for his project.

However, on the day the call came for money on the table, none of these so-called friends were anywhere to be seen. This let down explains how profound the mistrust was. As it happened, Len Dyke's suggestion turned out to be a great idea and was the catalyst for black enterprise in various disciplines. It was clearly an error of judgment on the part of those who did not keep their word, which they openly regretted. Fortunately, Dudley Dryden, an old acquaintance, heard of Len Dyke's predicament and came to the rescue. Trust is a necessary first step in preparing the ground for ideas that can become the trigger for releasing seeds of thought processes that will germinate and blossom, if nurtured and pursued with determination. Good ideas evaluated and pursued, taking into account some element of reasonable risk, is something all entrepreneurs must take which will with time, grow into profitable enterprises.

It is this simple philosophical approach that occupies the entrepreneurial mind, an intrinsic mechanism that resides within each of us, and fires our individual innate gifts. These gifts, depending on application, will always, in some measure, realize your dream. Ask any successful entrepreneur and they will tell you that being action-oriented is necessary to realizing your dream.

Building a business of any size usually takes at least two to three decades and in most cases, will come to fruition through the thrust and energy of pioneers. That my colleagues and I were named as belonging to this select band of persons was a pleasant surprise.

And to what do we owe this accolade I asked? The answer was usually brief and to the point, either you not arrive or you influence change and made a difference. I offer a sincere thank you to all those who paid us this compliment, but will tell everyone that ours was a mindset in part, characterized by sincerity of purpose and an indomitable will to succeed which propelled our pioneering organization along.

Men of lesser courage and vision would have caved in under the sheer weight and pressure of the early problems we had to endure as we worked hard to carve out a toehold on the ladder of business success in Britain. This success was a matter of spotting a gap in the market at the time and we moved steadfastly to take advantage of it. Looking back, it was clearly beyond any doubt, and greatly to the company's credit that we identified a need and set about meeting it against huge odds. The black hair, and skin-care industry, today, provides thousands of jobs and a measure of independence for several of its stakeholders.

In those early years, help was not forthcoming from anywhere. It was a hard grind getting assistance from financial institutions especially banks; and credit facilities were not available from established traders. It was tough going and that we understood only too well, from the word go, that the world did not owe us a living, which meant that any achievement would be down to our own efforts—this is an important lesson, whatever your field of undertaking, be it in the classroom, at sport, or whatever we do, we have to become enterprising with a competitive edge—and at the end of the day, it will be our passion to win and succeed in our personal goals. It's the energy, drive and determination that will see you through in realizing your dreams.

Looking back, it is truly gratifying to see the growing trend of making wealth creation a focal part of community development. This trend fills me with a deep sense of satisfaction. I am particularly encouraged to see the Diversity Agenda starting to kick in positively throughout Britain, adding value locally and nationally.

Sources for essential reading in these changing times are books of encouragement and inspiration which provide outstanding examples of black success in Britain.

These include: *You Can Get It If You Really Want: Start your business, transform your life* by Levi Roots, *Portraits of Black Achievement* by Jacqui MacDonald and *How I Made It*, by Rachel Bridge. Rachel's book makes for essential reading, and in truth the work is a classic and a must read for anyone thinking of going into business.

National and International Recognition

Recognition of the Dyke & Dryden's pioneering efforts has been conferred by many well-wishers from many parts of the world. These came as totally pleasant surprises. One of the most treasured came in the form of a letter addressed to my colleagues and me from a Mr. Buzz Johnson, director of the Karia Press. His letter hinted at what was to be expected. It was an invitation to "An evening in tribute to the pioneers" on Friday 30 June 2000, from 7.00-10.45 pm. It explained further, that the background to the event is that we feel that our community should have the opportunity to honour our pioneers, personalities and activists during their lifetime to provide inspiration for other generations".

As it happened, both Len and Dudley were unwell and unable to attend. This left me to face what can truly be described as being spectacularly awesome. There were, for me, moments of embarrassment as faces popped up at every turn calling me by name, faces to which I could not put names, some of whom would interject with what turned out to become a familiar phrase, during the evening—"don't you remember?" Well, I could not remember which sent one unmistakable message to me—memory loss had arrived, or was knocking on my door!

In any event, the choice of venue, the Marcus Garvey Library Hall in Tottenham intrigued me and whether it was chosen by design was not for me to question. Suffice it to say, they could not have chosen a more appropriate place for, as it happened, Marcus Garvey had always been an inspirational hero for my colleagues and me. Another good reason, too, was that the company started life in Tottenham. This was the base from which we built our national and international linkages and reputation.

Host Juliet Alexander, who came from a media background, had done her homework well in setting the scene for some great entertainment as artiste after artiste poured out their souls in verse, song, music and storytelling. This was all punctuated by lots of jokes by the well-respected Mr. Ralph Straker from the Toastmasters Club. Every act was acknowledged with thunderous applause .The committee had obviously invested much time and effort in planning something wonderfully special, leaving me lost for words in saying thank you to the community for the tribute they bestowed on us. In closing, I declared that we accepted this mark of respect with great humility and for my part, this event would live forever in my memory. I reminded them of the words of the Right Honourable Marcus Mosiah Garvey, "Now we have started to speak and I am only the forerunner of an awakened black race that shall never go back to sleep."

Some years later, the black hair and skin care industry from across the Atlantic, in conjunction with Salon Strategies of London, had a similar idea to mark the achievements made by the pioneers of the industry here in the UK. Salon owners, manufacturers, distributors and senior executives from leading international hair care firms gathered at City Hall in London for a huge celebration party on 19 January 2007 titled, "A Tribute to the Pioneers: (the cover copy of the event flyer is shown on page 252). Also seen on the flyer is Madam C.J. Walker at the wheel of her Model T Ford 1912).

There was no letting on to me of the scale and scope of what was about to take place. My task was simply to turn up. And, in making sure that I did, a limousine, together with hotel reservation, was all taken care of on my behalf.

Guests were stunned by the similarities between the story of Madam C.J. Walker, the legendary innovator and entrepreneur and the struggles endured by the founders of the first black multi-million pound British company. The keynote speaker for the event was the adorable A'Lelia Bundles—a veteran television producer, journalist and author—the great-great-granddaughter of the late Madam C.J. Walker. What an honour!

As she spoke, silence like a blanket covered the room and it became clear to everyone that Madam C.J. Walker's success was due to her determination to create a better life for the black women of her generation through the benefits of her health and beauty products and the independent income it created for the hundreds of female agents who sold them. That conviction allowed her to thrive despite the tremendous odds that faced her in building the first successful black owned multi-million dollar business in America.

On Her Own Ground, the best, selling biography of A'Lelia Bundles, tells the nail-biting story of how her great-great grandmother built a huge beauty empire, amassed unprecedented wealth and devoted her life to philanthropy and social activism.

Event organizer Anne-Long Murray of Salon Strategies in her tribute to Dyke, Dryden and Wade, spoke warmly and echoed the feelings of many present:

"Have you ever stopped to notice the inscription on the side of a British two pound coin? It reads, 'Standing on the shoulders of giants' which could be the sub-title for the event. I'm so glad we decided to honour these heroes, to highlight the incredible contribution they made to entrepreneurship in the black community and the legacy they have built for thousands of people who are now employed in this industry. The racism they faced is almost unbelievable, compared to the issues black businesses face today. It's still not easy, but we are still much further ahead because of their sacrifices."

Lee Jasper, the special advisor to London mayor, Mr. Ken Livingston, explained why the event was so significant:

"We are all delighted to be hosting this event and supporting Salon Strategies on this important occasion, as we all continue to make a positive impact on London's economy and our own communities."

The attendees and sponsors came from all parts of society and, in particular, all areas of the beauty industry, especially from the US where the company has had a long and profitable trading relationship with its suppliers. It was good to see industry giants of the likes of Mr. Ned Washington of Avlon Industries, and Fred Luster and his wife founders of Luster's Products. Event sponsors Mr. Larry Mallory of Proline Corporation and Mr. Brendon McParland of Noble Silk. They all spoke warmly about their respective contributions to the industry and acknowledged the debt the industry owes to the UK pioneers in opening up the industry in Europe and Africa.

In response to the speakers and officers of the industry thus:

"I have to let you know that the event has blown my mind, to the point where I could hardly believe what I was hearing—the whole event left me almost speechless as I tried to comprehend the tremendous efforts made by the organizers and discovering that my colleagues and I were held in such high esteem—your tribute and its theme (In their Footsteps) that links the Madam C.J. Walker's edifice and Dyke & Dryden Ltd has had a profound effect on me. I have been deeply touched and recall how the visionary first lady of our industry has been my personal role model. I can also disclose that one of her products, 'Sweet Georgia Brown' , has been for years my personal hair dressing and conditioner, which also tells a little story about my preference in men's grooming needs—and in fear of running out, I always kept stock of half a dozen tins of the stuff.

This has been a great moment for industry building, for sharing and passing on new skills, developing new talents and networking, which strengthens our respective organizations in facing the future. I have to tell you that I will remain forever in your debt for this most gracious event, elegantly staged, full of surprises, fun and laughter in abundance. I crave your indulgence once more to repeat a million thanks to all the very kind people who have made this event such a memorable occasion."

Black Enterprise in the 21st Century

There have been many calls for my thoughts on enterprise in the 21st century. I am humbly gratified that people should care enough about my views and I will try to rise to the challenge.

To begin with, one thing is a must: The horizons of our educational and business ambitions must, out of sheer necessity, be in tune with the new discoveries in science and the advancing technological changes taking place around us; complemented by plenty of hard work to win the goals we set ourselves. Our eyes must be wide open to the fact that the world has changed and continues to keep on changing in a variety of ways. In this digital age, information overload is set to overwhelm many of us in its onslaught; there are 'chips' on the plate with everything—at breakfast, lunch and at dinner time. The internet has compressed time zones in a way that takes us all anywhere and everywhere all at once.

Secondly, on the business front, we must always remember that ideas are the raw material for business and being entrepreneurial is the vehicle that leads the way in identifying new markets, locally, nationally and internationally. There is nothing more satisfying than observing a business spark and see it become a flame and changing a community's attitude and its outlook on life with endless possibilities for the future.

Being entrepreneurial worked for me and I firmly believe, that as a community, we should aim to be more visibly active and become fully engaged stakeholders in all aspects of local and national community endeavours. We must set our sights on being more economically, politically and socially active, focused on achieving decision making positions in management and especially in areas of influence that provides for leadership in society. In this 21st century, it is absolutely necessary that we aim to achieve some of these key goals. Sharing and engaging in these activities are priceless lessons that I have learned and I strongly recommend that we work hard to be on the leadership train.

Hindsight is always a fantastic teacher! Interestingly, the calls for jotting down my thoughts came from a broadly based group of persons and organizations: universities, inner city researchers; reformers; social scientists; media organizations and a host of others, including budding young entrepreneurs in search of ways to improve their personal and business opportunities.

Providing Inspiration by Sharing my Experience

During a number of my speaking engagements, many of the questions put to me were pretty personal, down to earth and reasonable. Some folks, for instance, wanted to learn a little more about the backgrounds of my colleagues, myself and where we came from. Others questioned why none of the images of trophies bagged by the company over the years were shown in the first edition of the story. Pictures, they claimed, "speak louder than words." It would be our chance to share some of your moments in history. Yet others remarked, "It would have been nice, too, to learn and benefit from your acquired experience contained in your speeches." Such comments were quite understandable and truly touching. "Your courage," they said, "to start up a business in the early sixties, considering the odds that were stacked against the company succeeding in the climate that prevailed at the time, was quite a feat."

I decided to try and answer as many of their questions as I am able to in this edition. Indeed, wanting to share is a most reasonable request, for while an individual or the team takes the trophy and the purse, it is the community and the nation who share in the roll call of honour. Nowhere else is this better expressed than in sport where everyone loves a winner!

Not only is sharing the right thing to do, it is more so, a sacred duty which must be embraced and I dare say, that it is this duty which will help to set the strategic framework for collective efforts and partnerships that will lead to progress for the advancement in our multiracial and multicultural society.

Among the many things I have learned is that active participation in society gives voice, carries weight and authority to influence change. It must be understood that meaningful change requires that each of us must play our full part in the process that delivers opportunities for citizens to explore their full potential and share the responsibility it takes to build a well-rounded society. My personal experience through my involvement in various community activities taught me that striving to build community partnerships through the Diversity Agenda represents the bedrock of a society at peace with itself—we are each other's keeper.

Success breeds success and it is notable that some of the changes now taking place within the ethnic community can be credited to the company's vision and pioneering efforts which are slowly addressing some of the failures and shortcomings of the past. This nation has incurred huge losses on its social capital account, arising mainly from the politics of neglect and indeed attributable in many cases to weak moral courage on the part of some political, civic and business leaders, who were duty bound to face up to many of the racial and social tensions that threatened to tear the nation apart.

In responding to the question from where we came, I will start with Len Dyke as he was the architect of the original business idea, which got the project off the ground. He was partnered by Dudley Dryden in 1965 after being let down by friends who promised to support him, but failed to show up when a cash call was asked for. Len and Dudley traded as Dyke & Dryden for approximately two years after which the partnership was dissolved. A new company Dyke Dryden Ltd was founded in its place and at the same time, June 1968, Anthony Wade became the third partner.

Together, we shared a common cause in the struggle against the rabid racism the black community was experiencing. Len, Dudley and I were members of various organizations that together tried to find peaceful solutions to counter some of the prevailing problems that existed at the time, particularly in the field of race relations.

Len, as he was popularly known to his friends, was born in Kingston, Jamaica, but grew up in the village of Prospect in Clarendon, where he spent his earliest years. He attended the local school where his father was headmaster. He was a brilliant pupil, destined to make something of his life. As a boy, he was fascinated with electricity and it was clear to his parents that he would gravitate to becoming an electrician. This he did and became a certified craftsman. His ambition led him to become an independent contractor, supplying electrical services on demand. He became a visionary and understood only too well that the quality of his work would be the passport to a steady supply of contracts; and as such, his business prospered. He became a well-known and respected member of his local community and accordingly, enjoyed the trust of those around him.

Migrating to London was fashionable at the time and with the encouragement of many of his friends, Len decided to join them. In so doing, he gave up a comfortable home in the sunshine of Jamaica and together with his wife, stepped out into the kind of discomfort for which they were ill-prepared.

His niece, who was studying in London, visited them to see how they were settling in. She was astonished to see where her once prosperous uncle had ended up. It appalled her to find that he was sharing digs. What made her even more stressed, was that he had to obtain the landlord's permission for her to stay overnight with them.

Yes, there was "no room in the inn" in a fifties London for an eager and energetic workforce who came to the UK to fill the nation's acute labour shortage. The circumstances in which the sons and daughters of empire found themselves were ripe for re-education and change. This was a situation that concerned Len deeply, and he immersed himself in the struggle of drumming up some common sense into the bigots who made the lives of his people miserable.

He found work with British Rail in his field as an electrician, in his professional capacity, but soon got caught up in a strike dispute which ended with a walk out by militant members of the union. Not being a union member he stayed at his post and soon became the victim of violence to the point of being set upon with explosives that luckily missed him. This was a rude awakening for him about not falling in line with union radicals.

This incident, however, did not put him down. On the contrary, it mentally strengthened his resolve to prepare for business and a robust community leadership. On the business front, Len was a man with a mission and a vision to become a stakeholder in his adopted country. He acted on his vision and translated his ideas into action by organizing some of his friends to join with him in the business idea he had which got nowhere at first. A good friend however heard of his predicament and came to the rescue.

Len's ideas found fulfillment in many ways and I will just list a few of the organizations which were to benefit from his resourcefulness. Among these was the West Indian Standing Conference, where he served as chairman for several years. The Conference was the umbrella body which represented most of the Caribbean groups in the UK.

In the wider society, he was equally active and served as a mental health manager for the boroughs of Brent, Haringey and Enfield. He also served in the prison service on the advisory panel for prison parole and the Review Body, that dealt with matters connected with

THE PIONEERS AND THEIR DREAMS

immigration. These community commitments were in addition to his many business undertakings.

Dudley George Dryden, who hailed from Port Maria, famous for its fine furniture, helped to earn the town its brand name, "The Furniture capital of Jamaica". There was every reason that Dudley himself would become a star performer of the Port Maria "craft of excellence". He was the other founding partner of the company, that carried his name and a man filled with a deep sense of compassion and it will be easy to see why later on.

Dudley, on learning of the sad predicament that Len Dyke was experiencing (as a result of the failure of his friends to keep the solemn undertaking they had given to assist in funding his project), without hesitation, telephoned Len and advised him that he was willing to join him in his project, but as a sleeping partner only. Such was his sincerity of purpose and his keen sense of the importance of enterprise.

With Dudley's cash injection, the project was eventually floated as Dyke & Dryden and traded in supplying "pre-release" records without labels which carried a premium by the many mobile disc jockeys and sound systems of the early sixties.

Dudley Dryden's support for Len was the beginning of a new career and a major turning point that was to change his life of service to the community. He eventually resigned from his work as a master cabinetmaker and carpenter and moved into the business to support Len in managing the operation.

This new environment was to open fresh opportunities in the voluntary sector in areas for which his talents were ideally suited. His specialist skills were quickly recognized as someone with the gift to resolve disputes, between black youth and the police. He soon became a trusted friend of civic authorities and the community at large.

He became a tireless campaigner in the fight for social justice, spending countless hours, day and night, making a positive contribution to harmonizing race relations and was eventually appointed chairman of Hackney Race Relations Council.

His public trust credentials were of such that he commanded the respect of his local police authority and was recruited to be on hand as specialist liaison advisor on matters between black youth and the police where sensitivity was called for. It was quite amazing to everyone at a disturbance that the mere presence of Dudley Dryden could bring instant calm to an explosive situation.

He was practical, methodical and down to earth in his approach to the daily grind of life and very much at ease in whatever the world threw at him. He lived by a simple philosophy: "Do unto others as you would have them do to you." He was blessed with many gifts which included a keen sense of perception, flexibility and the ability to tackle intractable problems and came up with solutions. He was referred to as a walking dictionary of proverbs with one always ready to timely interject as appropriate in a conversation -leaving everyone present in spells of laughter.

Among his personal collection of trophies is the honour of the MBE bestowed on him by Her Majesty the Queen for his services to the community. There are numerous accolades which he received for his business acumen—all speak for themselves.

I would like to readily concede that it is always quite difficult for me to talk about myself. In conversations about the company, a question that always comes up is "How did you guys get together?" What I guess gave rise to this question is that unlike my colleagues, I hailed from Montserrat, one of the smaller islands and small islands always have been the butt of a running joke by some members of the larger islands.

I recall one of the earliest small island jokes told by a Montserratian school inspector on a visit to schools in Jamaica. The boys at a local school he was visiting wanted to know if the boys in Montserrat played cricket. "Yes, of course," replied the inspector, "but why do you ask?" Laughing their heads off, the boys replied, "Sir, we thought every time they hit the ball it would end up in the sea!" The inspector himself couldn't stop laughing at that bit of humour.

In answer to the question of from where I came, Montserrat my island home that I hail from is known as the other 'Emerald Isle', a name shared with the Irish settlers who were dispatched by Oliver Cromwell to the island in 1632. Its 391/2 square miles are regarded as an oasis of peace and tranquility, set apart in a turbulent world and described as follows:

"An island so lush and green, that it looks like a beautiful emerald lying in the crystal blue of the Caribbean Sea. High mountains rise from the centre of the island and taupe sand beaches fringe the Leeward shores. The foothills are dotted with luxurious villas, surrounded by exotic tropical gardens, where fragrant blooms and fruit-laden trees overload your senses."

I migrated from Montserrat to England in June 1954 to further my education and to find employment while pursuing a course study. My first job was to load and unload dishes off the conveyor belt at Lyons Corner House restaurant, Hyde Park Corner at London's West End. This indeed was as a means to an end. Next, I followed a course of studies at the Tottenham Technical College of London and years later, became a member of the governing body of the college.

After leaving college, I worked for the Smart Weston group of companies—a chain of some 200 menswear stores across the UK. My brief was to reconcile the daily gross takings for these stores and have the net balances on the desk of my boss by midday the following day. My boss, the Finance Director, a Mr. Louis Segal, impressed on me the importance of this task and especially the need for accuracy. He pointed out to me that as far as he was concerned, the cash balances on his company's books were the most important tool in managing the whole organization.

The wisdom embodied in that statement remained fixed in my mind. I was later to appreciate fully the intricate implication of the cash book balances as a key tool in the science of financial management. Entrusted with what, after all, was a major responsibility, I gave the task my best shot and recall my great sense of satisfaction when the postings of cash were reconciled to the penny, meeting to boot the demanding deadline. I struck a resoundingly good chord in boss's good books.

Meeting deadlines and targets greatly impressed my employers who were quick to recognize some potential in me and accordingly, promoted me with an improved salary package and greater responsibility within the organization. The additional role that landed on my desk was the implementation and monitoring of the debtors listing incorporating a credit control function. This area of work required secretarial support with authority to delegate. It was, in essence, a most useful training exercise with hands-on experience in communication skills which became indispensable in the events that were to unfold later in my career.

Under Louis Segal's tutoring, it soon became clear to me that I was destined to go into business on my own account. He was my inspiration. One of the great lessons I learned while working at the company was that nothing equals the priceless opportunity of learning on the job. I was fired up to change direction from following a course of study in public administration which led to a business career.

The experience gained at Smart Weston was invaluable as I made my first foray into the world of business on my own account. While still working for the group, I launched Carib Services, a trading company and market tested a business formula I labeled as the "CS Purchasing Formula" which I advertised as " improves" the bottom line for businesses.

This wonder formula was my new brain child and as it happened, had just come out its incubator and held out great promise with its first order which came in from Bermuda for the supply of stationery. The order was sourced, delivered and the proceeds paid into my bank account. I was so delighted that I immediately went off and shared my success with my friends Len Dyke and Dudley Dryden who were already in business.

They welcomed my news, wished me well and offered their congratulations. At the end of our conversation they disclosed to me that business was quite difficult and wondered whether I would be willing to join them in their enterprise as an equal partner .This disclosure threw me completely. We ended our conversation on a note of asking them to give two weeks to consider their proposal and to get back to them with an answer.

My head was now in a bit of a spin and my mind began to work overtime as I tried to comprehend and try to think through the permutations of reasonable risk, the evaluations of trust in partnerships and all that entailed. I was fully aware that I had choices and questioned myself about how much I valued my independence. At the end of this debate with myself, I concluded that I would go into the meeting with Len and Dudley with an open mind and make a decision on the basis of what came out of our discussions.

The meeting carried from where we left off: "Business was quite difficult." "How difficult was quite difficult," I asked. Arrangements were being made to get the figures out as soon as possible they explained. It emerged from our conversation that overstocking led to slow moving stock items which created the problem of poor cash flow, which was at the root cause of their difficulty.

"What could I bring to the table to reduce the losses and return the business to good health?" I enquired. The first need they assured me was for a cash injection; the second was for the business to benefit from my management experience gained at Smart Weston and thirdly becoming a willing and equal partner, helping to build the business.

I was completely floored by the obvious sincerity of these exchanges, but had one counter proposal to put to them. My answer to joining them both was yes, provided that they were willing to change direction from selling records to selling cosmetics. I then explained the rationale behind my thinking: records I believe is a good field to be engaged in, but I do not understand the business, nor did they on the basis of my observations from the outside. What I understand, and hopefully my suggestion, will prove me correct.

I proceeded to explain that there was a huge market out there for beauty products and no one was catering for it and that this could be our "light bulb" moment to get out there and give it our best shot. There was a unanimous agreement to press on with my suggestion of "out of records and into cosmetics" which I believed could change the fortunes of the business. The meeting ended on a positive note and with a decision taken, I gave up my Carib Service project.

A business career was always my first love. The idea was in my head all along, as I spotted the gap in the market. The need to meet the hair and skin care needs for the black community was steering everyone in the face. Luckily for me, I noted the opportunity and did something about it. The rest from there on is all history.

Inspiring the Community

The individual disciplines which enabled us to agree to work together as a team right from the start and resolve any personal differences that could arise may well be a fair way of learning more about us as individuals.

There have been many major spin offs for the community from the company's experience, in that it signaled that change was possible if you try and work hard that you can succeed. In fact, our formula started to replicate itself with members of our staff, who followed our example and launched out into businesses of their own. We are gratified that we were able to help others gain experience and create opportunities which started to broaden the community employment base.

Opportunities for me to put something back was particularly refreshing by way of using and sharing some of the many skills I've learned and exercised during my fulltime day job has been truly satisfying. These skills included directional leadership, hands-on administrative management and communication skills that led to getting the best out of the team around me. In this context, demand for my services was high and can be gleaned from Chapter 14: 'Dyke and Dryden and the Community'. These roles were great learning experiences and we were rewarded with the great privilege of serving the community.

Recognition of my services to the community has come in many ways, but one in particular stands out and came as a most pleasant surprise. A national search for The Black Enterprise Awards sponsored by the Colourful Radio Network and the Department for Trade and Industry for a black individual or company who can meet the specific criteria for the title of 'A Lifetime Achievement in Business Award 2005'.

Without my knowledge a loyal fan, Margaret Alexander, thought I measured up to the listed requirements and entered my name and advised me after doing so. It was a challenge I could hardly reject and duly turned up at the London Guildhall on the appointed date and time. The elimination process had narrowed the candidates down to three, which included my name. This was a moment of high tension among three nominees on the podium when the adjudicators called out my name as the winner and then proceeded to present me with a huge trophy with the letter "E" with the words BLACK ENTERPRISE AWARDS 2005 inscribed on it! I have to say that this was one of my career moments that meant something to me and one which I thoroughly enjoyed—and shared with my family and special life time friend—Margaret Alexander my sponsor.

I was completely blown away by Margaret Alexander, my sponsor on the night, and felt so touched that I was obliged that she should tell her side of the story on the night:

"Whilst listening one day to Smooth Radio FM, I heard that, in collaboration with the Colourful Network and others, they were sponsoring the first Black Achievement Awards. Nominations were invited. After hearing the various categories, I took down the details and submitted them online as requested in not more than 100 words. In 2004, quite by chance, I borrowed a copy of Tony Wade's book, titled, *How They Made a Million* and found it compelling reading and finished it within a few days. I was sold on the contents. I was overjoyed and delighted that the judges have all supported my nomination."

CHAPTER 2

RAISING THE STAKES

Encouraging Black Enterprise / Business

In the first place, I would like to acknowledge just how profound I found the vision of Jacqui MacDonald in chronicling *Portraits of Black Achievement: Composing Successful Careers*. This is a piece of work worthy of the highest praise and serves as the template for our 20th and 21st heroes to follow.

Her abridged biographies below, represents historical facts which puts to shame those members of society who are guilty of the denial of equal opportunity rights to members of a disadvantaged community which sets us up to fail in attaining our desired aspirations.

These bios are as it were, positive battalions of change, signalling a new determined direction in taking forward our place in all aspects of our national endeavours.

Among the big black issue is the subject of raising the stakes and the need of cultivating an enterprise culture especially as it relates to black economic development within the UK which is overwhelmingly critical. This draw back calls for urgent action in creating our own opportunities is of the greatest importance.

The realization of this need is clearly evident by the current wave of black start-ups in business. The importance of redoubling our personal energies at becoming self-employed and to be of independent means wherever possible is of paramount importance. Getting a handle on the provision of self-employment and become an engine for propelling our own prosperity is the surest way of safe guarding our place in society.

It is a way forward which I do believe holds the answers to many of our economic short comings- provided we are willing to work hard and engage in some element of reasonable risk and plenty of determination to win. As someone who has been down this road before, I advocate that creating our own solutions is the answer.

The acid test for the community is to apply ourselves at being the best we can be in whatever we do and let excellence shine through. It will eventually be the hallmark of a service or trade which cannot be taken lightly or overlooked. To be the best in whatever one does can often be the passport for success in whatever we do.

The Dyke and Dryden success story, while an inspirational one, was by no means an isolated case. There are many iconic examples of black excellence across a wide range of disciplines and the short list of biographies makes the point. The next chapter will also serve to share some of the outstanding achievements of members of our community who have been pillars of progress and an inspiration for other members of the community to follow.

The black community has been making its solid contribution across British society and in some areas we actually lead the way, especially in sport. Names that come to mind include Linford Christie, Frank Bruno, the man with a winning laugh like thunder, Lennox Lewis, Tessa Sanderson, Denise Lewis, Rio Ferdinand, Ian Wright and Mo Farah are all world champions, winning for Britain. Let us exercise our civil rights and responsibilities in equal measure, an approach where we cannot be accused of being drones or passive onlookers tuned in on the doom and gloom chorus.

The central community objective must be positive and patently clear. What is the winning formula? The answers come down to three basic facts: we must work hard and aim to play a meaningful role in the life of the nation and be an indivisible part of its infrastructure. We must aim, diligently, to convey without doubt our deep sense of purpose and our unshakable will to succeed. The key issue for black community development must be determined by the community itself. It must take on board the matter of tackling and bringing about manageable change in a similar way as other communities have done. Good models that work well are those run by the Jewish, Greek and Cypriot communities. The success formula these communities employ is to be found in the kinds and quality of the networks they have built among themselves.

Several publications attest to these facts and I will quote extracts from two which will illustrate the point I have been making for over two decades. Jacqui MacDonald in her work *Portraits of Black*

Achievement: Composing Successful Careers has illustrated a broad picture of what has been taking place and signposted a process which is set to continue and will hopefully shape the vision of the kind of British society of the future. Listed below is a broad sample of mixed academic attainment, skills and services which are making for the necessary changes and the quality of life we value within the society.

The following extracts from *Portraits of Black Achievement: Composing Successful Careers* present the perspectives of several successful individuals and represent the thinking that will ensure the kind of community development we must all aim for.

The Right Honourable Lord Bill Morris of Handsworth, O.J. General Secretary, Transport & General Workers' Union *is a former General Secretary, Transport and General Workers' Union.*

There is, of course, a long way to go. Black people are under-represented in positions of power and influence in Britain. Only 1.4% of MPs are from non-white ethnic minorities. Until the voices of all ethnic communities are heard in the Houses of Parliament, the decisions which are made there will continue to reflect only the experience of the majority community in Britain.

Discrimination in Britain is alive and kicking. Young black people are more likely to be excluded from school, more likely to be harassed by the police and less likely to earn as much as their white counterparts. In Britain, opportunity knocks less often if you are young and black and that is why many of us continue to campaign in order to make sure that it knocks more often. However, the most important thing is to ensure that when it does knock, our young people are ready to open the door and seize it with both hands.

When black people achieve positions of influence in British society, they have the ability to develop practices and structures which value ethnic diversity. What is more, they promote equality and ensure that the opportunities for black people are increased through positive example.

By the contribution of black achievers, both those in this book and the many thousands of others, we have demonstrated that we are not a community of economic migrants but a community of positive contributors to British Society. We have, all of us, given much more than we have taken from the country we call our home.

Keith Kerr *is general manager of Customer Services Development at British Airways, managing 20,000 staff and a budget of £2.4 billion. He is also involved in many voluntary activities.*

There's pressure that I bring on myself to achieve and to deliver to expectation. Then there's a secondary pressure from recognizing that I'm in a fairly unique position corporately, being black and so I'm carrying the cross or the banner for all minority groups. I'm breaking down a lot of barriers. There's a feeling that if I fail, I'll set the cause back ten or fifteen years. Being the only black person in this position brings tension because your friends think that you've changed. But the thing is that jobs like this bring a better quality of life. The fact that your children can go to a quality school, or go to the pony club or ballet classes is part of the rewards the job brings.

When I spoke recently to the African Caribbean Finance Forum I deliberately wanted to be provocative and talked about changing colours. This was a play on words because British Airways was changing its colours at the time. I introduced the concept that we need to change our colour on occasions as well. We just can't be "in your face" all the time and expect to achieve. Some black people became very critical and accused me of becoming white. But if you have that kind of attitude, you'll never succeed at the upper level because white people can always marginalize you.

Being the only black person in this position makes you incredibly strong and resourceful. You don't need anyone else's acknowledgement that you're okay because you know you've fought and you've got this far without anyone else.

Ziggi Alexander *is an Independent Management Consultant.*

I have always been interested in public sector work. After university, I thought I should be a teacher. There are too many black children failing in our schools, then and now. It is a national disgrace. However, when I did my teaching practice placements I thought, this isn't what teaching is about, it's about containment. So I became a community relations officer, with responsibility for education. At the time, I was the youngest CRO in the country. That job gave me a great deal of satisfaction and a really good grounding in community development.

After a spell working in Japan teaching English as a foreign language, I returned to the UK and entered local government as a community librarian. It was at this point that I realized my ambition to publish work on black British history. I co-edited the modern version of Mary Seacole's autobiography and co-researched the Roots in Britain exhibition comprising over 250 photographs exploring the history of black and Asian settlers in the UK from Elizabeth 1 to Elizabeth 11. During that period, I went to the USA for 3 months on a Winston Churchill Travelling Fellowship to look at African-American community education projects. From senior jobs in libraries, I moved sideways into strategic Personnel roles. Before I left London for a senior management post in the West Midlands, I was an Assistant Controller of Personnel in an inner city local authority.

Mervin Archer *is a business manager for NatWest Bank at Hendon Business Centre. His role is to manage a portfolio of diverse businesses with a turnover range of £100,000 to £1M and more, providing lending and advice services.*

My role in this job is to review business plans and match the needs of businesses to the branch's services. I've been doing this job for a number of years and with NatWest all my working life.

I fell into banking really. After A Levels, I applied for several jobs and banking seemed the best. I didn't have a particular affinity or love for it to begin with, but it's subsequently become a career. I passed my banking exams pretty quickly after joining the bank and obtained a law degree at London University in my own time. Since then I've had the opportunity to work in different areas of NatWest Group and to broaden my knowledge of the bank generally.

When I started, there were very few black people in the bank and many who joined at that time didn't stay on. The set-up then wasn't particularly supportive and there were barriers to progress. But I wanted to have options to different career paths. Focusing my energies in a certain direction wasn't part of any dramatic change: not a road to Damascus conversion or whatever. It was just the process of aiming at a particular goal and going for it.

The older and more experienced I've become, the more important I think that is because I've seen it work; from areas like physical attitude to moving an organization forward. The first step is always to have your aim, your goal, clearly defined in your mind. We all have tremendous potential that we never developed. But this process of goal setting and achievement is open to every single person.

Abiola Awojobi *is currently producer of Everywoman, a programme on the BBC World Service.*

Everywoman is an international women's magazine programme and the sister programme to *Woman's Hour* on Radio 4, which is where I worked previously. As a producer, you're responsible for putting the programme together and deciding what items are going to be on. There are just two of us on the team, but we try to get a balance, with a good spread of women's voices from around the world. The job involves researching, setting up interviews, finding the right guests, writing a script. I feel content with my career so far because I've progressed from local radio to network radio and now to international radio. *Woman's Hour* was very demanding to work on because of its high profile. There were about 25 of us at the table bouncing ideas around, inspiring each other. With only two it's inevitably more limiting, but at the same time it's more of a challenge and I've had the opportunity to act up as a senior producer on several occasions.

Over the years, in my capacity as a BBC Radio producer, I've often been told that I'm seen as something of an ambassador for the black community. People sometimes think that if they've got something to promote like an event or a book, I can automatically help out and get them on the radio—because I'm a black woman in the BBC. But of course, I can't always—one still has to use one's editorial judgment as to what makes a good story. But if I can't take a project on personally, I at least refer them to someone else who might be interested—that way I don't feel I've let anyone down.

I try not to let myself down, by being the best that I can—whether it's in my personal or my professional life. To me, success is setting goals for yourself and trying to achieve them. It's a mantra which my parents instilled in me and something which they in turn, as Nigerians, had brought with them from Nigeria. I do feel Nigerian first and foremost, but I also feel British. When I married, I deliberately kept my maiden name for professional use because I wanted people to know I'm Nigerian.

Andrea Levy *is a writer of five published novels, Every Light in the House Burnin, Never Far from Nowhere, Fruit of Lemon, Long Song and Small Island.*

What I try to do is work for the graphic design business in the morning and write in the afternoons. I do the administration so it's all invoicing, estimating and keeping books; all that sort of stuff rather than actually getting involved in designing which takes too much of our brain. This leaves me space and time to write in the afternoon, rumour has it.

I like having two different things to do. It's more stimulating. With books, there is always pressure in that you have to keep up a standard. I want to grow within so I'm always looking to better myself. Then there is pressure because people expect things of you. Sometimes I feel I've had such good luck and it's all going to evaporate. I have a certain sense that I've got to keep, like those plate spinners in the air at once.

Jessica Huntley *is a publisher and cultural activist. She founded and manages Bogle-L'Ouverture Publications Ltd.*

My mother was a very positive person. She taught me that no one was better than I was. Some person would say, *'Jessica would have been a nice girl if her nose was straight.'*

My mother would reply, *'Her nose fits her face.'* So I grew up feeling very confident about myself.

My first job was at a shipping company. Within two weeks, the manager told me that the bosses from the city didn't want a 'coloured' person in their office. I said ok. The manager was surprised how I took the news and said that he regretted it because I was a good worker.

One of the other jobs I had was at the Ministry of Pensions and National Insurance, Haringey Branch, London. At the interview, the manager told me that the post was temporary. (The Agency had already told me that temporary posts could be for two weeks or to two years). The manager said it was not worth my accepting it. I said I would still take the job. When I reached home, the manager who interviewed me was waiting at my door to see me. He said the job was only for a week and it did not make sense for me to accept. I said if it were only for two days then I still would. He stood at the door trying to convince me that it was not worth taking up the post; I spent five years there and became an active member of the union.

I got started as a publisher in 1968 after Dr Walter Rodney, a lecturer at the University of the West Indies, Mona Campus, Jamaica, attended a conference in Canada and was banned from returning by the Jamaican government. The people of Jamaica rioted, resulting in loss of life and damage to property. A group of friends in London decided to highlight what had happened to him. We held demonstrations and picketed the Jamaican Tourist Board in London. Walter was later offered a post at the University of Dar-Es-Salaam in Tanzania.

Lenny Henry *is an actor and comedian who works in theatre, television and film and sings with his own band. He is also involved in production and was awarded an Honorary BA by Warwick University in the early 1990s.*

I've never felt that I've done enough: I've always wanted to be the best I could be. I have a band and we'll practice half a dozen times just to get it right. I continue to strive to be the best I can. It's about having dreams and holding onto them, having faith in your abilities, having people around you who will encourage you and support you.

It's important to achieve your fullest potential and not settle for second best. Set out to get what you want from life. See the goal and go for it.

Kids need mentors: people who can give them support, someone they can look up to. When I was at school, the teachers didn't know what to do with me. I enjoyed some subjects, but generally school was not the place that I wanted to be. I suppose allowing me to do my own thing at that point was their way of 'containing' me!

It's not easy for black people to get on TV and to do what I'm doing, but it's getting better. It's a slow process, but it's happening. We won't have fully achieved until there are more black and Asian people in the position of directors, deciding the programmes we have on TV and radio. When we no longer see the usual faces on TV, then we'll know that we are moving on. It's important to me that my work appeals to a wide, multi-racial audience.

Denise Everett *is a senior embryologist at the Lister Hospital in charge of the day to day running of a very busy in vitro fertilization unit in the middle of London. She is the first black woman to hold such a position in the UK.*

My job consists of collecting, culturing and growing human eggs, sperm and embryos. These are used in a patient's treatment cycle. I've been in the field for ten years. My embryology career started at the London Bridge Hospital where I was for three years and now I am at the Lister.

After leaving school, I worked as a lab technician for an NHS biochemistry laboratory and then went into research for a drug company because I thought I'd like it but I didn't! I stuck at it for a year, though, so I could put it on my CV and in the meantime saw a job in *New Scientist* for a junior embryologist. I didn't know what it was and had to look it up. Then I phoned them, went for an interview and got the job. I've been doing it ever since.

I went to an all girls' school in Hackney. It was a traumatic time for me and before O levels, I missed nearly three months after having my tonsils out. I still got seven O level and then went to college to do A levels. I didn't learn anything in the classroom at college, but I learned everything socially! So I had to retake them the following year.

I knew I wanted to work in a hospital, but that I didn't want to be a nurse. I also didn't want to go back to university, so I took the job as lab technician, going to college one day a week to do the BTEC National Diploma. Then, foolishly, I waited until I was at the Lister before I decided to do a degree. I studied part time whilst doing a full time job. It was hard!

Janet Campbell *is director of human resources at SCO Limited.*

I don't have a degree, I left school at 16 with O levels and I found a summer job. I was supposed to go back to do A levels, but I'd had enough of education. So, I jumped at the offer of a full time job. It was in the merchandising office of the Scotch House store in Knightsbridge.

We had to check when things came in: do the paper work and make sure the right goods had been received with the right reference numbers. Then a friend who worked in an oil company told me they had a job opening in the legal department. I got an interview, but they felt I would be more suited to employee relations, so that's how I got into personnel. Where I am now isn't where I'd planned to be. I was going to be a nurse, but I spent two weeks of my summer on a geriatric ward and realized that nursing wasn't for me.

Had I done my A levels and gone to university, I think I would have ended up in law, but in personnel work, I do feel I have found my niche. I've done a lot of training on the job and I also have a diploma in Management Studies.

Yvonne Brewster OBE *is the Artistic Director of Talawa Theatre Company, responsible for the overall artistic decisions, planning and direction of the company.*

Talawa is 15 years old now. It began in those glorious days of the GLC (Greater London Council). I wanted to do something that I'd not seen in this country before; a large black production, properly funded, with top actors and doing something artistically important, but also sociologically and historically important, for the black community.

My job as Artistic Director is to look down the line, not to navel search. I've been quite careful in developing an artistic policy for the company. Some of the offshoots that have developed are the Women Writers Project, the summer school and our School's workshop. They're a vital part of the work that we do and so they're attached to every production. Audience development is extremely important because if you don't engage younger people, you are dead in the water. We're doing something that has come out of the process of living in Britain and we must make sure that it speaks to the younger generation of people who are essentially black British.

I was the first black woman drama student in this country. I arrived on the Queen Mary with a Chaperone. We arrived in Sidcup, she settled me in digs and said, *'Farewell my dear, I hope you have a good time!'* Then off she went. So there I was, in a ghastly little room with a one bar fire.

I've always been a fighter and I've always remembered that I can do it. In England, there was so much prejudice, as in pre-judgment, of what you should be trying to do, but I don't give up very easily. I felt that I was not going to give up, I didn't care what those English people thought because there were other places in the world that would allow me to work, like Russia.

Tony Wade. *Chairman of Dyke and Dryden. He pioneered the development of the ethnic hair care industry in the UK and introduced the Afro comb. Awarded an MBE in recognition of his contribution to Business.*

A business career was always my first love. My own business began when I spotted a gap in the market, to meet the needs of the black community for hair and skin care products. In the early 1960s, there was very little available. We imported cosmetics over from the States and made up a price list. In fact, the business really started in the boot of my car. I was going around to shops that were selling food and saying, *'If people are coming in for food they will also buy these things.'*

That was the beginning of the hair care industry. I was literally doing it all by myself, before I decided more staff was needed to grow the business. I oversaw the company's growth from a £35,000 turnover in 1968 to a figure of £4.7m.

The second publication from which I will select examples of excellence is appropriately titled *The Power List 2010* sums up some highlights, the 100 most influential black Britons. This list is appropriate in that, success breeds success and serves to stimulate the competitive spirit. This is a powerful message for diversity and builds the kind of confidence for an aspiring community working to play its part in nation building, where everyone engaged in this task are all winners. The list has ranked some of these trailblazers in a format which shows what qualifies them to be referred to as influential.

Rt Hon Baroness Scotland QC is ranked number 1. She is the Attorney general, Britain's most influential of African or African Caribbean heritage. She is the chief legal officer of the Crown, representing the Queen and government in court and advising the government on complex legal matters that can have international ramifications. Indeed, her advice could decide whether or not the country went to war.

Of course, this is far from among her first of firsts. Patricia Scotland has spent her life being No 1. She was the first black woman in Britain to take silk, which she did at the age of just 35, making her the country's youngest person to become a Queen's Council since William Pitt the Younger (1759-1805); she is also the first attorney general since 1315 when the post was created; and she was the first black woman to be a government minister.

Tidjane Thiam *chief executive, of Prudential is ranked No 2.* His appointment as the boss of Britain's second largest insurance group makes him the first black chief executive of a FTSE 100 company and is the latest step in his meteoric rise. More than that though, his appointment sends out a message that says it is possible to get to the very top rung of corporate Britain regardless of the colour of your skin. The Ivory Coast-born engineering MBA graduate is Prudential's chief financial officer. He previously held a variety of senior executive posts, including chief officer for Europe as his fellow insurance heavyweight Aviva. Further back he was a partner of McKinsey & Co in France, CEO of Ivory Coast's national Bureau for technical studies & Development. His post identified him as an imaginative financial strategist and future blue-chip chief executive, a point not lost on the world economic forum who subsequently named him one of the 100 global Leaders of Tomorrow.

Dr Mo Ibrahim *is ranked No 3*. Founder and chairman of the Mo Ibraham Foundation, Dr Ibraham is a Sudanese-born British national and a self-made billionaire. As a former BT engineer, he transformed the lives of millions of people in Africa with his telecommunications company Cetel. When he started his company in 1998, there were just 2 million mobile phones on the continent. When he sold seven years later, there were more than 100 million.

Much of that transformation was down to his vision. But it didn't stop there. In his continuing desire to see Africa progress, he set up a foundation in his name and launched the Mo Ibraham prize for achievement in African Leadership which goes to a former head of state who demonstrated excellence while in power. The award of £5m is the largest philanthropic prize ever. The foundation also publishes an annual index to benchmark how well African states are being governed as Dr Ibrahim believes progress is possible only when good governance is in place.

Damon Buffini, *Chairman of Permira is ranked No 4*. [He is] considered the undisputed king among the private barons. He grew up on a council estate in Leicester and heads one of Europe's biggest equity private equity firms. During the past 10 years Permira has grown funds under management from £1bn to £21bn.

Buffini developed Permira's buyout strategy, funding and new business. Although the recession has meant private equity within a very different financing environment, Buffini's stewardship has ensured that most of Permira's Portfolio – including fashion chain New Look is holding up well. Buffini is a member of the Prime Minister's Business

Council for Britain and is president of Fairbridge a nationwide charity that works with marginalised young. He is also founder of Breakthrough, a social investment initiative and is an avid Arsenal fan.

Olisa is ranked No. 5. The extraordinarily well connected Olisa's day job is at the helm of the boutique merchant bank Restoration Partners, where he advises entrepreneurial IT companies on business and capital strategies. But hc is also one of only two people of African or African-Caribbean heritage to serve on the board of a FTSE 100 company, which he does for both Thomson Reuters and Eurasian Natural Resources Corporation, all of which means he is a very influential man.

Known for his quick wit and creativity – not to mention his taste in bow ties – Olisa always found time to give something back and he is most proud of his last ten years as chair of Thames Reach, which has grown from humble beginnings to become a £20m charity dedicated to ending street homelessness in London. Over the years, he has at various times been an early NHS Trust director, an inaugural postal services commissioner and the first black governor of the Peabody Trust. He is married with two daughters.

Trevor Faure is ranked No 6. He is global general counsel and partner of Ernst &Young. Trevor Faure redefines the term high-flyer. He was appointed to his present post in February 2009 and leads a worldwide network of about 300 legal staff and is involved in all aspects of legal management, advice and strategy for global accountancy firm Ernst & Young. Since his last power list placing, Faure became The Lawyer Magazine's Corporate Council of the year 2008. The team he developed won the Legal Business team of the Year Award 2008 and the development process itself won the Lawyer HR 2008.

Faure created and negotiated the 'profitable partnership' fee model with Eversheds which won the *Financial Times* 2008 innovative Lawyer of the year stand out award. In addition, 'SMARTER' legal integration model he created has been adopted by Harvard Law School as part of its 2009 programme. Faure taught one of classes personally. A great mentor to many young people. He is married to fellow Powerlistee, Sharifa Faure.

Claire Ighodaro is ranked No 7. She is an independent director and trustee. She is one of the best connected and most influential women in corporate Britain. As an independent director, she sits on and chairs the audit committees of some of Britain's largest and most prestigious organisations including Lloyd's of London the world's leading insurance broker, the Open University, the UK's largest university for part-time higher education; the Banking Code Standards Board and also UK Trade and Investment.

She is also a non-executive board member of BEER, a trustee of the British Council and chair of the London Region Learning and Skills Council. Her background is equally fascinating. She was the first female chair of the Charted Institute of Management Accountants and former finance director of BT Broadband. Somehow, Ighodarbo also finds time to be actively involved with several charities that support education skills and development.

Vivian Hunt is ranked at No 8. Director McKinsey& Co. Hunt is one of the most senior women in leading strategy consultancies and boasts a 15-year career serving clients and health systems across major markets in the UK, Europe and the USA. She is head of UK pharmaceuticals and medical products practice for the leading management consulting firm McKinsey & Co and leads its commercial pharmaceuticals practice for Europe, which means she advises chief executives and presidents of major pharmaceuticals and medical-device companies on strategic and healthcare delivery issues.

Vivian Hunt has supported the commercial strategy of and developed the operational plans for more than 20 leading ethical and over-the-counter drugs affecting for example, , diabetes, asthma, smoking cessation, thrombosis, hypertension and depression. Hunt has an MBA from Harvard and now sits on its alumni interview board. She is married and has two sons.

The examples of the successes quoted above fill me with a deep sense of pride and I believe they will do the same for all those who read this book. These accomplished dreams are inspirational reminding me of the old adage, '*where there is a will there is a way*'.

It was that self-same innate spirit and creative genius that drove many of our ancestors of generations ago to shape and fashion artefacts which today adorn museums around the globe. Among them is a handmade stone axe found in the Rift valley in Tanzania 2000 years ago. The safe keeping of this amazing historic all-purpose tool is to be found on show in the British museum. It remains the prototype, copied and used the world over ever since its discovery. Scientists believe that the self-same genetic gene is rooted in our veins and remains a part of black heritage.

Solidifying and building on the gains we have made thus far, in the current circumstances are major mile-stones in community building blocks. Black enterprise however, cannot be limited to the present or measured, by our recent history in the British Isles. Out of necessity the extensive history of our ancestors dating back for over thousands of years must be taken into account. African civilisations have existed since the dawn of history and it is also a truism that mankind began on the continent of Africa.

African-Caribbean people achieved much before, during and after subsequent periods of physical enslavement and colonialism. It will be recalled that prior to the invasion of Africa and the consequent enslavement and displacement of many members of African society, our ancestors administered and controlled their countries and resources through a vibrant commercial and trading system.

Raising the stakes, in the widest sense of the word, is a rallying call to all the people across the Diaspora to awake to the vision of redeeming the fatherland and make the twenty-first century the Africa century. Recent research points to pertinent facts that the time is right for investing in the continent's rich mineral resources and its forestry, to mention but two items of natural wealth, that are the envy of many nations.

May 26, 2013, is a landmark day in the African calendar of noted African events. This day celebrates 50 years of the founding of the OAU (Organisation of African Unity). Clearly African Renaissance is great news and music in the ears of every one of us especially of the African race. The performance by Sierra Leone with a whopping growth rate of 35 per cent is dazzling. Further, between 2000 and 2010, six of the world's fastest growing economies were in sub Saharan Africa. This is a part of the world that the *Economist Magazine* dubbed 'the hopeless continent' a decade ago.

The (IMF) International Monetary Fund in its World Economic Outlook noted that sub Saharan Africa has performed strongly and should continue to do so. Output grew by an average of 5.1 per cent in 2012 and is projected to grow by 5.4 per cent in 2013 and improve by 5.7 per cent in 2014. Inflation dropped to 7.9 per cent and continues to trend down.

Poverty has been falling and between 2000 and 2008, secondary school enrolment has increased by more than 50 per cent. Foreign direct investment has moved from less than US $10 billion in 2000 to US $80 billion. Government debt has slid from approximately 80 per cent of GPD a decade ago to approximately 40 per cent currently. Foreign direct investment has risen from less than US $10 billion in 2000 to US $80 billion.

Consumer expenditure is expected to leap from the US $600 billion in 2000 to US $1 trillion by 2020. The World Bank's most recent annual Country Policy and Institutional Assessment says the region's macroeconomic performance is now on par with other developing countries. Some predict that Africa will overtake Asia in economic performance by 2040 or even before. Suddenly, a lot of respectable voices have become bullish over Africa.

In June 2013 the Japanese government expressed their intention to invest billions of dollars in Africa in an effort to catch up with the Chinese.

These intentions all signal that all eyes are now focussed on exploiting the rich mineral wealth of a continent that was not so long ago on its knees unable to attract investment capital.

I, like many others, share the vision that this century will be the African century. It has also been my belief that the black race has learnt the lessons of exploitation and will at all costs protect what is left of its heritage. In concluding this chapter, I feel very confident that all the signals of this century appear very much to be on track.

With President Barack Obama hosting and presiding over the third working session of the USA-Africa Leaders' Summit at the State Department in Washington on Thursday 7th August 2014. This occasion gave him opportunity to address his guests as follows:

'*I stand before you as the president of the United States, a proud American. I also stand before you as the son of a man from Africa.*'
He added, drawing applause:
'*The blood of Africa runs through our family, so for us, the bonds between our countries and our continents are deeply personal.*'

CHAPTER 3

INSIGHTS INTO BLACK LITERATURE AND THE ARTS

The heroic contributions made by many black British citizens have not had the kind of publicity they deserve. It is, therefore, fitting to make every effort to provide opportunities for bringing about some awareness of these talented persons who have subscribed to black enterprise. The contributions are not limited to politics, business, finance and entrepreneurship but also to the Arts. In this chapter, we continue to celebrate outstanding black exploits, focussing on those individuals who have distinguished themselves in this arena.

In writing this chapter on literature—the written word—I am reminded that this book itself is concerned mainly with black enterprise in the United Kingdom and this includes our contribution to the universal intellectual sphere, sometimes referred to as the 'intellectual enterprise'.

Deriving from their colonial history, the Caribbean and the greater part of continental Africa have various dialects. The Spanish, French and Dutch-speaking communities have English as their mother tongue. To give justice, therefore, to such interesting developments will require elaboration which this chapter cannot fulfil.

Writers

Because Caribbean writers have the opportunity to travel, they are less inclined than most to settle in one place permanently so there is no clear distinction between West Indian literature and black British literature. The early generation of writers in the 20th century worked from England where publishers were accessible and where writers interfaced with each other. Yet, they chose to write mainly about the West Indies and in many cases, for the region's population.

When Trinidadian political activist and writer C.L.R. James died in 1989, several impressive obituaries appeared in various publications paying homage to his enormous contribution to history, politics, literature and sports. His unique achievement, however, has seldom been mentioned in literary reviews. That this Caribbean icon excelled in different fields, is indicative of the originality and creativity of West Indian self-expression which has been directed into specialized channels and which is in conformity with the more established societies.

In the flowering of talent in the years on either side of 1960, C.L.R. James, wrote *The Black Jacobins*, which became an instant classic on black history and literature. *Beyond the Boundary*, also by James, is still rated as the best book on cricket ("what do they know of cricket who only cricket know"). It is a unique historical study of cricket, as a social and cultural form, which is in part a sustained attempt to repair this neglect.

Only Jamaica's late Prime Minister Michael Manley's refreshing *History of West Indian Cricket* equalled this classic. Dramatist Errol John, whose father was a famous cricketer and whose brother (they were both called George) played a pivotal role in Caribbean journalism and also made an attempt on literary development in the black community.

C.L.R. James had an itinerant career. He left his homeland in the early 1930s and made his name as a journalist in England covering cricket, before spending a number of years in the USA. As an avowed Pan-Africanist, he worked for some time with the late President of Ghana, Dr Kwame Nkrumah. When James returned to Britain, he was one of few remaining Marxist ideologues associated with American lawyer, singer and civil rights activist, Paul Robeson, in the years leading up to the outbreak of the Second World War. James spent his later years in Railton Road, Brixton, which after the events of 1981 became the 'frontline'. As a great literary genius of the century, James' works have not only attracted fellow West Indians, but also sections of the European intellectual community; several members have analysed his works in the context of modern times.

Other Trinidadians, who have produced Caribbean classics, are V.S. Naipaul who achieved international acclaim for his prize-winning novel, *A House for Mr. Biswas* and Earl Lovelace who won the 1997 prestigious Commonwealth Writers' Prize for his latest novel, Salt. The judges described the book as '*a Caribbean novel of huge vigour and vitality, written with dazzling energy.*'

The Jamaican, Professor John Figueroa, too, combined literature and a love for cricket. He is a distinguished academic. In his book *Through the Caribbean* Alan Ross describes the Professor as, '... *that Johnsonian, extravagantly-bearded figure, John Figueroa, poet, professor, educationist.*' The Professor has taught and lectured in Jamaica, the USA, West Africa and Britain. He is a popular commentator wherever the West Indies cricket team plays. Recently, he settled at Milton Keynes close to the Open University.

Writers George Lamming of Barbados and Andrew Salkey of Jamaica had established their careers in the United Kingdom before moving to the USA where the tradition of black writing and the theatre offered a wider scope. Their departure has not diminished the influence both men still have in the artistic talents in the black community in Britain.

Guyanese, Wilson Harris, is a prolific writer. His first novel, *Palace of the Peacock* was published more than 40 years ago (it won him the Guyanese Prize for Literature in 1987). Since then, he has published over a dozen novels and two books of literary criticism. Harris has held many positions in academia, including Associate Fellow at the Centre for Caribbean Studies, University of Warwick. Edgar Mittelholzer who left the then British Guiana to England in the first half of the 20th century is an outstanding literary artist. Before committing suicide several decades ago, he had published a series of illuminating publications—*Swarthy Boy* and *Corentyne Thunder*—which evoke pain, frustration and delight. They celebrated his authentic and ingenious form, derived from his own Amerindian-African Creole ancestry.

By the mid-1970s another Trinidadian writer, Samuel Selvon, emerged having written ten novels including *A Brighter Sun* and *The Lonely Londoners*. BBC television screened *Home Sweet India* as part of the Commonwealth Season, while BBC radio had broadcast 12 of his plays, among them being—*Highway in the Sun, The Harvest in Wilderness, Milk in the Coffee*—set in England, and *Zeppi's Machine*. Radio has been generally a more effective medium for communicating the Caribbean experience in Britain, as well as the memories of the older generation in their formative years 'back home'.

Novelist Joan Riley is perhaps at the forefront of a new and more self-confident generation of women writers. Grenadian Jean Buffong's emerging literary talent should not be underestimated either. Noteworthy, is the increasing number of loosely knit black writers' groups and workshops across England, most of which are led by black women. In the md-1980s, the University of the West Indies cited the dominance of female writers in journalism and professional writing. Women are combining blend of innovation and drive with enterprise unheard of prior to the last decade.

Distinctive in his 'Dub' style and appearance Jamaican poet Linton Kwesi Johnson, the editor of *Race Today*, is the poet with the largest audience through his public and television readings. His originality and consistency are unequalled in British literature today and are an inspiration to the black community. Desmond Rutherford summed up the inspiration which has fired many to poetry by dedicating his first book to 'sufferers' of the word, but he and others who wish to give expression to their feelings have had to publish their own initially or give readings through the local government and adult education classes. Johnson has the singular distinction of being the second living poet and the only black poet to have his work published in the Penguin Modern Classic Series. Johnson's high profile serves as an example that even a poet can succeed in his own age.

Grace Hallworth has put her childhood interest in folk stories to good use in her books such as *Listen to This Story, The Carnival Kite* and *Mouth Open Story Jump Out*. As a director of the Bogle L'Ouverture publishing house, Jessica Huntley was responsible for opening the Walter Rodney Bookshop and for being the first to publish Linton Kwesi Johnson. Amryl Johnson, another Trinidadian, has published books of poems including *Sequins for a Ragged Hem, Watchers and Seekers*, and *With a Poet's Eye*. She is a lecturer who has assisted pupils throughout Britain.

Trinidadian Faustin Charles, who has been residing in Britain for more than a generation, is an accomplished storyteller, novelist, poet and editor. He studied language and literature at University of Kent. His readings are done in schools, the Commonwealth Institute and an annual Caribbean Day celebration in London. He believes that oral traditions must be developed into a viable industry so that succeeding generations of African Caribbean heritage will be able to uphold strong values. In 1970 two of Charles' books of poetry were published. *The Expatriate* is an account of the experience of Caribbean people exiled in England.

Established prize-winning poet, James Berry gleaned further honours with his collection of short stories for children — *A Thief in the Night*. He was born in Jamaica, but has lived in England for more than 40 years. He has worked for both radio and television. His best known publications include the selection of poems — *Lucy's Letter, Bluefoot Traveller* and *Fractured Circles* — and for the prize-winning poem, *Fantasy of an African Boy* in 1981.

Berry served on the Community Arts Committee of the Arts Council and the Literature Panel of the Greater London Arts. He received a Minority Rights Group Art Award for his writing in 1979. Towards the end of the 1980s, creative writing began to flourish in the black community and Berry was part of this rich tradition. He was to be followed by Guyanese John Agard and Grace Nichols. Through his magical poetry and short stories, Agard published the richness of Caribbean folklore, while Nichols whose first book of poetry, *I is a Long Memoried Woman* and *The Fat Black Woman's Poems*, communicated the versatility of language and the creative power of the Caribbean artistic industry.

Publishing

In 1966, Trinidadian John LaRose founded New Beacon Books. His commitment to bring books to the community began, literally, with him taking them in a Marks & Spencer carrier bag to meetings. This developed into bookselling from his home until the business moved to Stroud Green Road in Finsbury Park, North London. A characteristic New Beacon title, *Jamaican Airmen,* by Martin Noble recognized the need for black people to record their history to Britain.

Bogle L'Ouverture Publications began two years later, with perhaps their most influential title *How Europe Underdeveloped Africa* by Guyanese historian, Dr Walter Rodney. This company also had its origin in the private home of founders Jessica and Eric Huntley, after which they acquired premises in West Ealing (with the business renamed the Walter Rodney Bookshop after Rodney's assassination in 1980). Both Beacon and Bogle L'Ouverture were specialist outlets pioneering a tradition of community-based shops supplying black and Third World literature to readers in Britain, Africa, Asia, the Caribbean and North America.

Anxious to publicise the work of black women writers, Cheryl Robson founded the Aurora Metro Press in 1981. She became a recipient of the Pandora Award by Women in Publishing for her work in developing, publishing and promoting women writers in 1992. The Arts Council subsequently awarded her the Raymond Williams Publishing Prize for the success of seven plays by women—*Female Voices, Fighting Lives*.

It should be noted however, that Britain's burgeoning black book trade had its genesis in the 1960s. Two decades on, the flow of black poetic talent grew stronger. Linton Kwesi Johnson, Grace Nichols, Benjamin Zephaniah, Valerie Bloom and Marsha Prescod, to name a few, often used 'nation language,' groups of individual artists and writers to organize and develop their own publishing outlets.

Typical of this trend, was Akira Press, started by Desmond Johnson who came to London from Jamaica in 1988. A poet and publisher, he was inspired by the Black Writers' Workshop and the Black Ink Collective in Brixton. In eight months, Johnson sold 5,000 copies of his poems, *Deadly Ending Season*, causing the *West Indian Digest* in 1985, to describe him as a poet and publisher 'who sells poetry like hot bread.'

Other new publishers included Yvonne Collymore's Arawdi, with books for Caribbean children, Lorna Miller's *Inky Fingers*, a collection of her poetry, and Sandra Agar's Obatala Press and Karnak House.

Verna Wilkins of Grenada is bent on maintaining Caribbean literary excellence in Britain, with the establishment on Tamarind Limited, set up in 1987. Based in Camberley, Surrey, Tamarind is a highly respected publishing company dedicated to children's literature. When Wilkins first set up the business, she was advised that books with black children would not sell. One popular title, *Dave and the Tooth Fairy*, has sold 50,000 copies. It is now part of the national curriculum. The confident businesswoman believes that children learn from pictures before they learn to read.

The proliferation of independent black publishers at the time reflected the mood among writers who were determined that their creative contribution must neither be ignored nor fall prey to changing fashion. A parallel necessity was also to include more black people in the organizational mainstream of the printing and publishing industry.

Theatre

Black actors and actresses, though excelling in the work of Jean Genet and the Shakespearean classics, have been hampered for years by the lack of dramatists, producers and directors from their own community. That situation changed somewhat when persons such as Michael Abbensetts, Mustapha and Barry Beckford, became a part of a growing artistic tradition in Britain. *Calypso*, a play in 1948 by Hedley Briggs with music and lyrics by Ronnie Hill, was accredited as the first true West Indian play in London.

Eric Conner, who died prematurely 20 years later, starred in this play and his multi-faceted career as an actor, singer, author, composer, producer of film and television and broadcaster, represented several landmarks in stage productions, including *Junction Village* by Douglas Archibald presented on the same bill with his own *Caribbean Revue* medley of music, dance and spectacle. At the time, the Trinidadian was almost alone in maintaining the spirit of West Indies drama in Britain, though the year before he died, BBC television gave impetus to potential artists by encouraging new talent in the Rainbow City series.

There were other important developments in the early 1970s. Jamaican playwright Barry Reckord explored the harsh realities of unemployment in paradise with *In the Beautiful Caribbean*, while contributing to the *Empire Road* series and *Black Christmas*. The television plays tended to be two-dimensional, but at least authors were beginning to establish autonomy distinct from the previous importation of shows direct from Africa, the USA, and occasionally from the Caribbean. Their potential was limited still to the expectations of established producers.

Trinidadian playwright, Matura, came to prominence in 1971 with *As Time Goes By*, presented at the Theatre Upstairs and confirmed afterwards with *Play Mas* and then *Rum Coco Cola*, staged at the Theatre Royal for three and five years respectively.

Much drama originated from the community rather than from the established theatre. Jimi Rand produced, directed and acted in *No Cotton Pickers* at clubs, community halls and private venues and later became artistic director of the Brixton Arts Theatre, the Lambeth Ensemble Theatre and the People's Art Company. Before him, Frank Cousins, who studied theatre administration at the London Polytechnic, founded the Dark and Light Theatre in South London and took producers on tour to several European cities. He was the principal member of The Black's cast.

The Black Theatre Cooperative produced *Welcome Home Jacko* and *One Rule by Matura*. Though foremost, but not alone, these theatre groups matured in the 1970s and the early years of the next decade. The Keskidee Theatre in Islington, North London hosted *Remembrance* by Saint Lucian Nobel Prize laureate, Derek Wacott; *The Throne in an Autumn Room* by Lennox Brown, as well as Edgar White's *Lament for Rastafari*. *Mister Biko* and *Theresa* were probably the works best associated with the Temba Theatre Company at the time. At the dawn of the 1980s, awards for acting, writing and directing became popular.

Horace Ove, a Trinidadian who studied painting in Rome, became known initially through his direction of the film *Reggae* that focused on the Caribbean Music Festival at Wembley in 1970. From there he went on to make *Pressure* and *Hole in Babylon* (which looked at the Spaghetti House siege and in which T-Bone Wilson and Archie Schepp acted). *Pressure*, in particular, is accredited with giving most poignant emphasis on the conflict from within and without in an oppressed community. *Yet Black Joy* and *The Harder They Come*, starring Jimmy Cliff, are two black productions which had the greatest impact on the outside world.

Better known for his talents as a playwright, is St. Kitts born Caryl Phillips who received acclaim for the novel *The Final Passage* which was later adapted for television by Sir Peter Hall and screened by Channel 4 in early 1997.

Phillips is described as one of the finest and most important novelists of his generation. He and his parents left the island of St Kitts when he was four months old. In his book, *The European Tribe*, he asserted that: *'Black people have always been present in a Europe which has chosen either not to see us or to judge us as an insignificant minority, or a temporary and dismissible mistake.'* Phillips is the recipient of numerous awards including the Martin Luther King Memorial Prize. He is Professor of English at Amherst College, Massachusetts, USA.

Guyanese Norman Beaton, who in 1995 was a doyen of television entertainment in Britain, brought a clean, sober and instructive approach to the performing arts, possibly because of his educational background and appreciation for Caribbean values. As a qualified teacher, he left his homeland to further his education in Britain. After finding difficulty with the education system, he turned to entertainment, mostly acting beginning first with the Liverpool Poets group. He later acted in plays—*The Empire Road* for instance. He even acted with English actor, the late Sir Laurence Olivier on stage. Beaton featured in the films *Black Joy* and the *Mighty Quinn*, which included actor Denzil Washington. At one time, the Guyanese starred with Bill Cosby, a leading American black entertainer.

Yet it was the BBC Television series, *Desmonds*, which portrayed Beaton's sheer brilliance portraying Ambrose the egotistical barber and family man. *Desmonds* was a big hit in Britain and elsewhere and at one time, in the early 1990s, had a viewing audience in excess of ten million. His support comprised fellow Guyanese, Carmen Munro and Ramjohn Holder of *Pork Pie* fame. Holder has promised to continue the standards of excellence that Beaton bequeathed.

While researching this topic, I came across the names and addresses of the following African-Caribbean theatrical, dance and artists groups listed in *Third World Impact* published by Hansib Publishing. I would like to mention a few to show the range and extent of black involvement in the literary arts industry in Britain. Nottingham: Black Velvet Dance Group, the Early Start Project and New Booker. Wolverhampton: L'Ouverture Theatre Trust and Ekome Arts. Bristol: Kutamba. Manchester: the London Youth Dance Theatre, Rainbow Art Group and the Sam Uriah Morris Society. London: Talawa Theatre Company and Phoenix Dance Company and various youth steelband groups.

Ray McLean, a powerfully built, but supple man, taught many young dancers at the old Dance Centre in Floral Street, London, and showed himself to be a lithe entertainer at performances in Britain and abroad. Like many artists of his time, McLean is a Trinidadian. To be fair to his contemporaries, however, he was among instructors who created a lasting impression on students, most of whom later achieved excellence in their respective pursuits. Ray was in business long before the television series *Fame* caught up with reality.

Limbo dancing straddles the borderline between cultural art and popular entertainment. There are fewer competent professionals in this field than is often realized. Captain Fish and George Henry are two performers whose work is remembered best over a number of years. They had the ability to hold an audience, no matter how many times they appeared. Yet Henry and Fish gave much credit to fellow dancers for their success. Harry Girad who combined fire eating with (Eastern Caribbean) dance in the 1960, returned to Saint Lucia where he manages the Green Parrot.

Gloria Cameron played a vital role in preserving West Indian folk culture through the Caribbean Drama and Folk Group, which she formed in 1965. She produced several of her own shows, primarily in Lambeth, South London and the group performed at charitable functions. Her involvement in community work included the formation of the West Indian Parent Action Group, and her membership on the boards of several drama, cultural and community relations groups.

After its decline in the 1970s, black women's theatre shifted emphasis from the exploration of serious drama to the treatment of art form as a commodity. Since 1982 however, the Theatre of Black Women (TOBW) was the vanguard of black women's theatre in Britain. That same year, playwright and drama director, Yvonne Brewster, OBE, became the first black woman drama officer in the Arts Council of England (she formed the Talawa Theatre Company in 1985).

Bernadine Evaristo, Patricia Hilarie, Paulette Randall, and Kadiji George are the founders of TOBW. After performing a series of plays, media interest in the organization heightened in 1985. It has produced plays such as *Miss Quashi, The Tiger's Tail, The Cripple* and *The Children*.

In spite of having its grant withdrawn in 1988, the TOBW is one of few groups responding to the needs of non-white women in the British artistic field.

Randall also worked as a director in Repertory Theatre where she gained much experience. She directed several plays, including *24 Per Cent* (about the percentage of black women in British prisons) and *Headrock*. He has been a consultant director on Lenny Henry tour and was, at one time, the sole producer of the popular television series, *Desmonds*.

Music

While it has been accepted for some time in America that black people have contributed extensively to classical music—in composition, instrumentation and opera singing—the breadth of achievement in Britain is being understood and appreciated even more. Perhaps the more supposedly ethnocentric musical forms of reggae and calypso have distracted the attention of our neighbours from the fact that many middleclass black families like their young daughters to play the piano or take ballet (dancing) lessons. With our more recent colonial past, we are probably more proficient in these Victorian traditions, unlike our white neighbours.

Samuel Coleridge-Taylor, the son of the famous surgeon, Daniel Hugh Taylor, became one of Britain's most popular composers. His choral compositions, *Hiawatha* is set listening for thousands of school children and their teachers, who are unaware that the composer was black. Coleridge-Taylor was not content to let his work alone represent his struggle for social equality. He became a founding member of the League of Coloured Peoples which was established in 1931 by Jamaican Dr. Harold Moody, who practised medicine in Camberwell, South London. black singers have participated at the Glyndebourne Festival featuring the renditions of Coleridge-Taylor.

Rudolph Dunbar was a familiar conductor in England until he moved to the USA, where he later died. His flamboyant nephew, Guyanese Professor Ian Hall, came to public notice after performing in different artistic and musical roles. He attended Keble College, Oxford University and is reputed to be the first black musicologist to be trained there. Very intelligent and exceedingly talented, Hall spent some eighteen months in Ghana where he taught music to President Jerry Rawlings and other Africans. He has been director of music at several schools and an organist at concerts and recitals on radio and television. He is head of the Bloomsbury Society which was set up in 1971 to promote the arts in universities. Hall's compositions are usually dedicated to events or particular individuals. He is the author of published essays and verse. It is indeed a great pity that this musical genius is not popular with the mainstream media.

Ivan Chin's band was an important feature of social events that became a classic. Chin served in the RAF at the end of the Second

World War (1945-1947) and as a member of the West Indian Ex-Servicemen's Association. While working with his band at concert throughout the European continent, he promoted Caribbean tourism and participated in meaningful community activities. He served as both secretary and treasurer of the Carib Housing Association, South London and was founder of the Guyana circle. Chin died in early 1997.

In July 1997, at the opening of Mahogany Limited, North-West London, junior minister of health, Paul Boateng, MP, reminded the audience of the vast contributions by Cy Grant to black British culture. Yet, while Grant is famous for his talents as a calypso man and an actor, it is often forgotten that he qualified as a barrister in 1951. He was co-founder and chairman of the Drum Arts Centre in 1974.

Grenadian-born Alex Pascall, the broadcaster and former Chairman of the Notting Hill Carnival Arts founded the Alex Pascall Singers and recorded the Anansi stories for broadcast. As an exponent in the performing arts, his understanding of the spectrum of African and Caribbean culture is beyond question. In 1974, he was invited to host the first black radio programme in Britain— black Londoners on Radio London, In early 1997, he was awarded an Order of the British Empire (OBE) for community development, including arts and culture.

Media and Communications

More recently, black journalists from media institutions, frustrated by their inability to move up the success ladder and eager to enjoy autonomy, have established private companies ranging from management consultancy to training and public relations. One perfect example of this new development is the well-known, but graceful television presenter and journalist, Jacqui Harper, who is the owner of a rapidly expanding management training company. She is known for her work with the BBC, GMTV and Sky News. In the mid-1990s, Harper founded Crystal Media to make an impact on the world of communications training. Her clients include firms such as Abbey National, HSBC and Norwich Union.

Brenda Emanus, who arrived in Britain from Saint Lucia in the 1960s, is a dynamic communications specialist. She freelances with various publications, mainly the Voice and develops program ideas for media production. She worked for the BBC on the black magazine programme *Ebony*, as a researcher and presenter, whilst presenting other programmes, including the *Clothes Show* and *Travelogue* for Channel 4.

Recently, black women have combined their talents in an effort to provide a sustained quality of service to their community. The BiBi Crew was formed in 1991 and consisted of Joanne Campbell, Judith Jacob, Janet Kay (who has since left due to recording commitments), Suzette Llewellyn, Josephine Melville, Beverley Michaels and Suzanne Parker; each actress has at least 10 years' experience in theatre, television and film.

The company is dedicated to producing high quality new writing from an African Caribbean perspective and to introducing the black British experience to a larger cosmopolitan audience. Campbell is on the board of directors at the Theatre Royal, Stratford. Jacob appeared in *Eastenders* and *The Real McKoy*. Kay has released an album entitled 'Love You Always' in Japan and her success in the record industry has meant she has had to leave the BiBi Crew. This group represents a new trend in the performing arts, where individuals from disparate backgrounds fuse their talents to realize each other's dreams.

Artists

Surprisingly, painters and other visual artists raised in the tropics of Africa and the Caribbean have retained their eye for colour, even after years in the fog and rain in Britain. Illustrations of the sun, the trees and the water, seemed sharper in contrast to the actual first-hand experience. Few painters have depicted the tropical nights which in many ways are more impressive than the day, with the stars being overhead and seemingly so low that you could reach out and pick them. The heavenly bodies there are not obscured by the elements.

Ossie Murray, a Jamaican, who has spent years in the London boroughs adjoining Essex, is a specialist in defining the wooden landscape of his homeland. He has an eye for attractive ladies and came to public attention some years ago for his lively portrait of Jennifer Hosten who, as Miss Grenada, won the Miss World Beauty contest in the early 1970s. Ossie also designed the pennants for the Commonwealth Sports Awards at Islington Town Hall. He has illustrated books and has taught through the now defunct ILEA and through his local borough administration.

Sidney Gellineau who, like Murray, specializes in oil paintings, has been with Horace de Bourg and Errol Thorpe, amongst the best Trinidadian painters. They have exhibited at public and private functions, with encouragement from the Trinidad and Tobago High Commission. In spite of their years in Britain, West Indian painters maintain themes of their youthful days in the Caribbean. Yet black artists have not gained universal recognition or been adequately compensated financially, for their efforts, unlike their white counterparts. History has shown that only after death, the works of master-artists become best sellers.

De Bourg is unusual in that he favours water colours and includes themes from Britain and location pictures from his visits to West Germany and the Netherlands. He has a lead role each year in the Civil Service art exhibition Whitehall and was chosen to paint a portrait of the former Prime Minister, Baroness Margaret Thatcher. Spectators of fashion shows and beauty contests on the North Sea ferries between Britain and Holland have seen his paintings on exhibition prior to the main event. De Bourg's works are displayed at various places in England on occasions.

Writing, painting and music are more difficult than most other artistic activities to quantify because apart from the few professionals involved, they are conducted at evening classes and schools throughout the United Kingdom as a pastime for enthusiastic amateurs. There is also a very fine line, if any at all, between traditional art and the modern sciences, involving computer technology, in which our young men and women of today are excelling. Sir Christopher Wren observed for his memorial stone in St. Paul's Cathedral that the words should be *'If you want a monument to me, look around.'* A visit to local libraries, art galleries and town halls would serve the same purpose in respect to enterprise in the arts.

Boyce Drake studied Fine Arts at the Gloucester College of Art and picture restoration in both Bristol and London. He commenced his first course in the mid-1950s and a quarter-of-a-century later, he won a scholarship to study picture restoration techniques at Stuttgart in West Germany. Boyce is a picture restorer and retailer of artists' materials in Gloucester. He has chaired the city's International Friendship League.

There is no clear distinction between graffiti and mural paintings. The reason given often is that black youths in socially deprived areas, denied the usual artistic opportunities, brighten their lives by painting on available surfaces and stress their individuality in an otherwise anonymous environment through their highly personalized style. This argument could well be true. However, it is customary to paint pictures on wall of buildings in some parts of the Caribbean and this manner of self-expression could be passed down from parents to children.

Some time ago, Alex Pascall wrote in the magazine, *Saffron*:

> Black people have always had a medium of their own; that is, through talking to each other and passing the news along. The structure of the black media must go beyond what is put over the air or written on paper. Black people have a lot to talk about. I am a communicator, not a broadcaster. You must take any opportunity you can get to write for any paper or to carry out any research.

European art and literature have not always been as specialized as it seems today. Leonardo da Vinci, above all, and Michelangelo, mastered different fields of art and knowledge during the renaissance of classical European culture. The black community may well be experiencing a similar revival. There are, of course, important differences in artistic themes. European artists have been willing to portray their pagan past before accepting Christianity. African-Caribbean painting lacks a similar legacy in any depth—at least as far it concerns publicly exhibited works.

Much of the writings, especially poetry and drama of the 1980s, committed politically almost exclusively to the radical movements of socialism and where applicable, to feminism. It is easy to understand, therefore, the anger of the poor against what they see as inequalities in the society they live. The danger exists, however, that the anger may consume the art in a way that C.L.R. James, V.S. Naipaul and the writers of an earlier age managed to avoid, though it has to be admitted once again, that their social circumstances were considerably different.

The achievement of black people in sport, music and other popular art forms has worked against those who have the capacity to succeed in what society considers to be classic European arts. It is unlikely that a boy or girl from such a background would be taken seriously at school if he or she expressed an ambition to play the piano at concert recitals or to write a study on Jacobean drama. The ignorance of what our children are capable of achieving extends into other areas of scholarship or (for the purposes of this chapter) the intellectual enterprise.

Because Caribbean territories and African countries have been a colonial football, West Indians have a particular knack for learning languages. From their checkered history, the inhabitants of some of the Eastern Caribbean sub-region have grown up speaking French patios, as well as English, in the manner of traditional cultural value systems. Everyone engaged in commerce or administration needs to understand Dutch, French or Spanish to speak to his or her neighbours. There is a true story of a young lady, a model, who, while making a promotional trip to London, told her agent *'There was no need to worry. Why didn't you tell me they spoke Saint Lucian?'*

Yet in spite of their learning, many of the most educated immigrants had to accept menial jobs when economic circumstances forced them to leave their homeland. It was not unusual to find a multi-lingual lathe operator, or a cleaner who could recite whole passages of Shakespeare, Keats or Yeats. Poets would contend that it gave them an even deeper appreciation for life. African-Caribbean people are in the forefront of Bible study and that does not exclude traditional (professional) theologians.

Undoubtedly, there is a reservoir of talent born of education and knowledge existing in the black community, but it is yet to find acceptance within the British society. The time is therefore, opportune for Britain to respond intelligently and positively to such infinite resources.

PART TWO

THE JOURNEY OF THE COSMETIC KINGS

CHAPTER 4

GETTING STARTED

The Entrepreneurial Spirit

Quite often, people opting for a business career will tell you that getting started is perhaps one of the most difficult decisions they have ever had to make. Entering the world of business could quite easily be the decision of a lifetime. Surveys have shown that the major reason for getting into self-employment is an individual wanting to do things for himself or herself, or to be of independent means. A legitimate question that arises most times is: What are the factors that motivate and drive an individual to take on board an entrepreneurial route?

Some people are driven by a burning desire to prove to themselves and others of their ability to achieve amazing results of personal success. Some of these cases arise, for example, where siblings have refused to follow the desired parental paths in education, of accountancy, law or medicine etc. because they instinctively believe that they could achieve and be successful on their own terms.

Taking the entrepreneurial route puts such persons in a special group. The choice of a slot in business demands that you make things happen rather than waiting for events to happen for you. Being an entrepreneur is great, in that you automatically belong to a special group of persons whose ambition is to change the world; these are people brimming full with vision, people who are often referred to as being action-orientated

During my active business life, among the most frequently asked questions were *'How did you do it?'* or *'What does it take to win?* These were important questions with no simple answers. Looking at the second question first and based on my personal experience, a first question you must ask yourself is *'What is my mission in getting into business?'* If the answer is to succeed and realize your dreams and win at what you decided to do, next steps must be to cultivate a positive attitude to winning and understand that business is a game filled with fun and packed with lots of excitement!

Remembering always that you are in it to win. The trick is, you release the success formula within your dream, grasp it firmly and focus on it—for winning is the ultimate prize!

What is the success factor you ask? This is your instinctive creative entrepreneurial power source that resides within—always waiting to be released! It's a part of your imprisoned dream waiting and longing to escape and transform itself into reality. I know, I've been there. It's an integral part of you. It is a mindset, an ambition that signals a powerful message of confidence, of conviction and of winning. Only you the dreamer can recognize your gift and must act on it. What I am about to share has not been gleaned from text books or tutored in business school but rather an instinctive discipline rooted as part of your inner being, your personal source of strength and an abiding belief in your own capabilities to achieve your dreams.

With two colleagues, we succeeded in opening up new horizons to wealth creation activities for the black community which had not been seen before in Britain. We focused on our dreams and as a result built a multimillion pound company in the process.

On the question of *'How did you do it?'* my answer was really pretty simple: *'Regular doses of hard work, underlined with determination,'* I explained. What does it take to win? Much the same medicine, but mixed and spiced up by learning to work smarter, but underneath it all, it comes down to a matter of one's attitude. Describing attitude, I can draw on many examples, but will use a true Caribbean story of a cousin, who was barely literate and whose story will illustrate how attitude and entrepreneurial genius comes together to make the point.

An estate on one of the islands came up for sale by auction on an agreed date and my cousin Wally duly turned up to the auction with no money in his pocket, but simply armed only with determination and a plan to out-bid everyone else—and he did. The laws of the island provided for seven days grace before settlement had to be made by the winning bid. During this grace period, he skillfully sold the peripheral parts of the estate and raised enough cash to settle his commitment for the estate within the time allowed. Here was a brilliant piece of entrepreneurial maneuvering that won the day.

This story did not end there, but kindled further business initiatives that were to change the lives of many families across the region. With the purchase of the estate, he went into farming several acres of Sea Island cotton, famous for its quality lint. His farming was again a major success which led directly to the purchase of two sailing ships, the *Morning Princess* and the *Evening Princess*. These ships traded among the islands. His successes were such that the whole island concluded that he was visited with the Midas touch. He further purchased more estates in other islands and diversified at this point into property development. Here, we have an entrepreneur in action whose drive and passion instinctively chalked up success after success in growing and integrating his businesses.

What emerges from Wally's character is his positive attitude to attain the goals he had set himself. He was absolute in his belief that he could accomplish his dreams, and he pursued them with relentless self-confidence, conviction and drive. Some psychologists reveal that the secret of success, to a large extent, depends on the love and passion with which an individual tackles whatever he or she is doing. It is suggested that it is this love and passion which keeps them optimistic and relaxed while pursuing their dream.

How Do You Harness Your Dream ?

You rationalize your ideas and follow your natural God-given instincts by adding new attainable goals to your list. You get into the habit of cultivating a circle of business friendships and mentors who could advance and give momentum to your ideas. You master new technologies which help with problem solving, read autobiographies of successful business people and you will soon discover that many of the big names in lights were once small.

Small Businesses and The Economy

• New entrepreneurial talent enters business through small firms.
• Small firms are a breeding ground for new industries.
• They are an important source of innovation.
• They are usually the optimum size for efficient operation.
• Small businesses provide the ideal opportunity as a starting ground for people who value their independence.

The role of small businesses in the economy makes interesting reading and quoted below are some key statistics on small businesses in the UK with extracts from the 2005 Warwick Business School:

- 2,200,000 businesses have no employees, that is (about 61% of SMEs)
- 1,450,000 businesses have an annual turnover of less than £50,000.
- 1,350,000 business have less than £10,000 worth of assets.
- 87% of SMEs are located in England (3,150,000 businesses)
- 38% of SMEs are located in London and the South East (1,400,000 businesses)

Percentages by Ethnicity and Region:
- 93% of businesses are majority white owned (3,400,000 businesses)
- About 7% of businesses are owned by individuals from the ethnic minority backgrounds (220,000).

What these figures explain is that the role of Small Businesses cannot be taken lightly—they are in fact the backbone of the economy. 98.6% of all businesses are considered small. A significant and major point to note is that of 1.4% of large business, each of them was small at some point in their history! Small, therefore, is distinctly beautiful and full of hope and I can share with you how small business has been a part of life over the years.

Not all entrepreneurs are primarily motivated by thoughts of making loads of money, or the love of money and quite rightly so. Wally certainly was a man moved by compassion and the love of those around him. He was generous and a very modest man. Some entrepreneurs are motivated by the satisfaction he or she derives by being in control and doing their own thing. With the excitement this affords, it keeps them stimulated to keep going. Some entrepreneurs are motivated by positioning themselves to change the circumstances of their families, friends, their community, the environment and the quality of the lives of their people.

Indeed, we see this happening in many large corporations who have taken their corporate responsibilities seriously and have allocated a percentage of their profits and created trusts to identify cases of need to administer the funds earmarked in the communities in which they operate their businesses. These benefactors may apply their gifts of money to natural disasters, in areas covered by their policies, in education sponsorship, sports training and the promotion of good causes and derive immense satisfaction in sharing their successes through the organizations they have created.

Great philanthropic organizations that come to mind include the John D Rockefeller Foundation, the Smithsonian Institution, the Rothschild trust, the Welcome Foundation and Shaftsbury Trusts. They are all great names that have shared their wealth with a number of good causes.

However, the most striking image of a successful entrepreneur that makes people sit up is the individual who is willing to take the ultimate risk by gambling all he owns in pursuit of fulfilling his dreams. The approach of the more cautious entrepreneur will chart his course of action while still working in their current employment. In fact, this was the path that I followed in getting started.

My mentor and inspiration was my last boss, the finance director of the Smart Weston group of companies for which I worked as their bank reconciliation clerk. Louis Segal was a man with great presence. He strode like a giant through his accounts department bristling with immense energy and wearing a permanent smile of contentment with his life. He drove a Rolls Royce and shopped at Harrods, the most distinctive store in all London, both symbols of taste befitting a man of his standing.

An Unexpected Offer of a New Partnership
that Altered the Course of History

As mentioned earlier, it was with a sense of great satisfaction that I shared the news of my decision to take the plunge on my own with a new venture I named Carib Services. With two friends, Lincoln Dyke and Dudley Dryden, who were already in business importing and selling pre-release records from Jamaica. It is worth pointing out that pre-release records carried a premium in that they had no labels, but a ready customer base. The sound system music promoters attracted regular party goers, who were always on the lookout for the latest music in fashion from Jamaica.

After disclosing difficulties that they were experiencing in their business and their desire for me to join them in their enterprise as an equal partner, I accepted their proposal after two weeks of much thought and consideration. My counter proposal to them (with a guaranteed yes) was to change direction from selling records and move into selling cosmetics. There was unanimous agreement with my suggestion. The meeting ended on a positive note and with that decision, I abandoned proceeding with my Carib Services project. The rest, from there on, is all history.

The partnership of Dyke and Dryden founded in 1965 was replaced by a limited liability company in June 1968 with my acquisition of 33 per cent of the equity in the business. Changing direction became a major turning point in the history of the company. My new partners wanted to rename the business, Dyke, Dryden & Wade which I felt was quite a mouthful and unnecessary. *'D & D'*, I said, *'has nice a ring to it, and rolls off the tongue smoothly.'* I thought their suggestion was much too long and cumbersome and we all agreed to stick with the prevailing name.

Where we were headed could not be too strongly emphasized, I explained to my new business colleagues. It was very important that we accepted this fact up front as many businesses failed just after a short period of time. They failed mainly because there was no plan, and no focus. Yet this need not have happened if only their owners had not lost focus in spotting the first signs of trouble at an early stage and acted to prevent it. The watchword, we agreed, was to be vigilant and remain steadfastly focused on our objectives.

The original Dyke and Dryden project had been a big hit and Caribbean music lovers flocked to the new record store at 43 West Green Road from all over London to pick up their prized musical gems by their preferred artists. House parties were the order of the day for entertainment and relaxation during the long cold dark days and nights of winter and hence a huge demand for records.

However, the beauty needs of our sisters represented an enormous opportunity as at that time, there were no major suppliers or manufacturers catering for black hair products in Britain. It was, therefore, down to the community itself to do something about it. In doing so, it was simply a question of responding to the need and set about meeting it from our original store, at 43 West Green Road N 15, already well known for its business in the sale of records.

Changing focus from selling records to selling hair and skin care products was the first stage in moving the business forward in a new direction for goods and services for which demand already existed. The trick was to spot the gap—which I did—and then set about finding a way of exploiting it. Clearly, the change improved the fortunes of the old partnership, but not without immense hard work, many challenges and sacrifices. The all-round change in this new mode of operation presented formidable challenges which had to be addressed. This called for a spirited and innovative grasp of the situation to make things happen.

Having got the New Dyke & Dryden off the ground on a new course I can, therefore, offer some encouragement and empathize with some of the young entrepreneurs out there and invite them all to think creatively and above all, adventurously about the structure, scale and operation of their business. People who have never run a small business themselves cannot fully appreciate the problems associated with running one's own business and make it become a winner.

Unfortunately, some relations and friends always assume that because you own a business, you are loaded with money and assume that you spend most of your time on holidays and when you do visit the place, you do little more than give orders to employees—this is all a fallacy. Outsiders are often blissfully unaware of how much time and effort you actually put into building up the company. They would never know the long evenings you put in working over weekends, at nights and on bank holidays, whereas others are relaxing and having fun while you continuously beaver away on the job. My advice is to remain focused and remember your goals.

Early Challenges

My initial investigations at Dyke and Dryden highlighted what some of the previous shortcomings were. There was, for example, no stock management in place, which meant that at no given time could the business account for the stock held, its value and its age etc. When you consider that the company's stock holding represented the bulk of its wealth, it demonstrated, in part, one of the major weaknesses represented in the poor showing of the company's performance. Other factors associated with stock, included poor purchasing decisions and stock rotation etc.

The marketplace is ever shifting and changing and the successful entrepreneur is the individual who can endure and navigate through the many stages of growth and keeping track of an expanding business. Within two decades, by 1987, Dyke and Dryden was well on the way to becoming a multi-million pound business and creating an industry that provided a significant number of jobs and making a valuable contribution to the nation's economy.

A note of caution to always take into account in following a career path in business that it is often punctuated by highs and lows. Mastering the secrets of survival and challenges in winning is the satisfaction that fills the soul with a deep sense of fulfillment.

Carving Out a critical Base In The Industry

To begin with, the space constraints for this new activity, was a major challenge and induced the doctrine of 'making do with what you have'. The old records retail business unit at 43 West Green Road was used to house the cosmetics beauty products we introduced. Our total space was approximately 3,000 square feet. An area 24 x 24 allocated for retailing with an adjacent backroom doubling as an office for administrative staff. A converted old shed at the back of the building served as an improvised warehouse for storage, packing and deliveries. The foregoing would no doubt paint a rough picture of the location which remained for a time as the company's operating base. Space was at a premium, which meant that turning stock around quickly was an essential part of managing the space at our disposal.

It was from this humble beginning that Britain's first black hair care industry grew and operated for some considerable time, until we were able to find more suitable work space. The industry today, provides thousands of jobs and a measure of independence for some of its members. Looking back, it was clearly beyond any doubt and greatly to the company's credit that it identified a need and set about meeting it against great odds.

Despite the space constraints, we enjoyed an advantage in having an excellent location. West Green Road, located in North London N15, has been for generations a business thoroughfare. The road today, remains a strategic link connecting two major arterial roads. Green Lanes on its southern end and Tottenham High Road on the east. Access from West Green Road connects to the Victoria line underground network which snakes its way through the city to Brixton at one end and to Walthamstow Central at the other. These links make for excellent travelling connections around the city.

This area was part of prime industrial estates during the first half of the 20th century. Unfortunately, after the Second World War, the high cost of production in London forced many companies to take flight and relocate. Today, the road boasts a new and totally integrated community with families drawn from all parts of the globe exhibiting and sharing good and harmonious relationships. This rich mix of cultures brings together a wide variety of merchandise and foods to satisfy the needs and palates of its various community members.

The store was soon to become nationally and internationally known for the widest possible collection of ethnic hair care and cosmetics available in the UK, attracting customers from near and far. What followed was to lay the foundation for the ethnic hair care industry that changed for all times the plight of black people's impoverished choice of suitable hair and skin care preparations for their hair and skin types.

In the early years, the company had a situation where mixed container loads of stock imported from the United States was more than our retail stores could handle. It was, therefore, necessary to break bulk by selling off the excess stock to free up cash and reduce the pressure on precious space. This exercise was spectacularly successful and led directly to the expansion of the business and the development of a wholesale division out of the same limited space.

This initial wholesale pilot operation actually began out of the boot of my car. Armed with a box of samples, price lists and an order book, I motored around the local chemists, food shops and mixed bag stores, looking for shelf space and offering new opportunities for the owners to increase the lines carried and gave a guarantee that they would see their sales increase. There was little need for a bullish sales pitch, since entry was far easier than I had anticipated, as most stores visited were already being asked for the products. At the stores where some resistance was found, I offered to leave the merchandise on a sale or return basis as an introductory gesture, explaining that if the goods did not sell, I would return and collect them.

This introductory phase worked brilliantly, for the entire stock left was sold quickly with repeat orders flooding in. With no staff in place to handle this initial testing exercise, meant that all orders had to be personally picked and packed by me during the day, in an organised shift-like pattern. I was working the phone in the mornings collecting orders and assembling them in the afternoon or evening. Completed orders were converted into picked and packed lists, then taken home and invoiced at night. My kitchen table served as a makeshift desk for a portable adding machine used for computing my hand written entries of invoices made ready for delivery the following day. This successful pilot now urgently needed a structure and system to handle quickly local deliveries.

Initially, in making do with the premises at 43 West Green Road. The tea room, together with an old shed at the back of our building, acted as office, work station and warehouse all rolled into one and was home to the initial wholesale operation, while the shop front maintained its original retail status.

Tenants occupied the first and second floors which were residential and could not be used without planning permission. Eventually, these floors became available, but it also meant carrying boxes of bottles and jars up several flights of stairs day-after-day. My legs would give up at times, but my soul wanted to carry on.

Many of the drivers delivering goods would be roped into helping move the boxes up these flights of stairs, but even generous sweetener tips would not do the trick for their help, since they were used to fork-lift trucks and loading bays and would moan and swear in disbelief on seeing where their deliveries had to go. As leader of the pack, there was no escaping this back-breaking exercise. I had to be out in front, encouraging them all the way and at the same time conscious of weight and high risk of the boxes coming through the ceiling to land on the floor below.

A temporary short term answer was found by buying a nearby building at 126a West Green Road which helped to reduce the storage problem. However, this created yet another problem, that of moving goods between the two sites some of which conveniently got lost in these movements. Addressing this unworkable situation was a high priority. Estate agents were approached to assist in finding suitable premises and a 5,500 sq. ft facility was eventually found at 10 St Loys Road about a mile from our original location.

This was a welcome relief and a sense of much satisfaction to all concerned. State of the art equipment was purchased which made loading and unloading less of a tiring exercise and made the working environment as a whole a far more desirable place.

The move to St Loys Road was another turning point. It provided space to move about and all stocks were stored at eye level which made order filling far more simple, resulting in faster turnaround times for gathering and packing orders. This respite, however, was short-lived, for we had grossly underestimated our space requirement and within two years we had outgrown the warehouse. Fortunately, our agents found us a 16,500 sq. ft purpose-built building at 19 Bernard Road which we purchased in 1982. This new premises provided us with a superior working environment, with a proper kitchen and canteen together with excellent office accommodation to cope with the various departmental functions of personnel, accounting, sales and marketing, which perfectly met the needs of the business. In addition (and for the first time), there were decent offices for the directors.

Another superb spin-off to occur from this location was space for the opening of a cash and carry facility where hairdressers and some traders could walk in, browse around and help themselves with stock and cash out on leaving the section. This new facility aided the operation and made a significant difference in turnaround time and impacted on cash flow.

The immediate, all round gains in efficiency were remarkable in boosting our levels of productivity as never seen before. Progress continued apace and as it turned out, Bernard Road became the meeting place for everyone connected with the industry.

Different visitors had different objectives. Some American manufacturers saw the space as ideal for better exposure for their products and were keen to ensure that they were getting their fair share of distribution space and at the same time monitoring our manufacturing efforts which, after all, we were now competing with them with our own products.

Some of the guests were clearly spies wanting to see and learn how they might enter the industry. There were too, those who wanted buy into what was now a lucrative business niche. Manoeuvring through the many demands placed on us as a result of the company's success, became a delicate balancing act in deciding which direction we should take. My colleagues after much soul-searching, decided to sell their interest in the business which took place in November 1987.

Demand at 43 West Green Road grew to such an extent that a second location had to be found to service the retail segment of the market. One was found in the busy Ridley Road Market in Hackney, where large numbers of the black community gathered to meet, greet and share their news from back home and at times, would in reality, shopped till they dropped. As a matter of fact, the market environment for me was the perfect text book example for sales and marketing. The three Ps principle was very much in place—product, place and people. This was where the action was. The road was also the strip along which the infamous racist Oswald Mosley conducted his rallies to harass the Jewish and later the black community.

Acquiring the lease on 40 Ridley Road was another story. It was also like being put through an obstacle course. So extreme was racial discrimination at the time that it took the good offices of a great Jewish friend, Harry Lester, to front the purchase of the lease for us. This was a remarkable and noteworthy deed, one for which we have been eternally grateful. Harry also owned the adjoining leases for numbers 36 and 38 and on his retirement, sold them to us, enabling us to add new product lines to our stock in trade— namely toys. This product line was to test the mentality of some of our customers in many ways, but in particular, to highlight a popular trading myth, senselessly believed and rumoured by some people who should have known better.

Here is one of several incidents that stumped Dudley and me on a busy Friday afternoon. One of Dudley's childhood friend's daughter came by with her young son in tow to the toy counter and greeted Dudley warmly as you would expect from an old family friend of long standing. In the meantime, the boy was in agony drawing his mother's attention to the toys. His mother did not or could not respond to his tantrum. Dudley moved by the boy's agony, picked a toy and treated him to it. His tantrum turned to smiles and he trotted off with mother happy with his new toy.

As they moved along the parade of shops, I saw the lady stop at a newly opened store which was competing with us. I was anxious to see if she was supporting our competitor rather than us, but more importantly I wanted to check whether we were competitive and there was no better way of doing so than by having people we could trust to act as spies for us to ensure that were seen as giving good value for money.

From my vantage point, I could not help noting that our spy picked up and bought an item of stock we carried and I mentioned to Dudley what I saw. *'Your eyes must be playing tricks on you,'* Dudley retorted. *'Perhaps'* I replied, but in the interest of competitive trading, I will try to find out as she comes back this way to go home. As she came alongside our shop, I approached her and politely asked for her assistance in helping us to discover if we were competitive on the item she had purchased next door.

She was very helpful, producing the item. This was a jar of Ultra Sheen hair conditioner for which she paid one pound fifty-two pence. *'Well,'* I said, *'you could have saved yourself some money if you bought it from us. Well thanks for helping us to prove a point. We are competitive offering the same item for one pound fifty.'* She literally froze and explained that she simply did it out of habit! Make what you will of a myth that exists, that black shopkeepers are always more expensive! This was one of those slavery inflicted, destructive rumours that, somehow, still lives on.

The additional space was timely, for it provided us with a significantly much better display area, allowing us to carry much larger stocks, thus beefing up our overall trading position. Our customers loved it. The location provided the opportunity for one-stop shopping as we were close to the markets in which Caribbean food was sold.

Although Ridley Road was a busy and bustling market place and good for our business, it was also a rather lonely place. For years we were the only black-owned business in a market that traded millions of pounds weekly in produce consumed by the black community.

The absence of black traders was not as a result of our failure to try and obtain shops or market stalls. Our low trading presence in the market resulted primarily because of the discrimination by the landlords who owned the shops or the council inspectors who issued the street trading licences and denied access to both stalls and shops to community members.

In those early days, if there was such a thing as a prize for the tolerance and patience shown by the community, there was little doubt that we would walk away with the prize for the daily diet of insults and abuse which we had to endure. Damage to our properties was a regular occurrence, much of which was designed to try and drive us out of the market, but fortunately, the sturdy stuff of which we were made proved too much for them to handle.

Racial Challenges To Growth

Meanwhile, an attack from another quarter came as a massive bombshell. Some months after the purchase of the two additional leases from our good friend Mr Lester, a letter arrived from British Rail requiring the site of our three shops for a proposed railway station. *'Why us?'* we asked. We had been through so much hell and now Big Brother had stepped in to boot us out of a parade of over a hundred shops. This seemed, on the face of it, to have all the makings of some kind of Machiavellian plot, considering all the harassment and hardships that we had gone through before.

We questioned the logic of wanting our three sites and could get no reasoned answer and could not help concluding that this smelled like institutional racism. We decided to fight it, well aware that it was like David taking on Goliath. Our advisors could see no grounds for British Rail wanting our particular sites and with the support of our many friends, we rejected their demand outright and marshalled support for our position. The local Market Traders Association was approached for their support which they agreed to give in principle. However, when it came to their active support by way of signatures and petitions, attending meetings and campaigning, we were left on our own.

Again, our customers were marvellous, providing thousands of petitions for presenting to Hackney Council who would have to give planning permission for the new station. And as luck would have it, Dudley was Vice chairman of Hackney Race Relations Council and did some fine community networking in many areas in the borough. In particular, he succeeded in getting the support of Councillor Bob Blackman, the then leader of the Council, who supported our view and suggested a different site should be found by British Rail for their station.

In the meantime, British Rail was still determined to kick us out of the market and offered us premises outside the market which, in our opinion, was unsatisfactory and would substantially reduce our trading position and after due consideration, we rejected their offer. The matter then proceeded to tribunal, where the Council rejected planning permission and with solid support across the borough we eventually won the day.

Yet, again, racism reared its ugly head once more when, in 1982, we decided to open a new store in the up-market Wood Green

Shopping City complex. We made three applications, meeting in full all the stated requirements, but failed even to get a response. Vacancies were still being advertised and we applied for a fourth time, this time through our solicitors who cited discrimination. A prompt response with a listing of the available units was duly received, from which we selected a site which became the company's flagship store.

These episodes are merely some examples of the many shameful and unnecessary road blocks which were all deliberately placed in the way of an emerging small black-owned community business bursting with energy and an appetite for hard work and commitment to realize and win the dreams that occupied their sleeping and waking hours.

Identifying and finding sites in these two busy trading places saw our business grow and prosper. Despite the road blocks of Ridley Road and Wood Green, it would be true to say that we were filled with a sense of purpose and nothing would stop us from pressing on, or deflect us from the goals we had set ourselves. Another five stores were subsequently opened in other London locations, together with a unit in Birmingham which doubled as a retail and wholesale outlet.

The retail sector of the business had now grown to eight stores which called for focused attention and divisional status. In addition to the specialist items carried, our customers and the public in general required all the associated toiletries such as tooth paste, deodorants and the like that make up the complete bathroom collection. Responsibility for building this product category of the business fell on the shoulders of Dudley Dryden and his team, which turned out to be superbly complementary and productive. The experiment of crossing over into the general market cosmetic sector neatly got rid of a negative which existed for some time, much to our disadvantage.

White customers, who wanted to support us, complained that there was nothing for them in our stores. In so doing, they overlooked one important fact that our route into toiletries was via an unfulfilled niche left by the general market. Catering to the general market, after our initial experiment, became standard company policy within the limits of affordability without being to the detriment of our core business, a policy which was extended to all our outlets.

The retail outlets also served as locations for paying for or collecting airline tickets to the Caribbean destinations which were purchased through our associate travel business, Dyke & Dryden shipping and travel, linked to the Inter-Caribbean Social Club, which handled our charter flights operations from time to time and gave us a stake in this segment of the travel industry.

Quite apart from the employment opportunities provided by the stores, they acted as meeting places for countless organisations engaged in community matters of mutual interest. These sometimes included social gatherings, cultural expositions, supplementary school programmes and some of the issues connected with black youth and the police, a problem with which Dudley was heavily engaged. Service to the community was in many ways central to the company's corporate responsibility to thousands of loyal customers who showed their appreciation for our services by supporting all our commercial activities.

CHAPTER 5

COMING FACE TO FACE WITH CUSTOMERS

'Hard work and perseverance yield great dividends. There is no short cut, no alternative route, to greatness.'
—Professor Charles Anyanwu.

'A one to one conversation with members of your customer base whereever possible, more often than not, always helps to build and strengthen your trading position.'
—Anthony Wade

Coming face to face with customers takes me back to the start of where, in truth, my business journey really began. It was the place where all the fun started to happen. Unlike many of my contemporaries of the day, my vision and place in society was seen as being daring, considering all the odds that were stacked against my adventure into the fierce cut-throat world of trading.

With literally no start-up capital; no chemistry skills, finding one's way around in the jungle of the market place for contacts and supplies was at first a gigantic challenge. One might in those early days describe it as a feat of courage, or perhaps one could put it down to the acid test of the spirit of the entrepreneur and the resolve to prove to oneself, that you can be a winner if you try. Whatever it was, this was a serious attempt to make our presence felt and provide a service that was desperately needed by our community.

Entering the industry at the retail end as I did was a stroke of good fortune for me. I was soon to learn that the shop floor was the ideal place in which to learn and gain a broad understanding of the marketplace, the sources of supply and of putting together a workable structure of developing my ideas. I was soon to discover that it was the place to meet the public, who would tell me what their needs were and from there on, it was up to the entrepreneur to make every attempt to satisfy those needs and in the process build good customer relationships and at the same time simultaneously build the business.

The shop floor turned out to be the perfect place for information gathering, to earn their trust and respect. In fact, it was the front line where the real action was, for a course of intensive lessons on which business decisions would be made. My career in the industry started on the shop floor and progressed through its many different segments: buying; selling and marketing; wholesaling; distribution; exporting; manufacturing; and gathering opportunity for practical hands-on management of the business and a rounded understanding of the industry itself as a whole.

However much of a cliché, the saying *'Necessity is the mother of invention'* may be, coping with the many areas of responsibility that landed on my lap, proved it true in my case. In truth, I was soon to discover that many of our clients shopped our markets from all parts Africa and getting to cater for the needs of these very important customers soon became my top priority.

Offloading part of my day-to-day responsibilities soon became an absolute necessity if we were to continue to make progress. The first area of which I needed to relieve myself of was the day-to-day management of our stores. It went to a very able member of staff, Mrs Elsa Robinson, a hairdresser by profession. She became our first employee in this department. Control of the main source of the weekly cash that fuelled the growth of the business was not to be taken lightly and Elsa brought to the table all the ingredients that made the business fly. Her all-round skills and dedication to the company were exemplary. Under her brilliant management and watchful eye, the retail division prospered. As a hairdresser, she was shrewd and able to handle all the very many technical questions about hair loss and breakage and deal with the ongoing obsession of what to use to make the hair grow, or what were the merits of one product against another.

It was a most interesting time, where being innovative and solution focussed in dealing with the many challenges that presented themselves in those early days, were stimulating. It called for good all round management skills, being versed in product knowledge that helped to put your customer at ease. The point was that most customers expected you to have ready answers to all their questions. One question that always aroused my sympathy came from white mothers of mixed-race children, or those with adopted black children, *'I am at a loss as to what to do with my child's hair. Please, can you help?'*

Cases like these were both sensitive and touching, and staff had to be trained how to handle them. Children with short hair presented little or no problem as products with a high glycerine content would always loosen tight curly hair, making it soft and manageable. On the other hand, those with long hair may need to have it cut, or treated with a specially formulated relaxer for children.

Elsa was a gifted communicator in imparting knowledge and among her many roles, was the induction of all new sales personnel for the stores and was responsible for the delivery of our ongoing educational training programmes, which were the hallmark of our brand.

Among the many items we carried were wigs and hair attachments which at the time were high-fashion accessories. It was always a delight to listen to Elsa spinning a great selling line in her sales pitch. *'Smart women's wardrobes,'* she insisted, *'should never be without a collection of the hair fashions of the day.'* She would also explain that, for a busy working woman, wigs were also a welcome necessity especially when there were countless demands on her time with none to spare for a visit the hairdresser. Wigs, she insisted, as she gave her convincing assurance to the customer, were the answer in keeping her hair appearances both satisfying and presentable. In addition to sale of wigs and hair pieces, were the accessories that went with them. There were three spray items, one for cleaning another for conditioning and the third was a holding spray to keep a particular style in place.

What is important about these items is that Elsa would always ensure that all of her customers would have the sprays. The items formerly traded as NP products owned by an English company. The company gave up supplying the products as a result of falling sales of wigs to European women who were their major customers. What NP products did not know was that Dyke & Dryden had a strong demand among its customers for their items and through an intermediary bought the brands and eventually managed to obtain the trade mark for our company. This acquisition was a fine piece of innovative footwork which worked to our advantage.

CHAPTER 6

MANAGERIAL CHANGES THAT
DROVE THE BUSINESS FORWARD

This phase of managing change is of critical importance for the company's future growth and prosperity and I have been keenly aware of the importance of surrounding myself with a good team. As good as my appetite and enthusiasm for getting things done, I soon realized that the strain and pressures of being a jack-of-all-areas of work soon began to tell.

Urgent help had to be brought on board. Eventually, after an extensive search and numerous interviews, someone from where I least expected, answered my shop window advert. The surprise was that the candidate was a white English young man who met all the requirements for the job, minus that he had no product knowledge whatever. I quickly advanced that this was not a problem as long as you are willing to learn and explained that I myself was in the same situation as he is now. I discovered during his interview that he had the right attitude and I on the other hand felt pretty good about my training skills. He shared my appetite for hard work and a willingness to be trained and had no hang ups about working for a black company. This situation challenged us both, for the order of the day in the early years was exclusively the other way round. The boss would be white, but never black and this was clearly a discrimination-testing exercise. Jeff's appointment was a test of my inter-personal skills and on the job management training.

In this scenario, working shoulder to shoulder was a foundation-learning experience at its best. I learned, at first-hand, what the employee was capable of delivering and on the other hand, I got across what the goal of the business was all about and what his role was expected to be, as well as his reward in helping to achieve the targets that had been set.

Transparency in these two areas of the workplace helped to create a good healthy organisation. Getting the principle of transparency right from the start brings to the forefront what can be expected in dealing with staff recruitment. This has been a factor which scored high on the company's questionnaire.

Transparency was among the many things that helped the company to grow and achieve its objectives. It became a core value in underlining the all important element of trust that led to the company's prosperity and encouraged that essential feel-good factor of 'being part of the team'. This policy worked in the company's best interest, with a low staff turnover and loyalty on which I could count on. This method of working assisted me in developing what was to become one of my most important skills: the ability to get things done by the people around me.

Retail And Professional Growth Segments

Several positive things were happening at the same time that led directly to the expansion of the hairdressing salon businesses. Black women had always taken a keen interest in their appearance and especially their hair. They would pay for whatever treatment was required to get the results and look that was in fashion. In fact, one of the most important company developments was providing the profession with choice of products and the service that went with them made a huge difference. Indeed, no self-respecting lady would ever want to be seen without wearing the latest hair fashion.

From the company's standpoint, hairdressing salons had sprung up in substantial numbers around the capital. These represented the single largest sector of black-owned businesses. Their role and influence were, therefore, of major significance and demanded my undivided special attention as I tried to get this group to work together for the common good of their profession and of the industry as a whole.

It was absolutely essential that an organisation to set standards and provide a code of conduct to work by and regulate an ethical behavioural pattern for the profession was urgently put in place. In this connection, I personally took the lead in facilitating the development of such a code. Getting the project off the ground was surprisingly simple. My secretary circulated invitations to all known hairdressers across town to attend a meeting at our warehouse. It was truly gratifying to see the response of an excited turnout for this meeting which led directly to the creation of CASH, the Caribbean Afro Society of Hairdressers.

The next phase of the development was the implementation of London-wide delivery service to meet the needs of the profession. This was then followed by a national distribution network outside the capital to cover towns with large black populations. By 1982, our growth explosion was so phenomenal that it overwhelmed the current management structure of the company. Urgent steps were needed to cope with this surge in activity. A professional management team was desperately needed, together with adequate warehousing and management systems to keep pace with the company's growth.

Formalising of the Company's Management Team

Of equal importance, too, was to need consideration to the overall management structure of the company. In the first place, it was necessary to formalise the directors' individual managerial responsibilities within the organisation. Our auditors, Newman Harris & Co., were invited to deal with what was, after all, a delicate undertaking, in that my colleagues were founding members. When I came on board two years later, we simply carried on with jobs which we considered ourselves best at doing in an ad hoc fashion.

Len Dyke had assumed the role of Chairman with Dudley Dryden as his Deputy while I was as the new kid on the block, assumed a Secretarial role and fitted in wherever help was required. Yet for all intents and purposes, I was what you might call the dogsbody, with my nose in everything that was taking place.

Newman Harris & Co, acted as both judge and jury. Armed with an A4 writing pad and pencil, he sat us down around a big table and fired questions at each of us in turn about our day jobs in the business. Based on our answers, he determined what our respective formal titles should be. We all three accepted his recommendations which on the basis of my diverse roles, he determined that I become Chairman and Managing director of the company. His advice was readily accepted all round and we pressed on respecting and applying his recommendations.

Major decisive changes were to flow in all directions throughout the entire organisation with regard to policy direction and leadership. My failure to accept my partner's suggestion to rename the company Dyke Dryden & Wade when I joined had sent mixed messages to staff and the public at large. This had a negative effect in a number ways and in particular on the part of people wanting to do business with the company, but at times only wanted to deal with the names that appeared on the facia board which, of course, were my two colleagues.

Financing the Business and Financial Control

Our early low-cost financing operation now needed a much more rounded corporate structure, which was to further test the founders' staying power in the new environment, where substantially larger sums of money were needed to finance the expansion of the business. Recognising this need was, in itself, part of the answer, but funding this leap forward became a crisis. Up to this point, we were trading for cash with a nominal bank facility of £2,500—the sum borrowed at the setting up of the business. It is also appropriate to mention that the above sum was secured by way of a second charge on the homes of the three partners and the life insurance policies we had at the time.

With the help of our auditors, a reputable firm based at Cavendish Square in London's West End, we approached our bankers with a properly prepared programme for vans, increased stockholding and additional staff. Annual turnover at the time was £250,000 and cash flow projections showed quite clearly that the £10,000 we were looking for could easily be met. But our small borrowing request was rejected by the manager at Barclays Bank in Lordship Lane. This was a major blow and explains just how some financial organisations held back legitimate black businesses, despite good trading records.

In this particular case, all the evidence leaves us to come to only one conclusion, that of blatant discrimination because of the colour of our skins. On the suggestion of our auditors, we decided on a change of bank and succeeded in getting an offer of £15,000 almost twice of what we were looking for from the National Westminster Bank based on the same forecast offered to our previous bank. With new business funding in place from the National Westminster, steps were immediately taken to implement our expansion programme. A recruitment drive was set in motion to find people who shared our vision and values and were willing to make a solid commitment.

The Senior Management Team

Our earliest fulltime secretarial support was provided by a wonderfully creative friend Mrs Joan Sam, who was always bubbling with drive, energy and enthusiasm. She was in a word dynamite and a tower of strength in those early days, bouncing ideas off me all the time. She eventually confided to me one day that her true calling was to become a hairdresser and without any hesitation, I offered my wholehearted support and encouragement. I further explained to her that I would miss her, but instinctively I knew that she would do well in anything she had set her mind to do. On parting, I asked her to make me one small promise, that when she finished her training that she would come back and see me for a chat and she did.

This move, as I expected, was successful for Joan. With her grit, drive and ambition, she succeeded in everything she had set out to do. What I did not factor in at the time was what a coup it would be for Dyke and Dryden! That story will be revealed later on.

It took a while to fill the vacancy left by Joan's departure. In the meantime, to our great surprise, a dear retired friend, known to us only as Miss Dorman, volunteered to hold the fort until we found a suitable replacement to fill the post. She belonged to the old school of thoroughness and imparted some lessons which left their mark on the business. This act of kindness is a great and memorable one which will always be remembered in the Dyke and Dryden story.

The post left by Miss Dorman was magnificently filled by Mrs Pearl Goodridge who came on board as office manager and was later promoted to Resources Development Manager. She did a splendid job in putting together a superb administrative unit which made all the difference, in beefing-up the all-round office efficiency.

Her skills lent themselves particularly well to organisational issues, problem-solving, conducting interviews and report writing, all of which made decision-making for me much easier. She was an excellent team player, very dependable and with honesty beyond reproach. Pearl and I have continued to keep in touch and the following extract on the role I played in the life of the company. My proof reader was so impressed with what I had to say about her that she arranged for a statement directly from her:

A.E.S. Wade was my 'boss' for 10 years. He was an excellent example of a good leader, a visionary, in his choice of business. He was never afraid to 'break new ground' at the same time encouraging others to venture into their own businesses.

He was never too busy to become involved in government organisations which were set up to assist and develop members of the society/community. He is the epitome of one who serves his fellowman and country. He was my mentor, my inspiration; one who saw possibilities and made them become a reality.

On my return to Barbados in 1988, I worked as a human resources manager for American Airlines and in my interaction with the staff became aware of the need for a nursery facility near the workplace in the city.

After some research (a practice learnt from Tony Wade) I opened a day care centre, which caters for children between ages three months to five years. We have just celebrated 20 years in business and he was my inspiration.

Another great find in the early days of the business was Rudi Page. He possessed great marketing and selling skills and came on board as sales manager, leading and inspiring a small team, who together succeeded in opening up extensive territorial presence and brand awareness across the entire country. Rudi was later promoted to sales and marketing manager and was later to play a key role in the launch of the company's subsidiary Afro Hair & Beauty. He was full of drive and ambition and today runs his own company, Statecraft Consulting Ltd, a business that has built a good track record.

The next key post to be filled was for the company's own internal full time accountant to implement and manage urgently needed systems to control the business. This position was widely advertised and produced good responses from candidates from some impressive backgrounds. Included in the listing was a young, newly qualified black accountant. The sifting process was carried out by our auditors and after much discussion, they suggested that we recruit persons with emphasis on experience.

We respected their views which were valid. We were, however, acutely aware that among the many factors holding back the black community was the lack of opportunity to gain experience in areas such as the one we were offering. On that basis, we selected Kingsley Peter, the newly qualified black accountant. He was articulate and professional in his approach to his work and lived up to our expectations of him. He justified the faith we had placed in him. He was a 'whiz' with figures and soon earned himself the nickname, of 'boy genius'. He represented the company well, his advice was sound and he was eventually promoted to the Board as financial director. He has since moved on, with one of the most senior positions in British industry, that of area financial controller, South East Network Services Division, for the National Grid, one of the top 100 companies in the country.

At the centre of the company's progress was its warehousing, stockholding and distribution management. It was one of the many roles filled by myself, knowing only too well that stock was key to everything else and required prudent attention at all times. This meant constantly evaluating purchases of adequate stock levels, its safe keeping and the turns. In short, it meant keeping an eye on all the processes that determined the result on the bottom line of the company's balance sheet.

The final appointment to complete our senior management team was that of the Warehouse Manager which went to Mr. Grantley Hedley. Grantley came from a soldiering background and had developed excellent organisational skills and was strong on discipline. This was just one of the qualities needed to marshal the stock pickers and packers to keep the distribution lines moving.

On the front desk of the company's efforts was Mrs Evelyn Dyke, who I always referred to as the *'First Lady of Dyke & Dryden'*. At her desk, she was the first point of contact with customers. With her sharp communication skills, she was brilliant in putting customers at ease and could charm the most hesitant shopper into parting with some of their cash. Her performance earned her the position of export manager, working closely with me on anything considered to be a sizeable purchase. Her skill in getting the company's own brands included in the mix of any purchases was quite remarkable and significantly aided our market penetration of the company's own products.

With the new management team now in place, it was time to make sure that everyone clearly understood the company's operating philosophy: 'We must at all times conduct our business with professionalism, honesty and integrity; raise our self-esteem and awareness of the community we serve, understanding that our success will at the end of the day be measured only by the service we give.'

I cannot claim that it was all I wanted it to be, but suffice to say that it helped the process of building our brands and the profile of our organisation.

The marketing and PR functions were handled in-house. However, events that needed some specialist attention were contracted out from time to time. This method of operation worked well for us leaving senior managers in control of our overall plans. Closely controlled reporting sessions managed by myself ensured that we stayed on top of every priority project.

Taking On The World

Having filled all our senior management positions, it seemed that it was time for some respite from the rigours of the daily grind. This assignment, however, was an extremely difficult thing to do, not because I trusted no one, but more so perhaps because the matter of steering the ship had taken me over by being there first in the morning and the last to leave at night.

I discovered that staff nicknamed me 'Mr Go-go-holic', but never to my face. Kay Osborne, Senior Vice President at M & M Products, one of our major US suppliers, labelled me, *'The man from Dyke & Dryden with the globe on his head.'* I had never questioned what she meant, but believed it had something to do with us bumping into each other in world markets.

British industry was particularly slow in dealing with what was an obvious gap in our segment of the beauty care industry. Manufacturers like Cheeseborough-Ponds, for example, were exporting their facial cosmetics to the Caribbean and neglecting a local market segment right in their own back yard. We were re-importing their products back into the UK to fill the gap in the market and naturally we had a good chuckle at their lack of vision which worked to our advantage and led to us getting into manufacturing our own brands.

American companies were in the forefront of the development of Afro products suitable for the use by folks with tight curly hair and dark and brown skin types. The proliferation of their products had become increasingly available in our market, across Europe and in Africa and Dyke & Dryden was to play an important role in providing part of the solution to share in this activity here in Britain.

A key plank in our business plan was to ensure that we carried good stocks at all times, which meant establishing good channels of supply out of the USA where the industry was already well developed. To accomplish this part of the plan, it meant making direct contact with the key players and decision makers in the industry. An itinerary was put together by Pearl Goodridge covering five states that I was to visit: New York; New Jersey; Chicago; Tennessee and Atlanta.

During all these visits, my welcome was one full of warmth with everyone keen on broadening their markets and saw our meetings as new chapters in their company's fortunes. This became a reality. Links were established and purchases made from all firms visited and a one-to-one rapport followed, with senior personnel anxious to ensure their share in what was now fast becoming a global market in the ethnic hair and skincare industry.

Gary Gardener, President of the USA-based Soft Sheen Inc., shared with me his vision. He explained that his sights were set on the world as his market, reasoning that in the USA, his market was limited to a mere 30 million people, whereas in Africa alone he could have access to 200 million people. His vision and thinking made an impression on me and little did I know that in that first meeting he also had Dyke & Dryden as a target in his sights and eventually Soft Sheen bought a controlling interest in our company in November 1987 by acquiring the shares of my two colleagues.

Among the major players in the industry at the time was M & M Products Company that operated out of Atlanta, Georgia. As it happened Mr Therman Mc-Kenzie was a joint President of M&M Products. As luck would have it, he was slated to be the keynote speaker for the Black Business Promotion Conference in London, jointly sponsored by the UK Caribbean Chamber of Commerce of and the Commission for Racial Equality.

In his speech, Mr. Mc Kenzie dubbed the UK, as far as his company was concerned 'the fifty-first state'. His glee was certainly understandable because in 1986, when he made this remark, purchases by Dyke & Dryden from his company was in excess of $1 million dollars in that year.

The conference was a high profile affair, attended by the Rt. Hon Michael Hestletine, the then Secretary of State for the Environment and the Minister for Small Firms, Mr John McGregor. It was aimed at drawing attention to the difficulties black business people faced in their search for funding.

All the major UK banks were represented and the conference had as its theme, Ethnic Business Development and the Role of the Banks. Mr McKenzie's keynote speech as a self-made black American multi-millionaire, did much in highlighting some of the steps needed to be taken by the banks on this side of the Atlantic. It was, in part, a crusade pursued by Dyke & Dryden and the Chamber on behalf of the Britain's black community.

A survey of the Chamber's membership after the conference showed that little or nothing had happened to improve the desperate need for funding. The outcome was a dismal disappointment for the Chamber and its members.

My initial American trip had laid the foundations of the ethnic hair care industry in the UK and changed for all times the plight of black women's impoverished lack of choice as far cosmetics were concerned. The company was to play a most important role in this unhappy situation, by launching out into manufacturing our own brands in the Britain.

Fuelling the pace of development in the industry was the breakthrough in the chemistry of hair which had a liberating effect for millions of black women the world over. The contention that women are never satisfied with what they have could not be truer than with hair, be it white women or black women. People with straight hair, change their hair formation by the use of thio-glycolic acid on rollers to make it curly, whereas black people's natural curly hair is processed with sodium hydroxide, a chemical used to make it straight.

In the mid-1950's, George E Johnson, of Johnson Products Company, developed the Ultra Sheen chemical straitening process for black hair, which revolutionised the industry. He made a fortune for his company and was the first black-owned company to be floated on the New York Stock Exchange.

The late 1970's and early 1980's saw another revolution with the reverse use of the thio-glycolic formula for processing naturally curly hair which ushered in the internationally acclaimed hair fashion of the 'wet look', 'dry look', 'curly look' and 'wavy look', and a whole host of other variations which made fortunes for many companies.

Lessons Learnt

There were very many lessons learned in looking back. Dyke & Dryden was to gain enormously from our early entry into the industry, but at a glance, we could see some of the many errors we made. Most of our agency distribution arrangements, for example, were concluded by way of a handshake rather than by documented formal contracts. Here was lack of experience on my part for, as it turned out, once the manufacturer's brands we introduced were established in the market, loyalty went out of the window.

Another fatal mistake was our policy of heavy discounting to some of our sub-distributors who would later became our major competition. The market had by then expanded significantly and by 1986 company turnover had reached the magical figure of £5 million, which at the time was quite an achievement for a black owned business in the UK. Len, Dudley and I always regarded modesty as a virtue and the credit for this performance always went to our staff, which were in truth the backbone of the business.

Time For Diversification

Our business was by its very nature organic and some hedging in a market that was maturing called for action to safeguard our position. Our success had spawned some big fish who were vigorously swimming after us. An urgent structural review was, therefore, once again necessary while we were still ahead of the game. Two options were considered. One was to diversify into property, which we did by buying up some of the freehold retail properties we occupied. The other, was to try and control our destiny by getting into manufacturing. This was a major turning point for the company in that it removed our total dependence on imported products. More about this subject later.

The overall market place needed to be looked at however and for this exercise we engaged the services of a consultant whose brief was to identify our strengths and our weaknesses and provide a road map for the next five years. A brief with time-scales was agreed upon and signed by both parties with 50 per cent of the fees paid in advance and the balance paid on completion of the assignment.

Two weeks before we were to receive the consultant's report, I went on a short visit to one of our major suppliers in Atlanta and was invited to lunch by the Vice President of sales. To my horror, my host produced a copy of the report we had ordered which was offered to them and others at a price. I gasped in utter disbelief at the betrayal of the trust we had placed in the consultant.

Stung by this treachery, our well laid plans were now in ruin— frustrated in our attempt to stay ahead of the competition. Unknown to the consultant, however, an alternative plan was on the drawing board which only needed refinement. This was put into action with immediate effect and saved us from a certain catastrophic demise.

We were always concerned that total reliance on American products was not in our best interests and that steps need to be taken to have similar items manufactured in the UK. Preparatory work had already begun in connection with registering trademarks, product formulation and locating suitable packaging contractors to do the work.

Some good fortune was on our side. Enter Mrs Joan Sam my previous secretary who went off to study hairdressing. We now have a home-grown hair professional in the person of Joan Sam, who earlier served the company as a loyal secretary and now a proficient hair artiste, coming out of our own stable as it were, to carry out product testing on trial runs and to monitor usage results and provide educational seminars. This was the scenario I envisioned when I asked Joan to come back and see me when her training was through and she did.

It was hard to believe, seeing the picture I had in my head unfolding before my eyes; the birth of Supreme School of Hair Dressing had arrived in which our company became part shareholder. This was a tactical move which served us well as we moved into manufacturing. Joan's intervention was pivotal in strengthening and consolidating our position in the industry. It was a happy and enjoyable working partnership with Joan that helped to lay the foundation stones of the UK black hair care industry.

CHAPTER 7

A STRATEGIC MOVE INTO MANUFACTURING

Self-confidence, vision and a creative mind are strengths among man's finest gifts. Understanding your gifts and having the confidence to share them with others is central to attaining one's goals in life. It is sharing your gifts that, in turn, often impact the lives of others throughout the ages. Whatever one's station in life, it is by being action-orientated and stimulated that satisfies the thirst of an enquiring mind.

On my rounds of speaking engagements, one of the most frequently asked questions that I am asked is *'What led you to get involved in manufacturing, especially since you had no background in that field, nor any working experience with chemicals?'* This is a great question and one that I often answer with a schoolboy's relish: What made the chicken cross the road? The simple answer is of course, to get to the other side. Seriously, you educate yourself about what you want to do or alternatively you buy in the expertise you require.

Partial self-sufficiency was the true thinking behind creating our own brands. In the first place, this was the result of some visionary thinking—looking ahead and with a sense of protecting our backs—to try and ensure a measure of independence and sustainability. I was mindful that once we had carried out the initial cost and opened up the market that our suppliers would move in and capture our territory, which was exactly what they attempted to do.

A good example of this tasteless behavioural pattern, I observed by Soft Sheen in less than one year after purchasing two thirds of the equity in my company. They were undermining the expressed reason for which they bought i.e., to grow and strengthen Dyke & Dryden's base. But they were soon to discover they were losing us what was our major strength—by selling to our customers behind our backs.

Another major consideration was my belief that we should start laying the groundwork for black hair and skin care products made in Britain to meet the needs of a young and ever increasing population, rather than importing tons of water from across the Atlantic. Additionally, there were other long-term benefits to be derived from such a policy. The development of the relevant skills and the creation of a pool of labour for employment and export opportunities.

With this potential in mind, work was already in progress for the preparation of formulas, trademarks, the engagement of graphic artists for packaging and a search for suitable contract packers. There were, as usual, a number of considerations to take into account in going down that road. In Britain, there was no history of the skills in manufacturing products suitable for lack hair and skin types. There was, too, the question of the risk that our customers may not be willing to change from the use of items to which they had become accustomed. This was a major challenge and a reasonable risk I was prepared to take.

While this was all going on in my head, I was also thinking of opening up new markets. Situations in business sometimes force you to wear several hats at the same time. In this connection, I have to say that it was also a period during which I succeeded in persuading some of my American suppliers to accord my company decent credit facilities to enable us to open up a market that was still virgin territory. In return, I suggested that I was willing to act as their unpaid salesperson for opening up the market from which we would all benefit.

This gesture was a tasty appetiser and met with the prompt approval of all present. It was with concealed delight that I saw my proposal accepted by all the key players with no reservation. Looking back on this feat, it was one of those situations in which tact, assertiveness and conviction-driven arguments seized the moment and won the day.

The great thing about this deal was gaining access to stock. It was a strategic move in every sense of the word, for it held the keys to getting around funding problems the company was experiencing by the lack of support from my bankers in the UK. After firm all-round handshakes on the deals and once out of sight, I couldn't stop myself smiling on the plane all the way back home to unload my soul of the good news to my partners. This was a tremendous turning point for the company with a twin solution for the future and a confident message for the industry.

Stock availability is the lifeblood of the company and I was always able to honour the undertakings I gave to my suppliers which ensured a regular flow of stock. On the other hand, it became easier to sell in our new in-house brand on the back of well established brands which already existed in the market with better margins for ourselves as suppliers and were able to offer more competitive prices for our customers.

Paul Davis of Tor Chemicals and Joan Sam of Supreme Super Curl Were the Team Who Perfected the Dream

I recall with immense satisfaction, what has been one of the most enjoyable episodes during my entire business career and which indeed as I worked alongside two of the nicest people I had ever met. I had been dreaming and carrying around in head for the longest time the idea of having our own brands and it was Paul Davis and Joan Sam who were the two persons to make my dream a reality.

Joan worked with me as my secretary for about three years and together we made a great team . She was always bouncing ideas off me and I instinctively knew there was something special about her. One day she confided to me that enjoyed working for the company but her true calling was to be a hairdresser. I thanked her for her service and wished her well. I explained that I would miss her and asked her once she finished her training to come back to see us and she did.

In pursuing my product development idea, I struck up a friendship with Paul Davis, the owner of a young and ambitious recently established chemical company trading as Tor Chemicals, based in South London. He was a man filled with the spirit of adventure and after confiding in him what I wanted to achieve, he wasted no time in getting to work experimenting with formulations he had not handled before. He was later to become my guru and great friend.

This bold new stride into the world of manufacturing came with the launch of our Supreme Super Curl brand, which as the name suggests, was a product designed to cater for the 'curly' look and represented a major breakthrough for the company. Timing was of the essence and a key factor in the brand's success, lay especially in that hair fashions at the time were changing. Luckily for us, we were carried along on the crest of the wave! This was a significant breakthrough for British industry for this was the first gel perm formulated and developed in the UK. It was branded and trademarked under the brand name of Supreme Super Curl.

I offered my congratulations on her new vocation. *'What are your plans now I enquired?'* *'Well'* she said, her voice quaking with emotion, *'I would like to open a salon,'* she replied, but had no money. *'Money is not everything,'* I responded, *'provided you are willing to have my colleagues and me as partners, go and find a suitable place and you can consider this a done deal on the basis of a 25 per cent share each of £100 capital.'* In a matter of weeks Salon Supreme was up and running with Joan both as company Secretary and also a Director of the business with me as Managing Director. Len and Dudley agreed with my ideas and were happy to go along with the deal I presented.

The jigsaw of this project was in my head all along and now it became a reality. It was the first stage of an action plan, followed by a product line branded Supreme Supercurl. From my years of working alongside Joan I knew, instinctively, that anything she had set her mind to she would make a success of it. Joan Sam shares her perspective of her journey with Dyke & Dryden:

Anthony Edward Samuel Wade was instrumental in the early development of my hairdressing career which was encouraged by all three directors of the company when I started working for them in the early 1960's in West Green Road, Tottenham, North London. During my employment there, I expressed my wish to qualify as a hairdresser and then open a hairdressing salon and school. I was encouraged to take the first step towards that dream and I enrolled in the well-respected Morris Masterclass in London's West End. After graduating with honours, Mr. Morris asked me to become a tutor, which I readily accepted, as that experience was invaluable to achieving my ultimate aim to go into the beauty business.

I enjoyed my teaching job immensely, but, eventually, I knew I had to return to fulfilling my goals. I always kept in touch with Dyke & Dryden and especially with Mr. Wade as I had recognised a special like mindedness between us. We had the same positive approach to business development ideas and there were many things I could learn from him and maybe vice versa. My huge problem at that time however was lack of enough finance. Tony and the other directors decided to become my partners and Supreme Hair Salon and School of Hairdressing was born.

The business flourished, gaining recognition from Local Government offices, enabling us to win contracts to train unemployed young people and adults. Apart from locally, we were getting applications from abroad and had a healthy influx of overseas students.

With that going well, Tony and I started to work on product development ideas with our chemist, which resulted in us travelling to The Bronner Brothers Hair show in Atlanta, USA and visiting the home of the founder of the M&M International Hair Co. and meeting a few celebrities on the way.

Tony and I were invited to Nigeria to take part in the first Oyo State Hair exhibition. There, we successfully demonstrated our own products which ultimately became one of the most popular curl imports from the UK.

There is so much more to my business experiences with Tony Wade and his positive influences on me, firstly as my boss and then as a business partner and now friend for always. He is a man with a vision which develops into a mission; a man with integrity and a strong sense of fair play to other human beings. I have been a better person for knowing him and honoured to be called his friend.

Research and Development

It follows that our research and development breakthrough was a big new stride for British industry as a whole. In the first place it removed our total dependence on US manufactured products for the black community. Commenting on our mutual success, Paul had this to say: *'We will always be indebted to Tony Wade for his vision and drive in pushing us into this direction, which provided much rewarding work and employment for our company.'*

Paul's factory was situated just off the Old Kent Road where some fabulous eating houses were located. Paul, Joan and I made frequent visits to these establishments to celebrate after seeing at first hand the progress during our visits to the factory where we were filled with excitement as Paul walked us through the many stages of products coming to fruition. These were moments filled with a deep sense of achievement and the sweet smell of success as we witnessed the products in which we had invested our ideas, time and energy come off the filling lines.

The range comprised a gel perm, a neutralising solution, shampoos, conditioners and hair pomades. At the same time, John Cobb, a design consultant, was brought on board as part of the development team to handle our graphic designs, layout packaging and marketing requirements including press releases. This was a time of great excitement for everyone throughout the organisation.

The brand performed well beyond our wildest dreams to the extent that Tor Chemicals was unable to cope with the demand. Another contract packer had to be found in an effort to satisfy the enormous demand and also to ensure that we experienced no shortages in our supply chain. Getting this situation reconciled proved a little delicate to handle and great care had to be taken not to upset the original and painstaking technical development work carried out by my good friend, Paul.

A satisfactory solution was found by leaving the professional products with Tor Chemicals, the company who originated the brand. Thioglycolic acid, the active ingredient in the gel perm which breaks down the sulphur dioxide bonds of the hair, thus enabling change in its natural configuration from small tight curls to whatever the desired size and shape the patron requires.

To ensure effectiveness, the product must always be produced at the right pH balance and Paul, to his credit, had mastered this technique. Chemical processing of the hair, by its very nature, causes substantial moisture loss which must be replaced by daily doses of moisturising treatments essential for chemically treated hair. The net result is a large volume of retail sales of the after care items.

Manufacturing, as it happened, turned out to be another giant step for the company and our every move was being closely monitored by our competition both at home and abroad. The Americans now saw us a threat and became much more active in our market. We responded by making much of our home-grown brands and used the slogan 'Made in Britain', of which we were, naturally, justly proud.

DHL, a Bradford-based company, won the contract for initially supplying the retail items for Super Curl and eventually became our largest supplier, though not without some gentle persuasion. At our first meeting, we sensed some unease, which turned out to be the not unfamiliar reluctance of some companies not wanting to do business with a black-owned company. The owners, Donald and Tony Lang were about to send us away but gave each other a signal across the table and in their own words revealed later, '... *agreed to take a chance*' on us.

After agreeing on terms, work got underway for a trial run and to their astonishment, found they were forced to increase their staff levels to cope with the additional work we were putting their way. Months later, a much larger factory was acquired to accommodate our business. Their operational space by then had increased from 5,000 sq. ft to 48,000 sq. ft.

DHL's Managing Director, Tony Lang, an ardent cricket lover, had among his most treasured possessions a vintage cricket bat that carried the signatures of all the players who had taken part in the vintage Test Series England versus West Indies in 1984. He showed off his precious trophy to me and half-jokingly challenged me to a wager. If in any one year I were to spend £500,000 with his company, I could have his bat. Not one for refusing a challenge, I confidently accepted his wager! In the next year I spent £800,000 with him, and his precious trophy is now mine and takes pride of place in my collection of trophies.

Some years later, over lunch, Donald Lang, Tony's father admitted to me that they nearly lost a business opportunity of a lifetime simply by being bigoted. *'You taught us a great lesson,'* he said, that they would never forget. We built a great business friendship and I never doubted his sincerity, but one thing for sure happened. I opened their eyes and changed their negative thinking into a positive force for good and a case for promoting the diversity agenda—live and let live.

Manufacturing, as it turned out, became the company's major strength and earned the company much respect and recognition. It was manufacturing that earned for me membership on the Board of Business in the Community, the 'Captains of industry' club. This phase of the company's development provided not only the best margins, but indeed the measure of independence within the industry I spoke about earlier. In terms of recognition, producing goods for export is one of the principle ways of earning your stripes and slots and to be quoted in the *Working for Export*s magazine. I must concede that the magazine articles describing my export efforts remain a truly satisfying thought!

Natural Beauty Products

Apart from expanding the Super Curl range, we launched a second brand under the banner of Natural Beauty Products which enjoyed an even a much wider appeal by being more inclusive. It carried a full cosmetics range which included face powders, lipsticks, nail polishes, skin creams, soaps and lotions. Whereas the hair treatments included shampoos, conditioners, moisturisers, pomades and hair sprays etc. The introduction of these lines greatly expanded the products range thus reducing the need for imported products.

Completing this new range required a sodium hydroxide professional hair relaxer system for processing the 'straight look'. The launch of this item was not without considerable difficulty. The item, however, succeeded in making its mark and did well, particularly in East and West Africa.

Our curl products were so successful that, for a while, we experimented with a version called Curl Control under our Natural Beauty trade mark and secured two spectacularly successful slots of the curl market, both at home and abroad. For a time, the brands between them dominated some markets in Africa and whereas Curl Control remained the number one selling gel activator in Holland for years.

The Afro Comb or Pick

The introduction of what universally became a black hair accessory, the pick—better known as an Afro comb under our Natural Beauty brand—proved a tough endurance test in the battle against obtaining locally produced supplies. We imported huge numbers of these combs from the US and took a decision that we should produce a comb here in the UK under our Natural Beauty brand. This was a simple process, requiring merely a mould and a slot in a production schedule. After many months approaching supplier after supplier, we almost gave up out of sheer exhaustion in finding a company that was willing to take on our business.

With my attitude not to admit defeat readily, I was still constantly on the lookout for a factory that might just be persuaded to take on this business and as luck would have it, I spotted a company almost on my doorstep while shopping in Wood Green Shopping City. Atlas Plastics exhibited an austere air as I approached a smartly attired uniformed guard. His brass buttons glistened in the sunshine.

I explained to him that I did not have an appointment, but would be glad to see the sales manager if possible. He obliged and trotted off, returning with someone who turned out to be the works foreman.

I explained to the foreman what I wanted to talk about. He very kindly returned with the sales manager, a Mr Gooch, a most courteous gentleman. He invited me to his office to discuss the project and was quite amused with this fork-like thing called a comb which I demonstrated to him by simply combing my own hair. He was even more amused at the sight of this fork-like instrument being put through my hair. It was music to my ears as he agreed that he could produce the item provided we were willing to meet the tooling cost outright. His requirement was a minimum first production run of 15,000 units. I accepted his terms and invited him to provide me with a pro-forma invoice on which I would settle promptly. We got off to a splendid start, with orders building to such an extent that they were unable to keep pace with the volume of demand that came their way.

On one of my visits to the factory, I was tempted to ask the guard why, on my earlier visit, he brought the works foreman to me when I had specifically asked to see the sales manager. *'Well, sir,'* he answered, *'to tell you the truth, we do have a lot of blacks working here and I simply assumed that you were just another one looking for a job.'* This episode is yet another example of a perception held by many folks in our society. He duly apologised and promised me he would be more careful about making that kind of assumption in the future. In the area of manufacturing, the company suffered a decisive blow in its attempt to broaden its horizon with a move into the general market place.

Our Natural Beauty brand has universal appeal to both black and white customers alike, hence the choice of name. We signed a contract for specialist creams and lotions with Thomas Christy & Sons of Aldershot to manufacture to our specification cocoa butter creams and lotions which at the time turned out to be unique in skin care preparations.

There were two new major hurdles to cross: the first of which was to find a white distributor with nationwide distribution outlets and secondly the project needed some additional funding.

The return on investment in the products was good and the distributors approached expressed a willingness to take on the line, provided they could be assured of regular supplies. We were, it seemed, on the dawn of a new day getting into the big white market place, with what was a win, win situation with a unique product for which there was unmistakable demand and with distribution in place.

Sadly, although being involved in every detail of the project up to the point of satisfactory market testing of it by our bank manager's own female users, his wife, his daughters and close friends, our bank still failed to finance an additional sum for the project. This was without a doubt the deadliest blow of them all and an event that really stank, especially in that the bank was earning handsomely from our account — needless to say, we were devastated.

Some months later an identical product line, including the text I wrote, appeared under a different brand name which today is to be found in every high street store in the country. This could so easily have been the Natural Beauty brand, had our bank supported us. The pain of this episode still haunts me. Once again, this explains, in large measure, how the banks have failed the black community.

From the outset, it was patently clear that there was little or no risk involved. The bank held a fixed and floating charge on all the company's assets, which, at the time, were two unencumbered freehold shop premises, a 16,500 sq. ft warehouse with a small mortgage and several prime leasehold properties, together with a charge on stock and debtors. We were being held by belt and braces; this was in addition to the collateral, there was also a second charge on the directors' homes.

Despite the company's many challenges, its manufacturing efforts have had a significant impact on employment in many parts of the county, first, through Tor Chemicals in South London, Wendover House in North London, Hanworth Laboratories in Cambridge, DHL Products in Bradford and a host of other suppliers of packaging and sundry related items. Together these suppliers enlarged our ability to create a significant workforce within the economy. There is no doubt that the failure to embrace the principles of diversity and give opportunity to people with ability and a willingness to produce where possible has cost the nation dearly in lost productivity. Manufacturing became our best move along a path of self-sufficiency and an independent role in the industry and much respect.

CHAPTER 8

MARKETING THE COMPANY'S BRANDS

'Success requires that you work hard, have total commitment and be prepared to make sacrifices.'
—Dr S Prince Akapabio OBE

A challenge I have always contended is that 'intrinsic something' within that always brings out the best in human beings—perhaps by perfecting an invention, by winning a game or testing one's ingenuity at succeeding in doing something remarkably well. Manufacturing our own brands and the effort expended in doing so is a case in point. The entire history of the company has been one loaded with challenges of one kind or another. Pioneering the industry has been a major test of the company's survival instincts, in the face of the many barriers that we found in our path. Winning in this struggle is underlined by the fact that our brands, at the end of day became our major strength in terms of independence and a measure of sustainability.

It might be useful, therefore, to look now at the importance of marketing in the light of the role it will play as one of the key components in our business plan. However, let us first ask the central question: *'What is marketing?'* Marketing is a whole range of activities which include: planning and the introduction of new products; advertising; packaging; salesmanship; public relations and sales promotion; price planning and the provision of an after sale service. This marketing mix complemented each other and has played an important part in our brands success.

With products of our own, a strategic marketing programme with elements of all the above was an absolute necessity if we were to build our brands and carve out a market share. A variety of focussed marketing campaigns were put together—one for the local market and another for overseas markets in which we had connections through our re-export of imported products from the US and from Jamaica.

Soon after we began manufacturing, highly qualified university graduates were coming on board. Among them was Francis Okwesa, who came for an interview in preparation for his thesis in marketing. He liked what he found out about the company and the industry and later joined us as brand manager. He excelled in this role and brought an entirely new dimension to the company's branded projects. His marketing skills were responsible for establishing our brands solidly in some of our most important markets. It is with great respect that I acknowledge the contribution made by Francis.

Jane Hammond of Trident Public Relations Consultants spun a great line in our press releases on the new products. *'A beauty secret known to generations of Caribbean women is now available in the UK to pamper the delicate skins of English women, thanks to Dyke & Dryden,'* she wrote. Jane's spin was bang on cue and produced excellent feedback from our target market, the white population. Among the regular users were our bank manager's wife and daughters who were regular users and loved the creams.

Our generous sampling campaigns did well at creating demand. We knew, too, that we were on to a winner, for the women working at the factory where the product was produced were all white and switched to using our creams, in preference to the ones they used before.

Event Marketing

On the home front, some marketing campaigns took on the feel of great party occasions, full of fun, with events that attracted a large following of young person's bursting with energy to soak up the entertainment which was always an important ingredient in keeping the party spirit fully charged up. Included in the mix were a number of young and beautiful professional women with an eye for the business potential on offer, and who were, therefore, eager to be selected for inclusion as models in what was regarded as the premier fashion and beauty event of the year in the black community.

The search for the company's own 'beauty queen' would inherit the coveted 'Miss Dyke & Dryden' crown, collect a purse, a paid holiday and be on hand to represent the company at suitable worthy events. A similar event was the 'Afro Hair & Beauty Queen'. These events proved to be invaluable marketing occasions for the company. Quite apart from the social networking which these events provided, some saw the exposure as good opportunities to obtain places in glossy magazines, or to appear on posters thus offering a possible chance of getting started on a modelling career, which some of the girls actually did.

Product Launches

Product launches had an air of what came to be known as 'The Show' at which specialist choreographers would be hired to pull things together. While product performance would be key to the big sales push and is always accompanied by some fantastic razzle-dazzle, which the public loved and enjoyed and would travel miles to be a part of, not only for 'The Show', but also for the wining and dining that was always a part of the event. These gatherings were great on-the-spot sales orders taking opportunities which our sales teams would make the most of.

Afro Hair Beauty: A Merchandising Trigger

The founding of Afro Hair & Beauty, the jewel of our marketing campaign, was in a way a 'merchandising trigger' the key that opened doors right across the industry and the international market place. What is Afro Hair and Beauty? Quite simply, it is a trading name that came about as a result of the scarcity of personal hair and skincare preparations to meet the needs of the black women in Britain during the second half of the 20th century.

Founded in 1982, as a subsidiary of Dyke & Dryden Ltd, Afro Hair and Beauty became the marketing arm that drove the black hair and skincare industry in the UK. This development brought choice to people of colour and led directly to opening up the market for black products specifically designed to cater for the needs of black hair and skin types.

The exhibition became known as the market place for drawing to itself manufacturers, traders, hairdressers and anyone connected with the industry. Businesses came from many parts of the world, including the USA, Europe, Africa, Asia and the Caribbean, attracting thousands of followers who had an interest in the industry.

Over a short period of time, the industry generated a huge following of people who were waiting to see this new development. There was a keen sense of interest which found expression by way of the demand for exhibition space among many of the large American companies who were already in the forefront of the industry. Equally, competition came from a number of new enterprises who wanted to be a part of the hustle and bustle, buzz words the event generated which continued to expand the business year after year.

Central to the thinking behind Afro Hair & Beauty was the need for a body dedicated to the introduction of hair and skin care products used by black people, and for the education and proper use of chemicals which can cause immense damage to unsuspecting clients. In a wider context was the need to create an industrial base capable of creating opportunities and employment and in short to aid the growth of related activities and skills within the community. These include arts and craft, presentations of fashion shows, designing of display stands and anything for that matter connected with the exhibition and community development in general. Rudi Page, our Sales and Marketing Manager, was asked to take the lead in liaising with potential exhibitors, exhibition contractors, hairdressers, fashion designers and models, and also to work with Jane Hammond of Trident Public Relations, to put together a project that was to change the face of the industry in the United Kingdom.

Dyke & Dryden had organised what was to be its first trip to the Bronner Brothers Beauty Show in Atlanta, Georgia, in the USA. This Show was likened to a Mecca for the black beauty industry. On show were not only product manufacturers, but there were also equipment suppliers, traders, hairdressers and retailers — the model on which the Afro Hair & Beauty show was based. As a reward for his performance during the previous year, 1981, Rudi Page was sent on a trip where he made the best use of his visit by observing the format and the steps that we might follow in an event in the UK for ourselves.

What did the British show mean in economic terms? In the first place, it meant employment and independence for thousands of people in a variety of ways. There are over 1,000 salons across the country each employing an average workforce of three, making a total of about 3,000 jobs.

On the retail front there were more than 2,000 stores selling black products, employing an average of two to three persons, which meant a further 4,000 to 6,000 jobs. In addition, there are hairdressing schools, manufacturing and developing products for ethnic consumption at home and for export markets. If we were to add the attendant services of management, accounting, sales and marketing, warehousing and distribution, one would quickly see the multiplier effect on employment as a whole and appreciate just how profoundly the industry had affected the lives of so many families.

The company's first exhibition, held at the prestigious five-star Grosvenor House Hotel in Park Lane, was a trail-blazing affair, welcomed by the industry and the public alike. This was a brave step by the hotel and ourselves, as neither of us knew exactly what we were letting ourselves in for.

Black people and their friends, responding to press and radio commercials came out in their thousands, eager to see at first-hand what this new and exciting happening was all about. For the first few hours, the sheer numbers were a cause for concern that we might be unable to accommodate everyone. Disappointing this crowd was the last thing we wanted to do. And so I was gratified that my fears were unfounded. The crowd behaviour was exemplary from start to finish. *'Well done!'* they shouted *'It was about time we had our own show.'* Jane Hammond of Trident Public Relations did a splendid job of creating national and international awareness, filling the venue to capacity.

Lady Dorothy Pitt, the darling of the community and a great supporter of black enterprise, speaking at the opening ceremony, paid a fitting tribute to all the participants from home and those who had travelled from overseas. She declared that the event represented a major landmark in black pioneering history and enterprise. She reminded the gathering that *'Black is beautiful and we must never be tired of saying so or showing how true that is.'*

Her remarks were indeed prophetic, for with 32 years behind it, the exhibition has become a cornerstone in building black enterprise in the UK. American companies saw the exhibition as the shop window for the industry and the ideal platform for expanding their businesses this side of the Atlantic. Lady Pitt was lavish with her praise for the high profile stand promotions which captured the imagination of all present. The media people had not seen anything like this before and commented favourably on the merits of this new development. The exhibition became a central meeting and dealing place for all the major manufacturers from the USA and for traders from the huge markets of Africa and the diverse ethnic settlements that stretched across continental Europe.

The event spanned three days with time set aside for breakdown and shipping away of stocks and equipment. After three full days, day four was naturally a welcome relief for everyone to get away from the hustle and bustle which, though exhausting, had brought satisfaction for most people, traders and shoppers alike.

While we were unable to quantify the volume and value of the business transacted at the end of each year's event, it would be safe to say that the business done usually ran into millions of pounds for the industry. Here was the opportunity to wheel and deal, make special offers and take advantage of the buying and selling activities which was the order of the day.

The exhibition has had an enormous influence on the development of many small ethnic businesses and on the expansion of several medium-sized companies. It has also provided a sizeable number of jobs in its wake. Afro Hair & Beauty became part of our community development policy, by always allocating a number of free stand spaces to small, new business start-ups, enabling them to display their goods, services and skills in a variety of disciplines. Those benefiting included people in the fashion and design industry, in the performing arts, film making, music and dance routines.

As the fame of the event grew over the years, visitors came from all over the world. This influx has had an impact on the local economy by pushing up hotel occupancy levels and increasing the numbers of visitors sampling our fine restaurants and famous stores. The role of the event has been widely recognised at all levels of the establishment and visited by government ministers, Members of Parliament, civic leaders, captains of industry and celebrities of stage and sport.

While the exhibition's key objective was business focussed, it was also packed full of fun and was a great day out for the whole family. Creativity was high on the agenda, offering further opportunities for enterprise. There were competitions such as 'Battle of the Barbers' where barbers sculpted wild and wacky designs: where hairstylists demonstrated their creativeness with day and evening styles 'Battle of the Divas'; the 'National Free-Styling College

Competition' allowed young budding hairstylists to exhibit their originality; and the 'Avant Garde Hair Competition' extravaganza gave opportunity for stylists to allow free reign to their imagination.

In addition, fashion and hair show presentations by many of the exhibitors combined to launch the career of many young up-and-coming hopefuls, some of whom have gone on to become household names. To name a few these included, Mark Morrison, Celetia Cruz, Cardi Revere, Bruce Jeremy and Ade Bakare.

Highlight of the weekend was the 'Miss Afro Hair & Beauty Competition' sponsored by Air Jamaica, an integral part of a charity ball whose proceeds would go to charities such as NCH Action for Children, UNICEF, the African & Caribbean Leukaemia Trust , the Sickle Cell Society and the Caribbean Mental Health Association.

Spirited auctions conducted by the effervescent Garth Crooks, reigned in the bidding with items supplied by celebrities such as Lennox Lewis, Tessa Sanderson, Patrick Agustus, Saracen, Victor Romero Evans and Janet Kay, while others gave generously of their time in support of the many good causes named above.

Claire Jackson, Events Director for ten years and a central pillar in the organisation, says *'I look back on my years spent as Events Director of Afro Hair & Beauty Exhibition as a period of great joy and challenge.'* Claire was extremely hard- working, conscientious and perceptive and has made a most valuable contribution to Afro Hair & Beauty. She was ably supported by my wife Roslyn Wade and Marion Goldspink who together made a great team.

The vibrancy of the event continues to educate and excite, attracting its patrons from around the world like a magnet and remains a great outing for the entire family in the black social calendar and if you are young at heart, you can't afford to miss the Afro Hair & Beauty after Party.

Catering for the many thousands who make the annual pilgrimage to Alexandra Palace is always a sought-after contract for keeping the massive crowds well fed and watered and is in itself one example of how the event helps to develop the community from within. The employment opportunities generated by the event are considerable and included a number of annual contracts for activities such as lighting and electrical fittings, around-the-clock security services, scores of hair and fashion models, show presenters, press and public relations consultants, cleaning services, car park attendants and many others, which when all added together was a formidable army of workers.

For a time, the Miss Afro Hair & Beauty Ball was the place to be seen at and it attracted many young, black women all vying for the coveted crown which carried several super prizes along with fame for the winner. Sponsorship for the exhibition over the years was provided by Dyke & Dryden and has been a powerful marketing tool for the company which helped immensely in building its image and reputation by bringing its products to the attention of a world public.

My colleagues and I were gratified to see the fulfilment of the objectives for which the exhibition was founded. There is little doubt about the influence and impact it has had on almost every sphere of black life across the country, from food to music and fashion. One may also add the introduction of the heart-warming colours of the Caribbean and no doubt that this contribution will be reflected in the future social and cultural history of Britain.

The performance of Rudi Page, Jeff Whittaker and Anthony White, members of our senior sales team, were particularly noteworthy. They were always impeccably turned out and consistently scored well in keeping the organisation ahead in the field. Their contributions as key team players added greatly to the company's progress and has been duly recognised and accordingly rewarded.

Expanding into the African Market

Some of the successful marketing methods used in the UK were soon repeated on the international stage, in East and West Africa. Nigeria, with its huge population, was our first stop and became by far our largest market. I became a regular visitor to that country and was subsequently honoured as a Fellow of The Elegant Twins School of Hairdressing for services to the industry.

Our trek across Africa took Joan Sam and me to Ibadan to attend the first Oyo State International Trade Fair where we were hosted by my great friend Elizabeth Osinsanya, owner and Chief Executive of Elegant Twins School of Hairdressing, the oldest and most respected of such institutions in Nigeria. I record herewith a debt of gratitude which can never be repaid. Elizabeth was a great hostess. She knew all the key decision makers and invited them to be our guests at the trade fair. The visit was a resounding success and Dyke & Dryden from then on became a household name in the industry throughout the country. Nigeria became our largest export market accounting for approximately 30 per cent of our export business for a number of years. The Ibadan presentation model was requested by several distributors across the country who were eager to be part of the Super Curl magic.

Wherever we went, our hosts were tremendously generous. One in particular stood out from the rest—the Palmerston Trading Co. Based in Anambra State, the Palmerston Trading Co. had exclusive distribution rights for our Afro comb and also carried the Super Curl lines. On arrival at the airport, I was greeted by huge Super Curl banners emblazoned with the word 'Welcome'. I felt like royalty and it took me a few days to recover from the warmth of such a reception. More surprises were to follow at my destination. I was particularly moved by a reception in my honour attended by a cross-section of the community. The traditional kola nut as a sign of welcome and symbol signifying friendship was passed around before the meal. During these precious moments, I reconnected with my African heritage as never before.

The next day, with the party behind us, it was time to review our business with Mr. Palmer. He shared an observation he made that our Natural Beauty combs were coming from a source that he did not supply and enquired whether we were supplying anyone else in his market. I assured him that we were not and agreed that he should investigate the matter. He promptly reported to the police that his combs were stolen and directed them to where they might be found. Following the lead given to the police, they found some identical combs and found a man who was promptly arrested. He protested his innocence, claiming that he had bought the combs from a company in Hong Kong and produced invoices to prove it. Meanwhile, the supplier from Hong Kong turned up and confirmed that he had supplied the combs. He was immediately arrested and charged with counterfeit and fraud.

This was live theatre at its best and coming face to face with this incident and the manner in which it was handled was pure drama. In the meantime my immediate concern then was how many thousands of combs might have been copied in this way. Mr Palmer was left to pursue the matter in his best interest and from the volume of business that followed from him assured me that he succeeded in protecting his interest.

In the meantime similar promotions followed in other parts of the continent, notably in Kenya, Uganda, and Ghana which was our next stop after Nigeria. It was truly interesting to note just how meticulous Ghanaian women are about the care of their hair. Ghana, although with a much smaller population than their neighbour Nigeria, their expenditure on hair care products and grooming is significantly much higher per head than women in the UK.

The main purpose of my visit was meet as many of the professional hairdressers as I could, and in doing so, attended many seminars as was possible. The turnout at the seminars were among the largest, liveliest and most impressive I have ever seen anywhere in the world. The presentations were full of panache at its best and what was even more exciting was the use of our 'Natural Beauty by Choice' relaxing system which had become a firm favourite in Ghana. During the seminars where the product was used, I was deeply moved by a chant used by the technicians and spectators alike. The technicians would shout *'Natural Beauty'*, and a thunderous response from the crowd would be *'Not by chance, but by choice!'*. This was a marketing slogan coined by Francis Okesa our brand manager. For me, this chant was among my most memorable moments in Africa capturing a unique endorsement of our products. These presentations made me feel ten feet tall!

Prayers were always said before the proceedings began. The manners and dress code of all present were a delight. This rigid discipline and dedication to their profession conduct seemed to be the result of a very strong professional culture which gave rise to a healthy, disciplined regional organisation.

As in Nigeria, I felt completely at home easily relating to my roots and loving every moment of it and feeling a deep sense of belonging. Another interesting major market place where our products gained in territorial dominance for some considerable time was Uganda. Much of this fine work was down to Rose and Charles Lobago who opened up the market first with Super Curl and followed later with Natural Beauty by Choice.

In addition, our technical team, headed by Mrs Joan Sam's induction of step-by-step presentations, backed by media exposure and regular poster campaigns always made a difference. One of our most effective marketing methods, however, was the use of calendars. Product shots accompanied by suitably sublime calendar images were ever present in customers' homes throughout the year. This method first introduced by Dyke & Dryden proved so popular that it was copied by our competition.

Marketing the company's brands not only provided the satisfaction of opening up new markets, but it also afforded me joys of meeting my continental brothers and sisters on their own ground. I could not have done better. I have made many great friends in my travels and feel truly blessed for the opportunity to meet and share precious moments with so many people from the motherland.

CHAPTER 9

THE ARTISTIC GENIUS OF
BLACK WOMEN'S HAIR FASHIONS

An important feature of the Dyke and Dryden story, omitted in the first edition, was the integrated relevance and source of strength provided by the emerging black community's hairdressing businesses. This second edition seeks to update, acknowledge and put the record straight.

The creative genius of hairdressers is a skill which fashion conscious ladies from every walk of life are always on the lookout for. Men of all ages, too, admire a strikingly 'come and get me' hair style and very often get blown away by ladies wearing these creations. Such a professional stylist is always of a kindly disposition, blessed with innate gifts and skills that equip him or her to cater for all types of hair styles, contemporary or other.

Among the unique attributes of a first-rate professional stylist is his/her creative genius in producing that intrinsic something that satisfies the vanity of her patron by producing a wholesome fulfillment in a particular style and look that fits a mood or charms the dreams of her man! This ability leads to the type of bonding between hairstylist and patron which, I am reliably assured, leads the most reserved and secretive patron to confide and pour out her innermost thoughts and secrets of heart to the person trusted with the care of her hair.

Strictly speaking and from a business point of view, I was filled with an abiding belief that building an unwritten partnership with a targeted customer base of hairdressers could eventually lead to laying the cornerstone of a shared mutual business benefit for the company and the community. This was why the company was always referred to as a community business. There was so much common ground to be found in the aspirations of the community, the company and its supporters—in a nutshell it catered for the special needs of our sisters and provided product choices that satisfied the tastes of the customer base.

Identifying the yawning gap in the marketplace that had existed for professional beauty products in the hair and skin care sector and doing something tangible to fix it brought immediate and far reaching results to the black community. It led directly to the sourcing and making available the widest possible choice of beauty products to satisfy those needs. This move was significant in building self-confidence, developing a range of skills, opening doors and asset building. In short, many folks within the community started to become stakeholders in our own communities by investing in and developing a much rounded service industry.

It may come as quite a surprise for many to learn that it was our sisters who were the true heroes as they were the ones creating demand for products and firing the first shots for black business development in the UK. These pathfinder and business minded hairdressers, who were already skilled, were in the forefront of addressing black hair and skin care needs for themselves, their daughters, their friends and, as a consequence, spawned the largest numbers of black hairdressing business owners in the early 1960s and 1970s.

Prior to the 1960s, there were virtually no black hairdressing salons to be found anywhere in the UK. The trade was conducted in parlors established in private dwelling homes, usually without planning permission. Patrons were obtained by referrals or by passing on the news through the grapevine. This, in itself, provided meeting places for Caribbean and African nationals to exchange news on general issues relating to their respective regions. Indeed, long before the term 'networking' gained universal currency, black people had perfected the art of social engineering and in particular through 'hair fests' around the kitchen table.

The nature of the home working environment was such that it restricted many of those talented pioneers from exhibiting their skills to the general public. A good hairdresser's services carried a premium and when one was found, people would travel from far to take advantage of the service.

It is a truism, that women literally drove the beauty care industry in that they were never satisfied with what they had and were always on the lookout for something new. Black women with curly hair will go through endless processes to make it straight, whereas, white women with straight hair will go through the opposite process with perm lotions to make their hair curly.

By the early 1960's, new black trendsetters were emerging. It was the beginning of a more enlightened and businesslike approach in meeting the requirement for suitable premises in which to carry on their businesses. Recognition by the community of the business acumen displayed by these exceptional pioneering entrepreneurs in the development of this remarkable service industry, had not only brought peace of mind to their clients, but has been accorded great respect for laying the foundations of an industry as we know it today. The list of names included here are merely some of the establishments that became household names: Madam Rose of Harlesden; Dame Elizabeth of Hackney; St Clairs of West End fame, owned by George and Lorna St Clair; Aquarius of Finsbury Park; Carmen England of Oxford Street; Enoch Williams of Glamourland and Winston Isaacs of Splinters of Bond street. Splinters is a brand that has currency and stands out in the world theatre of high black fashion for hair care and style and is widely regarded by many clients as the 'master'. The Splinters brand attracts clients from the top end of the society in every walk of life. It is important however, to point out that the names mentioned represents a mere sample of a much larger body of hair professionals.

Of a later era, companies like Supreme Salon, owned by Joan Sam and others, were fired up with electrifying enthusiasm, thus adding a new dimension to the industry by founding the Supreme School of Hairdressing. The school had a tremendous impact on the industry. While some of the establishments mentioned engaged in training, Supreme made a major leap forward, by trading internationally, enrolling students from many parts of Africa and continental Europe. When student recruitment on the home front was added, this placed Supreme in a quite different league and the school became a credit to the industry.

Hair professionals add the perfect finish to personal grooming which is an essential part of personal appearance, sometimes referred to as the 'final touch' for all social events or business appointments. This trend has remained much the same throughout the ages. Archaeologists have found hairpins, combs and adornments that date back to prehistoric times used by Egyptian women who had many hairdressing skills. The Egyptians knew how to curl hair and hold it in place with the use of hairpins, clasps and grips. The Greeks were also skilled hairdressers. However, in Western Europe France became the fashion centre of the world including hairstyles. Among the popular styles worn by French women of the time was the 'the pompadour' in which the hair was rolled back from the forehead, piled high and decorated with feathers.

Business names usually say something about what might be expected from the name of a particular salon chosen. The name Glamourland, for example, speaks explicitly of what one may expect of a treatment at Glamourland—a new and glamorous look of course! Located in the busy town centre of Finsbury Park sits Aquarius, a delightful 'house of beauty', a constellation and as the name suggests, it stands out. The warmth of the welcome to this awesome beauty parlor is wholesome and prepares its patrons to expect a makeover they will never forget and will for sure be always returning for more of the same.

Aquarius was founded by the late Denzil Parry and his wife Cislyn, both highly creative and talented hair artistes of the highest repute, trained at the internationally known Morris School of Hairdressing in London's West End. The proprietor's objective right from the beginning of their business was to set standards by which they would be measured—by nothing less than excellence. This dream became the hallmark of their organization. Denzil Parry was a great community man and a friend to all. He was filled with vision and drive that distinguished him in many notable ways—his acts of kindness and encouragement speaks volumes.

Many leading salons performed dual business functions. They were businesses as well as teaching institutions and thus they expanded the salon industry and its employment prospects for their many students. Student graduations became huge social events in the industry's annual calendars which were much loved and were looked forward to by the public. Admission to these events was by ticket sale and as the popularity of the events grew, this ensured that the halls were filled to capacity. These social occasions grew as more and more students graduated. This had a knock-on effect for a host of professionals in other disciplines, such as clothing designers, printers, entertainers, musicians, models, caterers, photographers and uniformed commissionaires. A new generation of entrepreneurs was emerging, promoting black community culture in areas where they were well qualified to deliver and put on show their skills and talents.

Proprietors with vision used these social events to good effect. They cultivated advanced public relationships with people with whom they were likely to do business in the future. Among these prospective investors were suppliers of services, bankers and other persons of influence in the society at large.

On the whole, the success of these social events was not lost on would-be promoters organizing similar community events to those provided by salon owners, as they sought to publicize community products and services to prospective customers.

Graduation ceremonies provided a new crop of hairdressers and stylists. Those presented by Madam Rose of Harlesden at the Porchester Hall in Paddington stood out, as this venue attracted a rich mix of prominent members across the society. They came to observe the high professional standards of the events, but also to enjoy the entertainment and fun a new generation had brought to the industry. The Honourable Marcus Lipton, the Member of Parliament for Brixton was a regular guest, among the thousands of supporters.

As demand for salon services grew, so too did the development costs of suitable premises, management, staff, furnishings, together with all the other related business costs. The black press, another embryonic industry that came on stream just behind the fledgling salon industry, experienced much the same difficulties as did hairdressing. It must also be said the arrival of the press was extremely timely and complementary in providing desperately needed marketing support for the hair care industry.

Publications such as the *Jamaican Gleaner*, *West Indian World*, the *West Indian Digest*, *Black Hair & Beauty Magazine*, and *Black Beauty Professional* were, in large measure, supported by the salon industry. In return, these publications profiled the work of the salon owners and improved their patronage. This trend continued through the 1970's and peaked approximately in the middle of the 1980's. Around this period, publishers offered free point-of-sale advertorials which targeted the upwardly mobile and fashion conscious young ladies. Both the trade and the press benefited in that, the emerging black patronage increased and at the same time the advertorials encouraged other businesses to follow the hairdressers' example. The strategic gains that were to flow from these new beginnings were immediate through the networking facility that was now in place and from which the businesses were to benefit.

There can be no mistaking the impact and influence the hair care industry has had in forging a first black business chapter and encouraging a number of new businesses which came on stream precisely as units of support to the industry. These were to expand, strengthen and broaden the black business community base and in its wake the emergence of a 'black middle class'.

Graduations kindled the special Caribbean flavour of joviality at these functions. Creativity and panache characterized the hairstylists' presentations that were all open to competition. In the meantime, the music of the famed Jubilee Stompers and Eric Clarke and the Debonairs were to set the scene for loosening up stiff joints by energetic dancing which has been remembered and talked about by revelers who shared in the fun.

The impact of the new lifestyles and self- assuredness displayed and enjoyed by many hair professionals triggered the ambitions of others to work hard and improve their status as the hairdressers have done. Self-esteem, independence and the promise of a better quality of life are goals these professionals have set themselves and a vast number are enjoying the fruits of their dream.

All in, the blossoming and importance of the Afro-Caribbean Hair Society cannot be overlooked for its role in initiating the professional approach by which its members should operate. Of equal importance too was its attempt to work with manufacturers to ensure that professional products did not circulate in the retail segment of the market in an attempt to avoid them falling in untrained hands that could cause immense damage to unsuspecting clients.

The Society played a major role in the annual Afro Hair & Beauty Show over the years offering salon education in the science of the hair, training in salon management, hairstyling competitions, client care and the evaluation of new products. These events gave widespread exposure, nationally and internationally, and served to showcase black British hairdressing skills to the many visitors who, year after year, attended the premier London Afro Hair & Beauty events.

Manufacturing

Another industry dimension that followed was the emergence of some hair technicians who developed remarkable specialist skills and moved into producing their own products. Among these enterprising hairdressers were George Sinclair and his wife Lorna. Their brands carried their trading name of St Clairs, building on their image of quality which was their trade mark. Their products proved popular and found a deserving slot in the market place. Enoch Williams of Glamourland fame, another celebrity hairdresser, also moved into manufacturing with his own brand, Sahara Products. The line performed well and clinched a niche in the market for its fine conditioning properties. The brand remains a firm favourite among its many users. The active ingredient of this product is aloe, well known among the black community where it has been in use for generations as a remedy for a multitude of ailments. Today, we find that aloe is refined and used as a key ingredient in a wide range of hair and skin preparations.

Salon Strategies, the umbrella organization under the leadership of its director Anne Long Murray and her team of policy makers, continues to drive this remarkable industry forward from its humble beginnings in 'home parlors' environment, to a seat at the top table where the interests of the industry as a whole is recognized, its operations discussed and actions taken to ensure its continued prosperity. This new body has, quite correctly, realized that if the black section of the beauty industry is to continue to grow and prosper, then education and skills training in all areas of the profession must remain a top priority. To that end, support from the national mainstream organizations was necessary and they were in full attendance at a City Hall Conference organized by Salon Strategies on 18 January 2007. The event was hosted by the Mayor's Office and supported by the Learning & Skills Council, the European Social Fund and the London Development Agency, through the Equal 11 Minority Business Diaspora interchange programme. Movers and shakers included officers from the GLA, LDA, the Health & Safety Executive and local authorities, with representatives from all these organizations in attendance to drive the Salon Strategy project forward.

This has indeed, been a great leap forward, considering the point from which the industry has come. Without hesitation, the industry is on the right trajectory to make its presence felt, adding continued improvement to the lives of all those who work in it and depend for their livelihood on its continued growth and prosperity.

It is with a truly deep sense of privilege and pride that I look back at the initiative in which I personally took part in helping to foster the founding of the Caribbean Afro Society by having my secretary arrange for a first meeting of as many hairdressers as we were able to have attending the meeting. During the meeting, I must confess that I took the liberty of proposing two officers, a chairman and secretary, to take the society forward. One may say this was a daring move on my part, but it was a way of getting things done and it worked.

There is nothing that I can say that will adequately express my profound thanks to all the people who make up the industry for their graciousness and kindness which would always remain for me a memory of a lifetime.

The Nigerian Connection

It would be unthinkable to conclude this chapter on hairdressers and the hair fashion industry without including the matriarch and high priestess of the hair care profession in Nigeria—my great friend Dr. Elizabeth Osisnya, proprietor of The Elegant Twins School of Hairdressing & Salon in Lagos, which became my second home in that country.

I first came to know Elizabeth when she shopped at one of my stores in London. I soon discovered that she was a most gracious lady full of boundless energy and with an engaging personality. She could quite easily have been an ambassador at large for her country. At our first meeting, she lost no time in inviting me to become her guest for the first Oyo State International Trade Fair in Ibadan. That first meeting with Elizabeth became a major turning point with huge ramifications for the growth of my business in Nigeria. Mrs. Joan Sam of Supreme Hair Design, as a part of my technical team, did a fantastic job in introducing and spelling out the key benefits of our brands and gave Dyke & Dryden a toehold in what became our largest marketplace in Africa.

Since that time, my travels across parts of that continent became for me an essential part of my education. I have had the good fortune of meeting and sharing my outlook on some world issues that face the black populations as it relates to our economic stake in the marketplace and trading the world over, a well-known situation that has been scandalously pathetic. For what it is worth, it was pleasing to note that the majority of persons with whom I spoke agreed with me, that they were of the same mind as me and needless to say, we agreed to do our bit to influence changing the balance where ever we can.

Elizabeth taught me many lessons, the first of which was that the world should be my market and as it turned out, on the very first day at the fair, all our stock were sold out with traders queuing up to place orders for thousands of pounds of combs and other products. This was a first and most important practical lesson for me. The Trade Fair was a great experience. Elizabeth was a wonderful hostess and knew all the key decision makers and had invited them to be our guests. The visit was a resounding success and Dyke & Dryden from then on became a household name in the industry throughout the country.

Elizabeth Osisnya studied hairdressing at the Morris School of Hairdressing in London and taught hairdressing in England. She returned home to Nigeria in 1962 and opened a salon and hairdressing school. The growth of her business was such that a larger and more modern establishment was required to provide the most efficient, scientific and modern training. She attained her goal and opened her new school on May 1, 1973. Dr. Osisnya is a member of the World Federation of Supreme Hairdressing Schools. She also holds a diploma from the London Institute and Morris School of Hairdressing. Elegant Twins celebrated its golden jubilee in 2003. During that year, I had the privilege and honour of being conferred with the Award of a Fellow of her school in recognition of my contributions and loyalty towards the development of her organisation. My trophy takes pride of place in my office.

In September 2013, this powerhouse of an entrepreneur celebrated her 80th birthday and the solid achievements she had under her belt in her lifetime. Once again, many congratulations and a big thank you to all the staff and friends we have made at ELEGANT TWINS!

CHAPTER 10

A COMMUNITY TRAVEL
AND SHIPPING SERVICE

In looking back at many of the industries which the community tended to gravitate to, some were services regularly used by the community. These were areas in which it was felt that they stood the best possible chances of success. A community travel and shipping service grew out of popular demand by many customers who expressed a preference for one-stop shopping and were keen on having these aspects of their business dealings done with the company. Being trusted and respected by the public in this way is no mean achievement. The endorsement of trust earned the company the seal of dependability, which is a priceless commodity.

These ancillary services were welcomed in that they added extra income at no additional cost to our core business and improved the bottom line. Each service was viewed as potential for growing a new business with time. The potential for doing so was already in its infancy as Caribbean people liked the idea of making periodic air journeys back and forth. At the same time, the traffic in shipping for personal and household merchandise was in its infancy, but increasing in volume all the time.

While there were other organisations showing an interest in these areas, the company felt it could possibly be best placed to deliver the service level in these two new fields to attract more customers. Shipping and travel operated from 43 West Green Road, squeezing use out of every square inch of the building and as I recall it was quite amazing how we were able to squeeze additional space in what was an already tight working surroundings at the time.

The mixed bag of our trading activities was the sale of records which represented the company's core activity at the time. Included also was a small section of cosmetics, together with the sale of airline tickets, travel insurance policies and making shipping arrangements for personal effects. The element of trust was quite remarkable with clients paying over large sums of money and returning later to pick up their tickets.

With the fullness time, the travel business grew to the point where it needed more space which resulted in the purchase of 93 West Green Road. From this location, the travel side of the business operated as an independent business unit with its own staff and overheads. Although we shared the overall management of the company as a whole, the day-to-day running of travel side business was left entirely to Mr Len Dyke.

Purchasing airline tickets for clients represented fairly large sums of money and it was therefore necessary to always exercise great care in its handling. Len was most particular about this, especially when it came to the movement of cash between the office and the bank. Tight security arrangements had to be made to cover this area. There was very good reason to be cautious following an attempted daylight robbery at the office after a number of customers had paid in substantial sums of money. Fortunately, the robbers were inexperienced and were scared off by the arrival of other customers.

The agency prospered and expanded its activity in line with the growing demand at the time for charter flights by residents in the UK returning from time to time to visit their relations and friends back home. During the holiday seasons, Easter, summer and at Christmas time, business was particularly busy.

The major company travel operations were its charter flights. These were sometimes handled independently, or at times shared jointly with other organisations in the same line of business. The flights were to all intents and purpose operated through 'members clubs' which offered its members privileged club fares, thus passing on substantial savings to members. There were a number of well-established and respected clubs. Among the best known names were the Jamaican Overseas Families & Friends Association (JOFFA), the Barbados Overseas Families & Friends Association (BOFFA), the West Indian Overseas Nationals Association (WIONA), and the Inter-Caribbean Social Club run by Dyke & Dryden Travel.

Between them, these clubs pioneered a unique way of substantially reducing the cost of travel back to and from the Caribbean. The operations were looked upon with envy by large carriers like British

Airways and Caledonian Airways who had a virtual monopoly on flights into the Caribbean at regular scheduled fares only. By working together the clubs were able to charter their own aircraft and pass on the benefits to their membership while retaining reasonable management fees and expenses.

This arrangement worked well for several years until some dishonest organisers became involved in the industry and many travellers fell victim to their scams. As a consequence, new legislation was introduced which ruled out the clubs and required bonded travel consolidation and special operators' licences to run them. While this change in the law effectively got rid of the cowboys, it also penalised the legitimate clubs.

Some Caribbean travel agents with IATA and ABTA accreditation have, to a major extent, only themselves to blame for missing out in obtaining consolidators' licences because of their failure to find a framework in which to work together and share in the current mass movement of people across the Atlantic. This was unfortunately a major mistake which caused them to lose out on this lucrative niche market.

The air charter companies were from different countries in Europe and the USA. Their terms of business were pretty clear and straightforward. The flying contracts were simple enough with the major condition to pay in full for return tickets to and return from members' destinations. Club members benefited from the sizeable discounts allowed by plane operators who were able to pass on part of the benefits to their members.

The Caribbean is today one of the world's fastest growing holiday destinations, and the hope remains that at some point, our travel agents will eventually become players in this lucrative market. A further area of growth in the market is to be found in the large numbers of returnees who, after reaching retirement, have chosen the sunshine of the Caribbean in preference to the cold of Europe. On the other hand, many folks have built strong English, African, and inter-island friendships and have become regular visitors and thus expanding the market even further.

With the loss of the travel club system of travel and the increased demand on management time within our company, our core business had grown to such an extent that it became necessary to drop the shipping and travel side of the business. The club operations were eventually transferred to colleagues in the industry. Our involvement has been satisfying not only from an earnings standpoint, but also from the composite benefits derived from the service the company gave to thousands of people who placed their trust in us, which had filtered through to other parts of our organisation. The experience has been both enjoyable and rewarding.

CHAPTER 11

CHALLENGES ENCOUNTERED IN BREAKING NEW GROUND FOR MINORITY BUSINESSES

As told by Kingsley Peters, Financial Controller, Dyke & Dryden.

The prudent advice and rigorous financial oversight of Dyke & Dryden's financial controller, Kingsley Peter, contributed significantly to the growth of the company. His work ethic of outstanding professionalism and the reputation of excellence he earned as a black professional, served as a sterling example of achievement for succeeding generations of black Britons.

I thought it important to include his perspective of some of the challenges we experienced as a company and a minority group in a highly competitive industry and an unwelcoming business environment. He shares his journey with Dyke and Dryden in this chapter. He begins with his attempts to build a life in the UK after Hurricane David devastated his native Dominica. Tony Wade

Hurricane David had a lot to answer, not only because it devastated my country, Dominica, in August 1979, but also because it frustrated my attempts to return home and left me with the task of building a new life in the UK. Pursuing accountancy studies and getting involved in community activity through the Dominica UK Association (DUKA) were the foundations of that task. My social conscience was alive to the fact, that my compatriots, like me, were faced with challenges of race, class and economic disadvantage.

During my early years in the UK, I dedicated my efforts, through DUKA, to providing support and creating opportunity to overcome these hurdles. So it was ironic that knowledge of the job of financial controller of a black-led firm came through DUKA. I applied for the job and succeeded in getting it. Even then, my knowledge of black business was limited to small hairdressing establishments and food outlets, but none with a turnover in the millions.

So it was with a sense of anxiety and excitement that in September 1983, a month after qualifying as a chartered certified accountant, that I walked into 19 Bernard Road, Tottenham, the home of Dyke & Dryden Ltd, the most popular representation of black entrepreneurship in the UK.

At the outset, my personal struggles were already in play. I learnt that my appointment as a newly-qualified black accountant was being opposed by the auditors, not for lack of competence, but on the grounds of inexperience, even though I had spent five years in reputable firms of chartered accountants.

This was typical of the challenges faced by black professionals daily in the UK at that time. So I was delighted that the initial friction among the three directors, caused by the auditors' concerns was overridden by their sense of history and their underlying mission to facilitate black talent. They rejected the auditors' view and sensibly decided to appoint me. This story is emblematic for Dyke and Dryden because it signalled the company's role not only in spreading the seeds of black enterprise, but in tearing down barriers to progress in the path of black professionals. Without that opportunity, it is debatable whether my professional advancement in the UK might have materialized. For that, I shall ever be grateful.

What followed was interesting. Within the first few weeks, I realized that more could be done to enhance the financial rigour of the organization. Consequently, I proposed that the auditors be sacked. This led to more angst in the boardroom because a couple of the directors' personal tax affairs were being handled by those auditors. There was strong resistance to my proposal, even in the face of clear evidence of weaknesses in financial control. In any event, good governance dictated that the long relationship between directors and auditors had become too cosy and required refreshment. In order to break the stalemate, I offered to resign. In retrospect, I recognize that this was a move of considerable temerity so early in my employment. But, it was a principled one. The auditors were duly sacked. Whether I would have indeed resigned is open to conjecture. Certainly, my views were motivated not by revenge, but by the injustice perpetrated by a firm that could have enhanced the financial systems, trained staff and facilitated the frequent provision of robust financial management information. Such a system would have informed executive views and facilitated more judicious financial decisions.

I made that task my own priority, the centrepiece of which was the introduction of a new IBM System 36-based financial and distribution application. Financial monitoring and financial planning then became a process, embedded in the management routines of the organization—a situation which pleased our bankers enormously.

What brought Dyke and Dryden into its ascendancy? It was the first black-owned company to kindle the true spirit of enterprise followed by the founding of the Afro Hair and Beauty Exhibition—an annual spring showcase of new and innovative hair and beauty products with live demonstrations of their application. Every year, over one weekend in May, manufacturers, distributors, hairdressers and thousands of customers, came from continental Europe, USA and Africa to participate in the vibrancy of this annual fest in the heart of Wood Green, in the iconic Alexandra Palace, once the home of the BBC.

The exhibition was managed by Afro Hair and Beauty Limited, a subsidiary of Dyke and Dryden which I had helped to set up. Its publicity value was incalculable. It led, in my view, directly to the catapulting of the company on the international stage, which later led to the acquisitive interest by Soft Sheen and Alberto Culver, two large American corporations in 1988.

I was immensely proud to be associated with the company. Dyke and Dryden Ltd, in the late 1980s, had no parallel. There were no black businesses with a turnover exceeding £3 million and with their own branded products like Supercurl and Natural Beauty, helping to boost margins, with retail outlets in North London and Birmingham.

Everyone, suppliers, customers and employees were eager to partake in the Dyke and Dryden offering. International interest mounted—as the influence of the annual exhibition gathered momentum. Exports rose as Nigerian and Ghanaian customers placed orders by the container load.

That the innovation, ingenuity and drive of Mr Tony Wade, the managing director with a third of the shareholding, was not recognized in the company's name was, in my view, a great pity.

His modesty precluded his acceptance of a name change to Dyke, Dryden and Wade Limited. I joined the three shareholder directors in the boardroom in December 1985, when I was appointed finance director. This made me vividly witness Mr Wade's catalytic influence on the company. For the first time, I was able to share the angst and worry and see at first hand, the many excruciatingly difficult decisions which had to be made.

By that time Messrs Dyke and Dryden were experienced figureheads with whom ideas were shared, but who had little to do with their delivery. The execution was left to Mr. Wade and me. It was always a source of regret for me that I did not pursue my desire for a small shareholding. At the time, I sacrificed weekends, late nights and family time to contribute to the company. Such was my interest and desire to contribute to the company's success.

Uniquely, of its 50 plus employees 90 per cent were of Caribbean origin. This was so because Dyke and Dryden had an allure and a reputation which resonated in the black community. I was clear that no bias or discrimination was applied and that all the recruitment procedures and practices were predicated on fairness and equity. Applicants for jobs were from a wide range of backgrounds but a dominant number were from African and Caribbean communities where the name of Dyke and Dryden was special.

Many times, the knowledge of the vacancy preceded the subsequent advertisement as employees were keen to let their friends know what the company had to offer. The attraction was not the salary or the benefits (which were limited) but the family atmosphere, the cultural connection and the coalescence around a common aim—to make the company more powerful.

Paradoxically, between 1983 and 1989, Dyke and Dryden recruited, trained and supported a host of black Caribbean or African employees—senior sales representatives, George Bacham and Cleveland Harris and warehouse personnel, David Stennett and Jonathan Cameron—all of whom were inspired by what they saw and experienced and left the firm within a short interval to set up their own businesses in the field of hair care manufacture and distribution. The entrepreneurial spirit which rocketed Dyke and Dryden to fame was infectious in the most positive of ways. This led to the staff members leaving, fired up by what they had seen and felt, keen to develop another 'Dyke and Dryden'.

Today, David Stennett has a flourishing hair care business called Headlines. It is the largest provider of the Affirm brand in North London, almost reaching the heights in this decade that Dyke and Dryden achieved in the 1980s. Jonathan Cameron through Clarendon Ventures had a thriving business in hair care distribution in East and North London for over a decade, successfully taking the concept with him to the USA where he now resides and has created a partnership distributing hair products from a South London base with spectacular results. Cleveland Harris, a former sales representative for Dyke and Dryden in the North, has a growing business in Birmingham. George Buchanan created a hair care retail establishment of great stature located for many years in Birmingham City Centre.

These enterprises now boast a combined turnover well in excess of the peak of Dyke and Dryden's and is testimony to the potency of the message articulated by Dyke and Dryden. The barriers of finance and credit access which dogged the initial progress of the company were less of an issue for these new businesses. Dyke and Dryden and in particular, Mr Wade, had publicly maintained a campaign against these barriers to finance over the years as managing director and in his civic engagements thereafter. This undoubtedly contributed to the smoother entry of a new black business class.

A major VAT (value added tax) crisis erupted, that affected Dyke and Dryden's export business in a way that remains questionable and regarded as nothing other than pure victimization by Customs and Excise (C&E) officials. Customers would physically come to the UK and purchase our products for export. They would arrange their own shipping arrangements and instruct their agents to include personal effects on the Bills of Lading. Exports were zero-rated and no VAT was charged on products sold as long as there was confirmation from an established shipping agent as evidence of shipment. By its very nature, the shipment evidence was received after the export had taken place.

The problem, however, was that the shipping agent would furnish shipping certificates long after the goods had left. The certificate would refer to the invoice numbers, but did not itemize the products. It described the entire shipment as 'personal effects', a description not acceptable by C& E. Written confirmation by the shippers that the goods were exported, foreign money transfers and other evidence of export were not sufficient and C&E retrospectively imposed a liability for the full value of VAT on all exports. What was disturbing in our case was that other companies, who operated in the same way that we did, were treated differently with no penalty.

To address this issue, we were forced to impose the VAT charge on all exports with repayment to the customer after a proper shipping document was lodged. This naturally upset the export customers who turned to other suppliers or sourced comparable products from the USA. Customs and Excise were made aware of other exporters who were exporting without detailed VAT documentation, but they were not investigated. Our exports declined, giving rise to excess warehouse stock which had to be sold at heavy discounts.

The double effect of the VAT bill and the additional discounting had an adverse effect of over £0.5 million on cash flow and profitability. This led to excessive reliance on credit from our American suppliers, in particular Soft Sheen products, who less than two years later, acquired Dyke and Dryden. I was personally troubled that I was unable to defend our practice. The case was an arguable one, but the cost of proving a fine technical legal argument on VAT law, was prohibitive. We had no control over the export customer's shipments as they gained excise duty savings in their country from declaring the goods as 'personal effects'. Mr Wade's call on the people of influence who celebrated Dyke and Dryden's success in the past proved fruitless.

They were either powerless or unwilling to help. To this day, I am convinced that the C&E had powers of discretion to limit the VAT they recovered, but they chose not to do so. They were intent on crippling a success story! The irony was that while government ministers were singing the praises of Dyke and Dryden, a department of government was pushing it to the brink of its existence.

In spite of the machinations of Customs and Excise, the company still maintained its appeal and was attracting the interest of US manufacturers of black hair care and beauty products, who were seeking a distribution arm in Europe. The stature and reputation of Dyke and Dryden was a prize to these US manufacturers who had no significant international presence and it was with that in mind that Soft Sheen products purchased a 33 per cent interest in the company.

I was at the centre of the takeover negotiations which were sometimes fraught with confrontation, but always business like. Mr Dyke and Mr Dryden's shares were fully bought and they remained ceremonial figureheads. Mr. Wade gave up some shares and retained his role as managing director. I was optimistic about working for Soft Sheen as a parent company because they were financially strong and had the resources to invest, with an enviable pedigree in the US manufacturing hair products marketplace. The fanfare which greeted their arrival was palpable and frightened the competition into thinking that Dyke and Dryden was going to be an even more powerful force in the black hair care market.

Instead, what took place was an acquisition without a plan, resulting in drift rather than action, bureaucracy rather than efficiency. An example of that was the purchase by Soft Sheen of a proprietary US system only capable of being supported by one engineer, based in the US. Prior to the purchase, Mr Wade and I visited Chicago to examine the system and seriously advised against its acquisition. We both suggested sourcing an alternative computer application in the UK, designed for our UK business with easily accessible localized support. Needless to say, Soft Sheen in their usual cavalier style ignored that advice and acquired US based system which was unable to cope with VAT and appallingly cumbersome, it frequently failed and wasted thousands of pounds in support costs.

Then, the promised marketing plan never happened. The objective seemed to be to send more products to Dyke and Dryden without any thought of its targeting to particular customers. Many of the key brands remained unsold. Frequent visits by the Soft Sheen top brass to endlessly discuss business strategies, marketing plans, contract manufacturing arrangements in the UK part of purchase agreement, without subsequently injecting resources was a sore point.

Then, the cultural differences began to surface. Soft Sheen officials viewed our annual leave provisions as too high, our benefits including company car, too generous and our working days, too short. This spilled over into excessive information demands, including daily reporting, from Soft Sheen management which meant that I had to work longer weekends, late evenings working with a US sourced computer system which could not cope. The

'Soft Sheen knows best' attitude began to frustrate and antagonize me. The Dyke and Dryden I knew, was beginning to stagnate under the watch of the Americans.

The crux came when, having planned a four-week holiday to Dominica, I was asked by Soft Sheen's CEO to cancel it, without compensation, just because he was visiting the UK and would need me to provide him with information at that time. I did not cancel my holiday. Relations with the Americans got frosty. It was not long after that I decided that Dyke and Dryden was losing its position in the marketplace and decided to quit. In September 1989, crestfallen by what I considered to be the failure of Soft Sheen to carry out their promised investment and their pursuit of a course set on destroying the legacy of Mr. Dyke, Dryden and Wade, I resigned.

CHAPTER 12

THE SALE TO SOFT SHEEN

In November 1987, a change in the ownership of Dyke & Dryden occurred which was to chart a new path for the company. My two colleagues, Len and Dudley, felt it was time to step down and agreed to sell their shares to Soft Sheen Products, a Chicago-based corporation which was the leader in the ethnic hair care industry with sales approaching US$100 million. At the time, Soft Sheen was eight times the size of Dyke & Dryden with sales worth approximately US$12 million. As it happened, both companies came from similar backgrounds, sharing an almost identical philosophy of using their best endeavours to contribute to building a black economic base within our respective communities.

As the news of the sale leaked out, many voices in the UK black community expressed their unhappiness that control would be lost to the Americans. For the record, I must let it be known that long before the sale across the Atlantic was even considered there was a conscious effort made to divest the shares within the black community in the UK. Unfortunately, those who showed an interest were faced with the old difficulty of being unable to raise the necessary capital.

At the time, the rationale behind the marriage made good business sense and offered new horizons of hope with projected potential benefits for both organisations. It made black business history. Here were two lack companies linking up across the Atlantic! It was something that had not happened before that I was aware of. My partners having expressed their willingness to sell went on to exercise their options contained in the partnership agreement. The first option rested with me to buy or decline, and I choose the latter. The deck was now clear to break the news to Gary Gardener, the President of Soft Sheen, who had earlier expressed his interest in purchasing the company if we were ever to consider selling. The timing to break the news to him could not have been better by way of timing, in that our brands were among the leaders in many of our markets including Nigeria.

Quite by coincidence, Gary Gardener and I were both on a marketing trip in Nigeria and as it happened were staying in the same hotel. We had time to explore his interest in my company and he confirmed that it still stood. On my return to London, I duly filled in my partners with the news which they both welcomed and from there on the wheels were set in motion to execute a deal which took 18 months to conclude.

During this time, the news of the proposed sale was leaked and attracted several offers. One noteworthy offer was one made by Dan Lewis, vice president of Alberta-Culver, who flew in on two occasions by private jet and offered over and above our asking price in an effort to secure the business. His offer was rejected. With hindsight we recognised that our judgement in putting our faith in Soft Sheen and stand by the undertakings they gave was flawed.

The media and the industry were rife with speculation about the deal and waited anxiously to see the direction in which the new management would take the company. Their anxiety was understandable as both companies were leaders in their respective markets and, naturally, the competition felt threatened and carried out various spying engagements, including listening into our telephone conversations.

It may seem senseless to the reader that we did not accept the best offer and with hindsight our decision did not demonstrate sound business principles. But, our commitment to black business development in Britain, rather than Dan Lewis' superior cash offer, was foolish to say the least.

The Americans foolishly gloated about the acquisition and in a press statement declared that *'by buying into Europe's largest distributor, Soft Sheen had stolen a march on the competition by profiting from them through their subsidiary.'* This boasting was a colossal error of judgement for which Dyke & Dryden was later to pay the price. This idiotic remark infuriated the competition. It must be remembered that Dyke & Dryden was a master distributor which carried the competition's products as well as its own. The response to that inept statement was immediate and severe. The first shots from our once good business friends were to squeeze Dyke & Dryden's supplies, while others refused to supply us at all. This was merely the beginning of the chaos that was to follow. Seconded management from Chicago came ill-prepared, without the faintest idea of the dynamics of the European marketplace and even worse, they were not prepared to listen.

Soft Sheen, as already mentioned, was the largest player in the industry and during the pre-acquisition the grand master plan, in brief, had three elements to it. The first was to use Dyke & Dryden's distribution network across Europe and Africa to dominate the market. The second, to expand Dyke & Dryden's retail chain in the UK and then move the Dyke & Dryden brands into other countries. The third element was to expand and build the brands and introduce them into the US market.

On paper, these were wonderfully visionary aspirations. The international director who was to implement the plan was equally bullish in his briefings with staff, raising the level of expectation for a meteoric take off. The first steps were to harmonise our computer systems and introduce modems with head office in Chicago to enhance the many benefits that linking our systems would bring.

In December that year, Kingsley Peter our finance Director and I visited Chicago to meet with our opposite numbers in the new set-up. The most pressing item on the agenda was the replacement of our old IBM36 computer. Kingsley, under whose portfolio this came, wanted, quite rightly, to make the purchase in the UK for ease of service and other practical reasons which I supported. However, the Soft Sheen people insisted on using the company they already worked with in the States. A compromise was eventually reached. We would purchase the hardware in the UK and they would purchase the software in the United States. This was our first major disagreement and it brought home to me the loss of my executive decision-making role.

As predicted, accessing the fixtures and fitting of the software presented nothing less than chaos. The equipment was inoperable for well over a year and ran up costs of just over £100,000. Kingsley's frustration boiled over on this and other related issues which forced him to resign his position with the company. This bungling had cost the company its most valuable member of staff.

He was a first rate finance manager who had served the company well and with his exceptional accounting skills he found a new placement as the area financial controller for the National Grid, one of the UK's top 100 businesses—this was proof of his calibre.

Kingsley's replacement was sent from head office rather than recruited locally in the UK and, needless to say, it was another inept decision over which I had no control. It was patently clear that the seconded staff were not up to the job and were letting down the organisation. Their reports to Chicago were misleading and did not reflect the realities on the ground.

What I was later to learn was that Garry Gardener (the then President with whom the take-over deal was negotiated) was relieved of his position. The fallout of the President's loss of office was to play itself out in that arrangements made under his leadership was unable to be taken forward. The net outcome of this setback was a further major testing time for Tony Wade. How he untangled himself is discussed in the buy-back of the business in chapter 13.

Despite this colossal daily pressure, I never lost my nerve and simply summoned up that reserve of inner strength called for in situations like these. I could not have done otherwise, for I was still the managing director, if in name only, to which everyone looked for a solution. Eventually, an independent audit was ordered and I quote an extract from the text which stated:

> It is our impression that the position of Managing Director Mr. Tony Wade has been obscured by the involvement of Soft Sheen personnel in the day-to-day management of the business. Overall responsibility for decision making no longer appears to be vested in the Managing Director, but to be diffused between Soft Sheen, the Managing Director and Soft Sheen personnel working at the company. The result is that the company lacks clear direction and decision making is a protracted and inconclusive process.

In the face of this unbelievable turmoil, my response was to offer to buy back the company and in 1994 I made an offer to Soft Sheen in Chicago which was rejected. However, in September the following year, a deal was struck and the company reverted to me— alas the poorer by a loss of approximately one million pounds.

In any event it would be fair to say that, although the deal had not worked out as planned, the intentions of Gary Gardener, the president of Soft Sheen, were, I believe, honourable in dealings with me and more so after learning that he had lost control of his office. I have to say that I was badly let down and learned an important lesson that I can never forget.

CHAPTER 13

THE BUY BACK AND
REBUILDING THE COMPANY

The power of positive thinking was always a major strength of mine. Nothing less could have prepared me mentally for the mammoth task that lay ahead in rebuilding the business and restoring the hard won gains that I had originally made. This was just another battle I had to win and I reminded myself that I had done it before and could do it all over again.

Confident in my belief, a restructuring plan was immediately triggered. This entailed getting right back, as it were, to basics by stripping the organisation of all its unproductive elements. With decision-making now back where it belonged, there was no one to answer to concerning how I should use my pruning shears.

I was never inclined to ruthlessness, though in reality I really should have been, given the behaviour of some senior members of staff who abused the trust placed in them to the detriment of the company's survival—and at a time when we were facing the most serious crisis the business had ever known since its founding. These members of staff were, however, seen off appropriately and with the proof that they were not indispensable.

A first step was to restructure my methods of operation and get the staff complement down to the bare essentials. This was followed by lopping off the retail segment of the company. Some units were sold to members of staff on easy terms, while others went to outsiders. The wholesale division and general distribution followed in similar fashion, leaving the company free to focus on its most profitable segment, the manufacture of its brands.

My new direction was communicated to my loyal members of staff followed by an announcement to the industry at large. From there on my devoted team bought into the new vision with an unshakeable trust, focussed on managing change driven by one objective—that of restoring the financial health and respect of the company.

This challenge was formidable, but certainly achievable, as long as we stayed focussed on the goals that we had set ourselves. To that end, a new creative manager with the right industry experience was found to implement the company's new direction. This new management team was led by Mr Tony Goodridge, an accountant who had under his belt years of working experience in the industry and knew most of the key players and customers well. He was adept at the mastery of creative accounting systems and customer relationship management in keeping everyone happy until we were in a position to deal with all our creditors.

The other key player in the new management team was my personal assistant and confidante, Claudia Newton. She was a first class all rounder providing me with support far beyond the call of duty. I will always be indebted to her super contribution in restoring the health and pride of the company.

Confidence returned once the industry received the news that I was back in the driver's seat. It was truly a source of comfort to find that so many of my old industry friends held me in such high esteem, for which I will be eternally grateful. They rallied round and offered the kind of support you would expect from good friends.

Funding the turnaround was, fortunately, not too difficult a process. It simply meant turning one of the company's unencumbered freehold properties into cash and with prudent and tight accounting policies we were well on the way to discovering new horizons.

A new and imaginative marketing campaign was launched to coincide with the 1996 Afro Hair & Beauty Exhibition, Dyke & Dryden's subsidiary, through which a clear and positive statement was made to our many customers and the industry at large. The market response to our vibrant new colour cosmetics range, designed by the Beauty Bar, went down like a treat with ladies of all ages and shades. Our 2-in-1 foundation makeup was an especially a big hit and, in the words of our consultants, Noella Mingo-Jones and Allison Edwards, *'We demystify but don't dictate.'*

The brands that stood the test of time were enhanced and improved in most areas with the introduction of a new Natural

Beauty four application kit. This item became a firm favourite with the professionals filling what was a missing item in our Natural Beauty relaxer range of products.

At this juncture, I cannot help but revisit the circumstances already mentioned which gave rise to the events that spurred us on to the development of the company's own brands. Manufacturing, as it turned out, was ultimately to become the cornerstone and pillar of our recovery and survival in a market that had matured with time. The fact that we owned and established our products gave the company a measure of independence and sustainability.

The challenge, then, was to sharpen our marketing and selling skills, linked to the best service on offer, which gave us an edge in swimming with the sharks without getting eaten alive. Vision, creativity and drive were the same old magic which, in the first place, had given the company a head start and a leadership role in the in the industry.

Being hands-on, once again, infused in me a new sense of exhilaration, a new freedom to explore, to be creative and innovative, with a willingness to take risks, qualities which were, in essence, at the heart of all achievement if one was to turn negatives into positives. In all this turmoil, I can surely conclude that this exercise has been a joyous experience with a soft landing — faith and confidence in one's ability will always see one through.

Black enterprise in Britain is still in its infancy. The future promises an increasing number of black entrepreneurs, capable of achieving the commercial success that Martin Luther King spoke of many years ago as the route to equal rights. Dyke and Dryden is a notable example of what can be achieved, when determination and hard work meet a market need.

I recall some of my trusted advisors as they counselled me saying, *'You've done it once, are you sure that you have the stomach for a second shot at it?'* They all meant well, that much I was sure about, but at the end of the day it was a question of whether you believed in yourself. Did I still have the fire in my stomach, the survival instinct and the winning streak in me? Yes, I instinctively knew I did and three years later after buying back the company from Soft sheen, I had an offer for the business which I could not refuse, proving to myself that once a winner always a winner.

This was a wonderful experience which I enjoyed immensely and one that has served me well in sharing my personal experiences with young entrepreneurs who looked to me for advice in difficult times. Getting out there and staying the course is a legacy for which there could be no price!

PART THREE

THE COMPANY AND THE COMMUNITY

Chapter 14

CREATING OPPORTUNITIES AND DEMONSTRATING THAT CHANGE IS POSSIBLE

Promoting Black Enterprise

Right from the start, the company was regarded as a community business, kindling a 'can do' attitude to succeed. This was at a time when success somehow seemed to have been evading the vast majority of the black businesses in British society. It was a period characterized by rampant racial discrimination which denied black people opportunities for commercial and social advancement in many ways, especially in the field of employment. The best paid jobs were reserved for kith and kin only and in many cases, where black persons were doing the same job, were paid significantly less than their white peers. As for promotion at work, forget it! This was the case even in situations where the black worker by reason of his experience and productive capacity, had at times to train new recruits for the same job that he was himself doing. It was even more painful to discover that the trainee would be better paid than the trainer. This added insult to injury.

As a launch pad for entry into the world of business at the time, music could not have been a more appropriate vehicle for the fledging black company. Music helped to provide that missing 'something' that was an intrinsic part of black culture. The enchanting rhythms of reggae, ska, soul, blue beat and calypso were sounds which most black people born in the Caribbean grew up with and loved.

A store offering these treasures was like a paradise where people could meet, socialize and share each other's music and company. This helped to engender a sense of togetherness which only the power of music could transmit. The following quote by Mr. Tony Mathews is self-explanatory:

Jamaica, an island just south of Miami, came under the influence of a radio station named WINZ. This station played music that appealed to listeners on the island and Jamaicans copied most of the musical expressions. However, although they copied the chord progressions and sang in a similar style as their favourite artistes, there was something lacking in the American music — missing was the power kick-in of the bass response. This discovery was first addressed by the sound system operators. The public wanted to hear the powerful bass note with more force and power as it had been in primeval Africa.

Slowly, they set about changing this aspect of the locally honed music. First step were to build their own amplifiers, followed by their own sound boxes. This then became the genesis of reggae and what is today popularly called dancehall. It took years of toil, trial and error to perfect this Jamaican phenomenon. By 1960, Jamaicans had established a real presence in the UK and this was where Dyke & Dryden came into the picture, by importing and supplying music from back home to meet and satisfy a demand which existed.

House parties in the late 1950s and early 1960s were the most popular mode for entertainment and people would travel from near and far to buy the records they loved, passing on the news to their friends and directing them to Dyke & Dryden who, by then, had built up a special kind of relationship with its public. This historical relationship remained a truly harmonious one throughout and the company was ever mindful of its own painful start up provided community support and assistance wherever it possible.

The absence of black people in the higher rungs of management has caused the community to pay a heavy price because most employers failed to promote people despite their proven skills and ability. Quite often, highly qualified black persons were passed over for promotion in favour of less qualified staff and at times with no experience whatever. Indisputable evidence exists to confirm this very disgraceful treatment of so many people within the black community. It is hoped that recalling these occurrences will serve to educate and inform people of the harm these situations created within society.

Various Acts of Parliament have improved many of the issues of racial discrimination in employment and other related areas. We now share the disciplines of becoming a more tolerant and law-abiding society which augurs well for the nation. There remains a long way to go, but clearly there has been some progress and this requires each of us to play a part in building the kind of society that we deserve.

The company practised good human relations with its staff and ensured for them the best possible provision of a healthy and a happy environment. There was always an unspoken assumption that the company belonged to the community. The company's employees never suffered the distress and indignity of being passed over for promotion by less qualified staff, as was the case with many white-owned organisations.

Influencing change by example was, by far, the most significant of all the benefits that have accrued to the community. In the first place, the company became a role model for thousands of our people in creating a 'we can win' attitude, which left an indelible mark on some members of the community, especially from those seeking business advice.

Secondly, the company provided a seedbed for the development of a range of skills, in the services it provided. Retailing became the first avenue that led into the market place followed by the creation of a sales force to spearhead and our distribution, wholesaling, warehousing, efforts and by the provision of all the attendant services in managing a business.

Product development, manufacturing and exporting came later. These varied experiences were to benefit the individuals their families, the community and the economy.

There was a further important economic dimension to this community self-start effort. It brought into play the multiplier effect with several past members of staff who, with drive, ambition and purpose, became business owners and managers in themselves. With their newly acquired skills, they too are engaging in the cycle of wealth creation activities and are positively promoting and extending the enterprise culture.

Seeing the spirit of enterprise coming to life among past members of staff is a source of great satisfaction. Names that readily come to mind are: Clarendon Ventures; Afrique, Headlines; TZ Enterprises; Statecraft Consulting and Supreme School of Hairdressing. These are new enterprises that originated out of the Dyke & Dryden stable and are now creating and further extending employment opportunities and the furtherance of enterprise culture within the black community.

Comments by Veronica Williams of Treasured Moments, a flower business, is a great example of what I see as excellent community networking, in action. Her story is particularly refreshing:

> We started trading in 1995 offering creative displays with exotic flowers and plants. We had approached a number of white British companies offering our services, but it was our relationship with Dyke & Dryden, that gave us the opportunity to be the flower and plant contractor for the Afro Hair & Beauty Show, which provided the most important springboard for our company.
>
> This opportunity helped to get us started in building relationships, a move that opened other doors for networking. These included Black Beauty & Hair, Pride magazine, Victoria Mutual Building Society, The Jamaica Gleaner, Lusters, Fashion Fair, Choice FM and others. Later, we were able to broaden the scope of our business to include areas such as bridal shows, the sale of plants and floral displays.

A vital area in which the company had a passionate interest was working with young people who wanted to follow a business career. The company let it known that its doors were always open to people with business ideas and welcomed them for discussions and advice. Several university students, for example, made the company the subject for their thesis while others used the industry.

There was also the situation where new graduates were offered placements within the organisation enabling graduates seeking opportunity for gaining experience in their efforts to find employment in the wider society were always helped to do so. It was a common complaint by many newly qualified persons, that they were often refused employment on the basis of lack of experience—we saw this as a sense of duty and in particular a privilege being able to assist in these circumstances.

In this connection, capacity building became a top priority for encouraging change, by bringing to the attention of senior managers in the establishment and showing captains of industry, the role of their responsibility to take the lead in ensuring that their organisations were not merely paying lip-service to equal opportunity. They needed to show, by their actions and employment practices, where they stood on this issue.

Membership of the Captains of Industry Club

My opportunity to pursue this course of action came at a perfectly appropriate time. As it happened, I was co-opted to the board of the Governing Council of Business in the community of which Prince Charles was president. This body included in its membership many of the senior leaders in industry and commerce. This elevation brought home to me for the first time how well respected and admired our company was within segments of the society. Stephen O'Brien, the chief executive of the Council and proposer of my place on the Board, was a man blessed with a double helping of energy. A seat at the top table of this forum of movers and shakers was not to be taken lightly, for it was the place where events were shaped and fashioned, and I was fortunate to have been invited to be a part of this organisation. It does sterling work, particularly in the inner cities, where members of the black community stand to benefit in many ways from its work.

My company was itself to become a beneficiary of the Council's work by way of being a member of the organisation and fortunate to have access to network with the membership at the highest level. An outstanding example was our Chairman's intervention on my company's behalf which resulted in getting our products into the Boots Chemists chain of stores. This was a major coup for Dyke & Dryden by getting our products sold in the largest cosmetics retail chain in the country. It encouraged other large groups to follow the Boots example.

Working at the grass roots is vital in getting a feel and a good understanding of the issues facing community members day after day. The principle routes of information gathering came from specialist groups monthly meetings, where issues of the day were highlighted and usually acted upon internally or referred to an appropriate body externally. The West Indian Standing Conference and its affiliate members drawn from different areas filled this role and was a perfect sounding board then. Another such grouping was the (UK) Caribbean Chamber of Commerce which provided a range of training placements and helped in filling the gap with some community business needs. This work was taken forward by the emergence of the North London Business Development Agency appointed by the Home Office to implement the recommendations of Lord Scarmans on the Brixton Riots of the 1980s.

This spell of community engagement was continuous in that an invitation to become a director of the (TEC) North London Training and Enterprise Council followed in quick succession.

New River Health Authority

Yet another board on which I was literally press-ganged to serve on as a director, was the New River Health Authority. At my interview, I declined the invitation on the grounds that I did not qualify as I knew nothing about health matters. I was quickly advised that what they wanted from me was to benefit from my business experience — with that response I had no choice but to cave in.

My first assignment, as it happened, was to look at the low staff morale the Health Authority was experiencing across the entire organisation. My initial findings were that poor communication between the authority and its staff was the root cause of the problems the authority was experiencing. I then submitted my report together with recommendations to address this situation. These were accepted by the board and acted upon with immediacy.

The Resources Director after carrying out my recommendations reported to the Board and advised that the situation had now improved. On hearing this news, the chairman's face glowed with relief. Instantly, he turned to me and enquired, *'What's next Tony?'* *'From now,'* on I replied, *'our organisation should aim to become an Investor in the People's Authority.'* This suggestion had an instant endorsement from the chief executive and the entire board which was to structurally change the entire working relationship for the authority and its employees. This for me was an outcome that was a truly satisfying first step considering my reluctance to get involved.

It would be remiss of me not to reveal that the time spent at NLBDA was a resounding success, having delivered thousands of training of places which has improved the life chances of many of our people. The agency assisted in helping well over two thousand new business start-ups with a survival rate well above the national average, which is no mean achievement. Several of these businesses are today significant employers and wealth creators in the local economy. This is dealt with more thoroughly in the next chapter which focuses on my work with that project.

In considering the subject matter of Dyke & Dryden and the community, it is evident from the foregoing that my contributions came as direct result of my leadership role at the company and in closing this chapter, it might be useful to show how the new challenge that presented itself was dealt with - the redevelopment of the Stonebridge Housing Estate.

Stonebridge Housing Action Trust

Stonebridge was an inner city area comprising of some 1,750 dwellings and 5,000 inhabitants in the London Borough of Brent. It was characterised as one of the poorest inner city areas in the country, overcome by poor housing, high unemployment and all the many social evils associated with such neighbourhoods. Brent Council, unable to finance the rehabilitation of the estate, applied to Central Government for Housing Action Trust status to deal with the problems of the area and this was granted.

In early 1993, I was one of several candidates interviewed for the post of chairman for a non-governmental body to deal with the redevelopment of the area. As it turned out, I was the successful candidate and was subsequently appointed by Sir George Young, the Housing Minister, in November of that year. It might be useful to share the press releases in several of the national dailies immediately after my appointment which read:

> 6th January 1994 — Tony Wade a successful black businessman has been chosen by government to lead their proposed Housing Action Trust (HAT) urban regeneration scheme for Stonebridge, a rundown estate in North London with one of the worst crime records in Greater London. His credentials suggest he will add significantly to the ability of the HAT to bring about real and lasting improvements to the lives of Stonebridge residents.

My brief was to redevelop or refurbish the estate, improve its management and maintenance, improve the social conditions by way of job creation through training, and improve the community and its leisure facilities.

This project had to be taken right off the ground. With the secondment of Lucy Robinson, a very able senior civil servant from the Department of the Environment, I felt confident in tackling this monumental task ahead of us. With an initial budget of £100 million of taxpayer's money, we were on our way and proceeded in laying the groundwork for a project which later came to be regarded as one of the most successful inner city developments in the entire country.

Our company's recognition on the business front at the national level was equally noteworthy. In February 1984, my company was one of 37 businesses invited to 10 Downing Street by Prime Minister, Mrs Margaret Thatcher to celebrate the country's best entrepreneurs. Further, in early 1985, Dyke & Dryden was one of five companies selected by the British Overseas Trade Board to share in their marketing campaign with a slogan headed, *'The World is Your Market'*. This project was aimed at encouraging small and medium-sized companies to get involved in exporting. My invitation to be part of the campaign was as a result of my company's performance in export markets with a whopping 30 percent of our sales.

On the 5th of November, a national conference was held at the Barbican in the City of London which showed a DVD of how the participating companies scored in carving out their respective slots in overseas markets. It was particularly satisfying to achieve another first, by taking a leading role in the field of exporting.

Working with young adults and giving them the benefit of my experience, was yet another wonderful opportunity of giving something back to the community. In this connection, I served as a Director of the Prince's Youth Business Trust, East London branch. This was another engagement in helping to encourage, inspire and point young people in their chosen careers.

Equally satisfying, was the time spent as a member of the Corporation of the College of East London as part of the decision-making body of the college in providing a quality education for its students. I have to say that this particular assignment, despite the many demands that existed on my time was special, for indeed it gave me a really warm glow, finding myself being able to share my journey with students at this institution. This is so because Tottenham Technical College was the place at which my education in the UK began and the place where I wrestled with subjects that were to prepare me to deal with some of the episodes in what has turned out to be really challenging, exciting and quite a colourful part of my career.

The company, through the efforts of its directors, has come a long way in helping our community to position itself for many responsible roles in the society in which we live and work and represents what I hope is merely the beginning of a page in black British history.

During an interview with Hugh Scully on nationwide television in the 1980s, one of the questions put to me was: *'What in your opinion was holding back the black business community?'* There were three situations, I explained. There was, in the first place, a lack of access to capital; secondly, the absence of opportunities for managerial experience by the failure of employers to promote black people in the work-place who qualified for promotion; and thirdly, the black community has had a weak political leverage.

Without doubt, there has been some improvement in all three areas, perhaps the most important of which is on the political front. According to a recent survey carried out by Operation Black Vote, it has shown quite clearly that the ethnic community holds the balance in determining what could happen as far as political leveraging goes by making black voices heard in some 100 parliamentary constituencies across the country. Using this newly found political clout could (it is believed) certainly make a big difference in getting the attention members of their constituencies need.

I regard myself as a bridge builder. I reject the politics of militancy and confrontation. I hope our new found strength in this area will help to ensure a more fair and equitable partnership role in all our national endeavours. I have been consistent in promoting my belief in the virtues of cooperation.

I am happy to note that our people refuse to wallow in self-pity, anger or bitterness. They are getting on with the job of carving out a better future, wherever possible for themselves, relying only on the priceless gifts of hard work, discipline and resourcefulness, insisting only on equal opportunity, freedom from fear and equality before the law. In my speeches to business related and other bodies, I have pointed out that it is not only governments which should be righting wrongs, whether these be race related or otherwise. Other influential sectors too, have vested interests as exemplified by the Diversity Policy of General Motors one of the world's largest corporations.

John Smith, GM President, sums up its quintessential rationale thus:

> In our industry, as in this nation, diversity is our strength. This diversity is more than a part of our national pride. Having people

of widely different ethnic racial and social backgrounds in our corporation has not slowed our pursuit of excellence—it has accelerated it.

In my business experiences since 1968, I have learnt that diversity is good for business and I hope that through these pages I will have convinced more people to embrace the Diversity agenda as others have already done. It may very well be the missing link in building 'Partnerships for Progress'.

CHAPTER 15

THE DYNAMICS OF CHANGE
AND COMMUNITY DEVELOPMENT

'Things that you do today, that are worthwhile, inspires others to act on sometime in the future'
— The philosophy and opinions of Marcus Mosiah Garvey.

Creating opportunities for a disadvantaged community, in response to Lord Scarman's report on racial disadvantage, is a subject that has engaged many brilliant minds. What was the key finding revealed by his summary? Anyone with an interest in the subject would be familiar with the answer. *'The lack of opportunity,'* he explained, was the major reason. And for the purpose of informed understanding, I will quote a paragraph from his statement.

> The encouragement of black people to secure a real stake in their own community, through business and the professions, is of great importance, if future social stability is to be secured. I do urge the necessity for speedy action if we are to avoid the perpetuation in this country of an economically dispossessed black population.

In the opinion of all fair minded people, the above statement was long overdue and was enthusiastically welcomed by all decent members of society. Lord Scarman's opportunity message, kindled a kindred spirit of compassion and activated the momentum for driving his message home.

It was quite coincidental at the time, that in the search for persons to implement the recommendations made by the judge, that my name was put forward and I was subsequently appointed by the Home Office into taking up the chairmanship of the North London Business Development Agency to carry out recommendations. In taking on board this role, I have to say that equal opportunity has always been among my passions and anyone who knows me well would be aware of that fact. As it happened, I was at the grass roots where feelings ran high and was therefore familiar with many of the issues of the day that led to conflict and confrontation by some members within the black community and civic authority.

In connection with my appointment, it might be worth noting that I was one of those persons who gave evidence to the House of Commons Select Committee with special responsibility for ethnic minorities under the chairmanship of Home Office Minister Sir John Wheeler. During my evidence, I warned of the possible consequences that could arise if the grievances were not addressed. It is quite possible, too, that my business profile as a bridgehead across the black business community and society generally, had much to do with my appointment. The other possible hook could have been that I chaired the UK Caribbean Chamber of Commerce and the chamber was very active in matters dealing with black business interests.

However, in looking back over the past two and a half decades, the all-important question to be considered is what has been the outcome of this assignment? I can state without hesitation, that the need to address the subject of 'lack of opportunity' in my view was correctly identified, though I cannot help expressing my personal conviction that political leadership was extremely weak in pointing the nation in the right direction was a long overdue and it took the courage of Lord Scarman to spell out that truth—something that was staring us in face all the time.

Establishing The Groundwork

After being appointed to lead the Agency, my first task was to put together a team and identify a suitable business name that would convey the objectives and aspirations of the Agency and its remit for North London—hence the North London Business Development Agency (NLBDA). This institution was established in 1985, under the sponsorship of Central Government, together with three local authorities namely, Hackney, Islington, and Haringey.

These three local authorities, together with a good number of national names from the private sector, were instrumental in helping to spearhead the agency's senior management. As if by design NLBDA became recognised as being in the forefront of the Enterprise Movement in the UK. I will now pick up the paper trail that will show the steps that were taken to bring about change and opening windows of opportunity.

In the first place, I want to acknowledge the very able support of Mr John Holt seconded from Business in the Community, who carried out much of the early spade work in preparing the ground for the very first session on the job with Robin Williams, a local bank manager seconded from the National Westminster Bank. My first impression of Robin was that he was someone filled with a deep sense of commitment for the task in hand. He was to be my personal advisor and sounding board and I can state that my assessment of Robin proved correct, as we settled into what was a formidable and challenging work load.

Our first meeting, over a working lunch in a City Road basement restaurant, provided the ideal setting that lent itself for us to focus our minds on the serious nature of our assignment in deciding how we were going to create opportunities for thousands of people who were caught up in the 'blame game' of political neglect, or rather, the failure to grasp and comprehend the nature of the problem facing the society through the lack of opportunity.

The agenda at our first meeting was to decide on a suitable site for offices and settled on premises at 35/37 Blackstock Road Finsbury Park, London N4, which was centrally located with good access for citizens of all three adjoining boroughs.

Secondly, we considered candidates for the post of chief executive officer and agreed that Mr Winston Collimore, who had good working experience with Haringey council, could fill the post.

Thirdly, we reviewed names drawn from a number of multi-national organisations submitted by Business in the Community who would double as board directors on the one hand and sponsors of the Agency on the other.

With the framework of our plans now agreed upon, all that was left to be done was circulation of a Mission statement that would give clarity to our intentions concerning change by involving everyone in a process who could subscribe to the work.The following was the text:

> The Agency will serve as an important vehicle through which Central and Local Government, the Private Sector, the mainstream and other community organisations can network, liaise and co-

operate, to address issues of common concern, which impact on people residing or working in the Inner Cities.' This will assist in the regeneration, of the local economy, through a continuous creation of new enterprises and the enhancement of job opportunities for those who are unemployed or disadvantaged.

It will act as a central source of enterprise and business support information and management training, as well as business advocacy for the local community and to co-ordinate various schemes and initiatives, which will bring benefit both to the local community and national economy.

The agency will adopt and maintain a proactive role in developing various initiatives, which would foster a positive entrepreneurial culture in the local community.

'It will implement creative and innovative programmes, through which the mainstream, the Private Sector, Government and small local businesses can work to address issues which impact on the Inner City, with a view to improve and enrich the overall quality of life for all.

It will continue the pursuit of successfully achieving these objectives by maintaining the role of a necessary, important, and practical means, for local businesses and in particular, those owned by members of the disadvantaged minority communities, thus enabling them to gain access, to fully participate, and contribute to the economic life of the nation.

These approaches were all aimed at creating opportunities through community partnerships. These partnerships were, I dare say, action orientated lessons that can only be garnered through the school of experience of which the entire board of directors were able to subscribe. The above ideas and thought processes were crisis related lessons, which the Agency was to be instrumental in pursuing.

Building partnerships with the community was the key solution that worked for us and, as it happened, they were enterprise driven. Well-defined strategic partnerships within communities became the solution and a method that was nine times out of ten always successful. I would now like to show in the following paragraphs what actually took place in bringing about civil order after the outbreak of violence.

Policy for the way forward was, in the first place, initiated at the central government level where task forces were created. These task forces developed project partnerships, which forged ways that drove change. These changes in turn, created opportunities which were the keys that brought about quantifiable outcomes. I will not dwell on the specifics of the various intervention packages, save to say that the Agency became a resource centre, using the formula I have just mentioned. It was a model that worked and one that has had other nations come knocking on our doors to copy our methods.

The question one may well ask is *'What has been the outcome and projected long term objective of the Agency's work?'* I can confirm that, in the first instance, the Agency succeeded in creating thousands of training places to fill gaps in the work force. Secondly, it helped to establish some 2,000 new businesses to become part of a productive workforce for Britain. In the long run, these newly trained persons and new businesses will, with time, help to create opportunities and grow the economy. The agency has impacted the black community development in significant ways.

Ground breaking research carried out by Mr. Eric Osei, a senior Business Development Manager, at the London Development Agency, a government body, has in 2005, shown that black owned businesses are now a rising economic force in London and also an unmistakeable trend across the country.

This research was supported by one of our largest financial institutions, Barclays Bank, which revealed that the majority of new businesses are now started by people from ethnic backgrounds, a large proportion of whom are black. The same 2005 report also showed that there were around 16,000 businesses owned by people of Caribbean and African descent in London—making up 4 per cent of all the businesses in the capital—and a further 27,000 black Londoners were self-employed, this represents an increase of 80 per cent over the past decade. The report also highlighted that black-owned businesses now generate a combined turnover of £10 billion and employ over 100,000 people, coupled with £4.5 billion spending power across London's black community. This is clear evidence that African and Caribbean people are now clearly wielding increasing economic power.

This economic transformation while not all down to the Recommendations of the Scarman Report, but in the main, must be credited to good government policies, for the many public interventions that flowed from the report which gave momentum in influencing the greater volume of the life changing improvements we see today—I think in particular of the role played by the Training and Enterprise Councils. Though however, their main thrust were to prepare the nation for globalisation.

I feel privileged to have been a small part of these transitional events. In fact, the minutes of the first North London Training and Enterprise Council Board meeting, held February 1, 1991 shows and acknowledge my name as a founding member of NLTEC Ltd. This body covered the boroughs of Enfield, Haringey and Brent and provided substantial support for the work of NLBDA.

As chairman of NLBDA, I made the following statement at our 10th year celebration held at the London Hilton, which summarises our achievements as follows:

> Clocking up ten years of sustained achievement in an organisation like ours does call for a celebration! The greater importance though, is our history and the circumstances that gave rise to our existence. Ten years ago, some of us responded to a call from Sir Leon Britain, the Home Secretary at the time, to implement some of the recommendations of Lord Scarman's report following the Brixton Riots. Our broad objectives were set out as follows.'
>
> Our first task was to increase the level of preparedness of ethnic people wanting to enter business. This we did by way of advice and counselling as a first step within our local community. Secondly, we worked with new and existing businesses and assisted in helping to find start-up and expansion capital and offered guidance as appropriate. Thirdly, we developed working partnerships with central government, local government and the private sector, to stimulate the enterprise culture and business development in general.
>
> How did we fare over the years? Our public accountability reports have shown both measurable and quantifiable results of which we could be justly proud. We have succeeded in translating objectives into action, action into facts and facts into statistics. Our business initiatives have moved from being local to national and from national to international involvement on behalf of some of our clients. At the core of our existence was the establishment of a resource centre, in all aspects of our work.
>
> In this connection, I want to acknowledge and thank all members of my board, my entire team for their loyal support throughout our

entire existence. I want especially to extend my sincere thanks to Emanuel Cotter our second Chief Executive and Elsa Redwood our senior counsellor for their dedication and leadership that was extended well beyond the call of duty.

In all this, we were conscious that we have done little more than barely touched a tiny part of the huge task of bridging the gaps in the economic life of our nation. Racial disadvantage is fuelled mainly by the level of unemployment among people from ethnic backgrounds and the effective response of dealing with this is the pursuit of fair and equal opportunity for all, if we are to win the notion of a 'one nation' battle in our society.

All the evidence we have collected points to some key facts: The need for ongoing education and training in business management; and re-skilling in all areas of activity with access to finance remain a critical factor for the development of the black community, enabling it to become more productive and self-supportive. Failure to do so will only serve to perpetuate poverty for generations to come.

The black community's willingness to work hard and contribute must be recognised and to that end, - under-representation of ethnic participation in national economic life, is not so much an ethnic problem alone, it is a national problem for our country as a whole. Ethnic business development must be seen in the context of the UK's economic future and I urge everyone in a position to influence this process to do so and to consider that it representsa a partnership for progress.

In understanding the scope of the transition that has taken place in multicultural Britain, from a business point of view, one only needs to look briefly at the situation which prevailed before the advent of business enterprise movements. The majority of black-owned businesses were concentrated in small scale traditional, ethnic sectors such as hairdressing, food retailing and catering and were limited to operating within the black community with little or no access to the general marketplace.

Following on the earlier trend, a later report has shown an increasing number of black entrepreneurs running multi-million companies in the mainstream growth sectors such as financial services, law, general business, the professions, media, fashion, property services and employment agencies. In large measure, due to the opportunities that flowed from the Scarman Report, but also from the awakened political awareness that followed.

The reasons for this shift are not too difficult to explain. Part of the answer lies in the generational changes occurring within the black community itself over the last 40 or 50 years. Many second and third generation black people now have greater economic opportunities available to them compared to their parents which has resulted in a major shift in their mindset and ambitions. It follows, therefore, that successful black entrepreneurs now possess a higher level of education and communication skills which leads to a much broader business base of opportunity and social networks, all of which has had the effect of impacting their entrepreneurial behaviour and business decisions. Breaking out into the mainstream sectors and markets has also been an important success factor, due to market size, growth potential, revenue and the profit margins associated with these markets. What we have seen here, is a trend that is set to continue and to grow in all areas of a new and enlightened progressive society and might be summarised as follows:

- Greater access to opportunities in education, training and commercial and social entrepreneurship.
- Fine examples of leadership and management integration in both our civic organisations, faith groups and our commercial firms.
- The development of all types of socialisation processes that inform and guide our behavioural patterns towards others.
- The advantage of being able to learn from diversity agendas or pluralism in terms of culture, ethnicity, religion and other creeds.
- Advantage of having access to the internet—has been more than a strategic bonus for the community, especially in taking advantage of winning business for and from the countries from which they came.
- Being able to network across national borders and or regional frontiers—politically and economically.
- The chance to access, improve and share experimental knowledge to enhance their knowledge in various professional disciplines and industry respectively.
- The election of Barak Obama as President of the USA is both an inspiration and a symbol that we can 'excel beyond the proverbial boundary' once we are able to seize the opportunities that exist.

- Signal progress has been made in relation to the plethora of literature (web-based and hard copy) on a range of subjects in all fields of human endeavours.
- Flexibility in terms of lifestyles, values, beliefs and traditions, individually or collectively.
- Greater prospects for wealth creation, altruism and other life chances are now open to everyone with determination, passion and talent.

The life chances created by better education is enormous and nowhere is this better expressed than in an article in the *Times* newspaper of 8 May 2003 written by Alexandra Frean, the social affairs correspondent, and headlined 'Black Africans in Britain lead way in Education'. Asian people born in Britain make up half of the country's non-white population for the first time, according to results from the 2001 Census. The figures, published on May 9, 2003 show that members of many ethnic minority groups are better educated and more likely to hold professional jobs than British white people and they are more likely to be in good health.

Commentators said the findings, which cover England and Wales, marked a significant milestone in Britain's cultural history. Richard Berthhoud, research professor at the Institute of Social Research at the University of Essex, said that for the first time, the majority of British black and Asian people, who were always being asked - *'Where do you come from?'* would now be able to answer, *'Here!'*

The influences brought to bear on black Britons by examples set by their American peers and role models are captured and high-lighted in recent press listings of Britain's most influential black people operating in all sectors of society. This list is not exhaustive, but unmistakeably points to the direction in which the black community is heading.

This leap forward is further emphasised by the recent phenomenal growth of ethnic minority businesses, now standing at 275,000 that contribute £20 billion to the UK economy. In London there are 66,000 ethnic owned businesses employing 560,000 people with a turnover of £90 billion in sales. Their business performance outstrips that of their white counterparts.

It is said 'success breeds success' and the current climate of independently minded individuals looking to pursue the twin pillars for success—enterprise and engagement in the professions—speaks to people across society generally looking to create their own opportunities whereever possible. There is no doubt in my view that these are people fired up by the same aspirations as the achievers they see and admire and the more we can talk about success and demonstrate it, the more we will improve the chances of winning the goals and objectives the community has set itself.

This leads me to explain my own personal beliefs about success. Where we succeed as individuals, in whatever our work or human endeavours, extends well beyond the boundary of individualism and finds a place in the archives of national pride—individual successes are therefore inextricably linked to nation building and becomes an integral part of a society at peace with itself.

It is remarkably refreshing to note how opportunity has set in motion serious enterprise awareness, releasing the competitive spirit and advancing the 'diversity agenda' which I believe holds the key for the advancement of a truly progressive society.

Since Lord Scarman's Report, overall community development has come a long way in creating an awareness and a sense of belonging—of partnership and the principle of a one—nation society where the interests are inextricably bound together. Sharing in the economic life of the nation now has a momentum of its own which is clearly unstoppable. There is of course much more work to be done and it should be borne in mind that opportunities created now represents an investment in the future of the next generation! There can be no argument against it. Furthermore, the prosperity potential for all people becomes dependent on the dexterity and creative productivity with which these assets are organised across the society at large.

Thousands of people through force of circumstance have migrated to greener pastures of the world. In the early twentieth century many Caribbean people migrated to places such as the USA, Canada and the United Kingdom. Migration takes place for a multitude of reasons and when added together, it all comes down to a single fact of wanting to improve their life chances. These life chances may have been to acquire certain professional qualifications, which cover all areas of national need and for example, management skills in an all-embracing manner. And appropriately, in this connection, for new nations this includes the maintenance of law and order, for education, tourism, agriculture and for that matter everything that helps to prepare the new nations to become efficient and take their places in macro world institutions. Whatever our vocation, those of us who left our native shores were in most cases the more able and in the peak of good health and usually better educated or well connected.

It has always been a matter of deep concern for families left behind and in most cases the moral fibre of support for them has always been forthcoming by way of regular remittances of cash, food, clothing and other supplies. Many emigrants in the new lands where they have settled looked at ways of creating their own opportunities and have established a significant and growing enterprise culture base for themselves. There is now clearly a case for focusing on building an enterprise network across the Diaspora to benefit our roots and to provide a much needed infrastructure for the development of partnerships to trade and serve a basic mutual community interest.

This idea seeks in the first place to create a climate for discussion and debate here in Britain and across the Diaspora as a whole. There is no doubt that among our various communities leadership talents and abilities do exist to kick start a pioneering project capable of creating a new dimension of helping ourselves in a novel and unique way. As a community and a people we must grasp a crystal clear truth, that unless we do some things for ourselves no one else will.

I strongly believe that we shape our lives through our thoughts and our dreams and fashion our lifestyles by the creative genius within us. Changes in the global economy calls for changes in the community's approach to the matter of wealth creation. Being multi-skilled in today's world is a significant asset. Preparedness to face new challenges is of the utmost importance, as it means what we can earn will very well depend on what we learn!

A question we must continually ask ourselves is: *'Are we making the best possible use of life's most powerful changing solutions for success which are at our disposal?'* These solutions are open secrets—information technology, communications and language skills—used by smart people every day the world over. These components are the tools for engaging in the rich, emerging markets of the world of which we must be part.

Knowledge, for sure, will always point the way but a note of caution is that failure to use knowledge correctly could lead to muddle and confusion. A good education no longer ensures success in life these days. Some of the world's top earners highlight that fact. Think of people like Richard Branson, Bill Gates, Michael Jordon, Madonna, Butch Stewart and a host of others.

Their successes were derived from their creative genius, powered and driven by their spirit of enterprise, and their willingness to take risks and a dogged determination to succeed and win. How are we going to win the goals we set ourselves? There is only one way is by being innovative, proactive and action orientated! Let us challenge ourselves to follow these simple rules and we too could all be winners!

PART FOUR

A SELECTION OF SPEECHES

A Collection of Speeches by Tony Wade

Selected by Margaret Bishop

The collection of speeches appearing in this volume by Tony Wade has the following themes: enterprise; community development; the role of diversity and in particular, the importance of the black community's struggle for a stake in the economic life of the nation. He believes that as a community, our only hope of improving our place in British society is by making our presence felt through sharing in the ownership of the means of production, streams of distribution and engage in asset building.

He advocates that the way forward is by attaining a solid track record of achievement in all areas of national endeavour. There are no magic or secret formulas for success in achieving these goals. Succeeding, he believes, is all down to the principle of being ambitious, action-orientated and bringing our creative talents to bear on whatever challenges we come up against. By turning negative attitudes into positives through dedicated and disciplined hard work to achieve whatever the targets we set ourselves.

These speeches were delivered at a number of public events, mainly in Britain and Jamaica between 1982 and 2011.Venues in London included The Queen Elizabeth Conference Centre, Westminster City Hall, and Wembley Conference Centre, while in Jamaica they included the Methodist Summer Camp, the University of Technology, the Small Business Association of Jamaica, the Heart Academy at Runaway Bay and the Jamaica National Heritage Trust in Kingston.

What these conversations (as Tony Wade refers to his speaking engagements) all have in common is the fact that they spring from the experience 'shared with readers' in his four books: *How They Made a Million* (2001); *Black Enterprise in Britain* (2003); *The Adventures of an Economic Migrant* (2007) and *The Cosmetics Kings* (2014).

It might be useful to note that this collection resulted from requests made by many of his loyal fans who found his journey fascinating and regarded his speeches as pointers for their personal journey. They also vividly illustrate to readers and audiences those paths trodden by people like Wade, a Caribbean migrant to the UK, who through self-discipline built a successful career and became a role model for thousands of people across the Diaspora.

Not all of his speeches, however, closely follow the pattern referred to earlier. A good example is his skill in blending historical facts. In a speech in Ireland, to honour Michael D Higgins the eminent sociologist and MP for Galway, he took the opportunity to put together historical facts about the Irish origin of his own name and, generally, the very interesting history of Montserrat, known as the 'other Emerald Isle' — facts of which many of us may well be ignorant. In another speech in honour of a young Jamaican artist, a student at the St. Mary High School, Wade examines the several manifestations of the word 'art' and the related elements of beauty in all of them.

Tony Wade is noted for injecting an early note of humour before getting down to the serious matters his address will consider.

The writer of the foreword to *The Adventures of an Economic Migrant*, well-known Jamaican businessman, Lascelles A. Chin, sums up his contribution in the following words that I find most useful to borrow for this introduction to Wade's volume of speeches, which, as was said earlier, are greatly influenced by his personal experience:

> The book reveals something of the inner man, of his Christian upbringing and the strength of his faith [even] in adversity. It unfolds the multi-dimensional spirit of the adventurer, entrepreneur, campaigner, influencer and author that makes for compelling reading.

THE OPENING OF THE MANCHESTER
BUSINESS DEVELOPMENT AGENCY

23 May 1985

Chairman of the City Council, officers of the Manchester Development Agency, ladies and gentlemen today, it is a great honour and a special privilege to be your guest speaker for this landmark event in your city. I say landmark, ladies and gentlemen, for after speaking to many of your officers earlier on today, I get a sense of the energy being transmitted and feel convinced that here we have something infectious and that your officers are up to the challenge of making Manchester a place filled with refreshing hope and opportunity for all its citizens.

By way of offering encouragement, I am happy to let you know that today, I celebrate 17 years on my business journey and I am happy to share the benefit of my experience thus far. I understand only too well that people go into business for different reasons. Mine was for economic independence, and motivated in part by my previous boss, Mr. Louis Segal, the finance director of the Smart Weston Group of companies, owners of 200 menswear stores all over the country.

Smart Weston provided my livelihood and looking back, it is clear that my colleagues and I were adventurous in the extreme, giving up our bread and butter jobs and moving, as it were, into the wilderness of uncertainty.

Our business, today, is represented by five retail stores, a cash & carry, wholesale distribution, importing and exporting, together with a travel agency and providing employment for 60 persons. These bold steps, I can assure you, were not without many risks and challenges on which I will enlarge later.

I can tell you, however, that risks and challenges are all part and parcel of the nature of business. Putting it simply, business, I discovered, is like looking after a baby. It is a constant process of meeting needs, putting them first and enabling it to grow. As the baby gets bigger, it becomes more expensive and there will come a time when, hopefully, it will stand on its own two feet.

The long-term objective of the proprietor is of paramount importance and will normally determine the strategy for obtaining this objective. In the process of so doing, one will encounter an unavoidable set of problems. How does one handle non-existent, but desperately needed capital? How do you exercise the various management skills that come into play — skills with which one may not be equipped? In my case the old adage held true: 'necessity is the mother of invention'. If the need to succeed is strong enough, then the learning curve for a particular skill shortens — his has been my experience. Clearly identifying the product and the market you are targeting is an important first step, followed by good strategic planning.

At this point, let us look very briefly at some of the factors which adversely affect us as a community. Immigrants, of whatever creed or colour, coming into a new society, are always faced with a number of handicaps, some real or perceived. It may be language, the level of certain skills, conforming to or the adaptation of local norms or behavioral patterns, all of which may act in some way as the basis for prejudice of one kind or another.

Prejudice based on colour affects the individual in two ways. The first through what I call a kindly, contemptuous tolerance and in the other more extreme case is abusive rejection. I, myself, like thousands of immigrants, have lived through and experienced some of the problems mentioned but will assure you that I often use such difficulties to strengthen my resolve to correct, as far as possible, the negatives encountered.

I have, over the years, been connected to various groups and organizations whose noble objectives are to bring about a more equitable and just society, by fostering good harmonious relations, and have at all times held and contended that here in Britain we have the finest opportunity of holding up a model society to the rest of the world.

Our capacity for tolerance, caring and understanding, the major ingredients of our model are unsurpassed anywhere else. These are qualities which we must collectively bring to bear on the needs of members of communities less fortunate than ourselves, particularly when this happens through no fault of their own.

The launching today of this Agency for Economic Development here in Greater Manchester, is a positive step forward and represents, ladies and gentlemen, the spirit of caring which I described earlier.

Now, I want to congratulate all those people connected with this bold and imaginative step forward. It is the cornerstone on which we are set to build a new economic base for the people of this region. I wish to offer a word of warning to the many young entrepreneurs who this Agency attempts to serve. The way ahead is long and hard: there are no quick fixes, no easy answers, none whatever. Building, as the Agency sets out to do, means work and more work; it calls for long hours and many sacrifices, for self-denial, sincerity of purpose and an indomitable will to succeed.

In addition, I want to say to my aspiring comrades, let us rise to the challenge we face, in the full knowledge that we cannot hope to improve our lot by sitting on the fence, on the fringe of society, remote from what is happening around us. We must, out of sheer necessity, make our presence felt. The need for a sound and strong economic base cannot be underrated. I urge you to stand shoulder to shoulder, with others in partnership for progress—together we win, individually we fail.

The emergence of a small black business sector in different in parts of the country is a most encouraging trend that fits nicely into the national need and, as I understand it, is part of the government strategy for restructuring the economy for jobs and growth, and surely here in Manchester we must be part of this drive and be in it to win.

At this point, I should like to put you in the picture about black business development in London. My personal experience gives me good reason for optimism. In my own industry, there has been good progress. In fact, it would be true to say that it is the single most important industry sector in which the black community has a stake, an industry that provides a good number of jobs and some measure of economic independence—an industry created by the community itself.

Other industries in which the community is making its mark in the south, are mainly in the service industries, the salon industry, property management, decorating, shop fitting, motor repair, insurance brokers, grocery stores, newspapers and magazine owners, music shops, restaurants, clothing and curtain manufacturers. Emerging, also, are some firms in the professions, especially in the legal field.

The pace of black advancement is, however, much too slow. Certainly, our being here today is, I believe, a realization and an understanding of the difficulties faced by ethnic business people in acquiring start-up or expansion capital and of the harm done in demoralizing and rendering to waste human resources that should be in gainful employment. Lack of capital where one qualifies not only denies ethnic people the right of equal opportunity, but it also denies the community the ability to develop and make itself self-supportive. Such a situation could also perpetuate poverty for generations to come.

Much has been written and a lot has been said, but being here today, ladies and gentlemen, I believe is evidence of translating good intentions into practice! My heartfelt thanks to you for listening.

CELEBRATING 25 YEARS IN BUSINESS 1965-1990

Master of Ceremonies, Mr. Ralph Straker, distinguished guests, ladies and gentlemen. It is a great privilege to extend, on behalf of our directors and staff, a warm welcome to you all, our supporters and friends who have come together to celebrate 25 years in the history of our business.

Tonight, May 26 1990, in this ornate ballroom, the Inn on the Park, is an occasion we do not take lightly, and, therefore, it might just be helpful to put you in the picture of from where our company has come. Our beginnings I can tell you are to be found solidly planted at the grass roots of our community, and we have been generously supported in our services by the community. The services we offer are well documented, and were well received and accordingly, recognized and together we carved out a toehold on the ladder of success for our company. Our community therefore has been our bedrock and the fertile foundation in which we grew.

Broadly speaking, our business emerged and grew through meeting and servicing some community needs. First we did so by providing the cultural assets of our the music, loved and adored by the community—music that satisfies the appetite of a fun-loving Caribbean people—music which helped to soothe and brighten up the long dark days of winter.

Our music store at 43 West Green Road in Tottenham became a regular meeting place for social interaction, for the exchange of ideas from which community business ideas were formed and gained neighborhood support, and which eventually became a hub of social and community activity. These early steps I hope, explains how our roots and humble beginnings crystallized, took shape and form into the kind of people we are today.

The second stage of the company's development was to broaden its industrial base by creating new skills that met other community needs and especially in the hair care and cosmetics industry. I need not, ladies and gentlemen, tell you that this move was a major and strategic turning point in the history of our company. It was the stroke which in many respects had a domino effect in moving the business forward.

It saw the company opening additional retail outlets, followed by the establishment of wholesale distribution and exporting. This business plan continued as we moved into manufacturing the company's own brands. This was in a way a well-honed strategy of a vertical integration processes that made for a measure of independence within the industry.

These steps were complemented by the founding of Afro Hair & Beauty Ltd, our subsidiary that had as its core task education in caring for the hair. Once a year, hair professionals would arrive from many parts of the world, and meet together under one roof to discover what developments and new products were coming to the marketplace. This was the big opportunity to learn and share in the professional use of new chemical products associated with the industry. This development had far reaching ramifications for the business and for the industry as a whole.

It is said that building of an industry usually takes at least a generation and in each generation there are always pioneers. Len Dyke, Dudley Dryden and I belong, I am told, belong to this select band of persons. Britain's black hair care industry is today the single most important sector in which the black community has a stake. It provides thousands of jobs and a measure of economic independence for some members of society, and created by the community itself.

It is beyond any doubt, and greatly to the company's credit, that we identified a need and set about meeting it against great odds, including a persistent inflexibility not only on the part of the financial institutions, but also from manufacturers, established distributors, and retail chains.

Considering the difficulties of the time, a question that keeps cropping up to this day, what was the driving force in moving the business forward? Without hesitation, I would say that it was sincerity of purpose and the will to succeed that drove us. Men of lesser will would have caved in under the sheer might of the many problems we encountered.

There was, for example, the situation which arose some years ago when the mighty British Rail, in their self-imposed great wisdom and without consulting the people of Hackney, decided that the new British Rail station at Dalston Lane should be sited in the middle of

Ridley Road market on sites 36, 38 and 40, all occupied by Dyke & Dryden Ltd. Call it what you may but in a street of 100 shops we were the only black presence in the street and was arbitrarily selected to be kicked out.

This plan came in for some strong criticism from shopkeepers and street traders in the area. Dudley led the campaign against the proposed closure and as a result the British Rail was forced to abandon their plan. Here you have it—it was as it were David taking on Goliath and we won. This episode illustrates perfectly the dogged strength of our determination of winning.

I have to tell you ladies and gentlemen, that the company takes its social responsibility function in the community with equal importance. Its support for various charities, and sponsorship of sports and education, are all seriously reflected in the goodwill that it enjoys with the community at large.

In 1982, the company won the Sunrise Golden Award for business achievement and the Revlon Service Award in 1983. In April 1984 it received the *Caribbean Times* Award for services rendered to the black community in Britain, followed by The West Indian World Business Award. Between 1984 and 1990 a string of awards followed. The Caribbean & Afro Society of Hair Dressers Award, and the M&M Most Distinguished Distributor Award, and the list goes on and on. I apologize for names not mentioned, but would like everyone to know that they too share a sense pride of place in our collection.

In 1984, however, came recognition for the company's achievements at the highest level when with members of staff we represented the company at a reception held at 10 Downing Street by Prime Minister, Mrs. Margaret Thatcher, for 37 successful entrepreneurial companies, whom she thought '... *were doing the country proud.*'

Being mindful of the reason for tonight's celebration, this very brief summary, ladies and gentlemen will merely serve to highlight just some examples of the sterling contribution as a community we are all making to the national economy.

In conclusion, I would now ask you to raise your glasses and drink a toast to a formidable shared community success, which belongs to us all. Thank you for attending and your kind attention and do please enjoy the evening.

THE UNIVERSITY OF TECHNOLOGY (UTECH)
18 May 2008

Ladies and gentlemen, I would like first of all to thank you for the opportunity to have a conversation with you.

The subjects about which I propose to speak are divided in two parts. First, I would like to explore the importance of building and strengthening our small business base, and secondly, how this feeds through into the nation's asset building blocks.

I believe it might be helpful to begin by telling you briefly what has been and still remains my personal philosophy about small business and its relevance for both personal and community development. I believe that the basic essentials in attaining an industrious culture, in the widest possible sense of the word, is education and training which creates opportunities, that generates ideas, and leads to prosperity.

My contention has always been that every community, whatever its make-up, needs to be assertive and innovative, ensuring that its talents and skills are put to the best possible use for the benefit of the individual and for the common good of the nation.

The question you may well ask is, does this philosophical thinking work in practice? The short answer is yes. And with a track record of achievements to my name to prove it, I will, in due course, detail some of them.

In conversations about business matters, one of the most frequently asked questions I get asked is this, *'How did you do it?'* The question usually comes from people I've never met before, but nevertheless I often understand exactly what they are getting at—but, for the benefit of those of you who do not know it's the little thing of how with colleagues we were able to pioneer the development of the black beauty industry in Britain from nothing and growing it into a multi-million pound industry which today provides employment for thousands of people. The industry is, incidentally, currently one of the fastest-growing sectors in the economy.

The Entrepreneurial Attitude

A frequently asked question: *'How did you do it?'* Frankly, there are no simple answers, but one fact to understand is that all things are possible and can be achieved once you commit to it. Jack Welch the former chairman and chief executive of GE (General Electric) one of the world's largest corporation spells it out in a single word in title of his book *Winning*. It is the one word which is on the lips of all successful people—winning is an inseparable mind set. Cultivating the spirit of enterprise to release the huge productive potential that resides in each of us as individuals is a gift. It is an innate part of the makeup of most us, and for entrepreneurs—people with natural business instincts gravitate automatically towards them.

How often you are with friends with a business idea they've come up with and will forever keep on talking about it, but do nothing about it. An entrepreneur on the other hand, comes along and will run with the idea and act on it—therein lies the difference, one is a talker and the other a doer.

There is urgency for the back community to harness our business ideas and find ways of promoting our entrepreneurial strengths. The need to build strong business partnerships and advance the role of mentorship are absolute requirements, if as a people we are to share in the business of wealth creation and prosperity.

Let me share with you my views on the importance of pursuing small businesses. Small businesses are the engines of every economy, whether in developing nations or developed nations. Let us ask ourselves the question, *'Why are small businesses so important?'* Small businesses ladies and gentlemen have traditionally been the breeding ground for new industries. Small firms are an important source of *innovation*. In some industries, the optimum size of units for efficient operation is small. Small firms bring into play the division labour by splitting processes which they are better at handling.

New entrepreneurial talent enters business through small firms which provide a seed bed from which new large companies will grow to challenge and stimulate established large companies in the economy. Small firms supply large firms with goods or services produced at a lower cost than large businesses could achieve. Small firms provide competition for ever-growing, multi-product firms and thus help the efficient working of the economy as a whole.

My subject, therefore, will touch on the role of fostering personal and community development, through enterprise, partnerships, and mentoring. I will try to show how this linkage helps in creating a more equitable and a more harmonious society.

In talking about enterprise, here is an amusing story that encapsulates what being enterprising is all about. A company whose business was in the manufacture of shoes and wanted to improve sales despatched two of their salesmen to a far off country to explore the market. The first salesman after two weeks in the country reported to his home office that he was catching the first plane back home as everyone there goes barefoot. The second salesman called home very excited saying, *'Send everything you can lay your hands on'* he said, *'for everybody here needs shoes!'* In those two reports, we see the negative salesman and the entrepreneurial salesman, the big difference between winners and losers.

In fact, it was enterprise in the first place that led many people of my generation to migrate to Britain during the last century where we found to be enterprising was an absolute necessity if we wanted to succeed. It might be of some interest to learn that many of us first generation blacks, by dint of sacrifice, hard work, dedication and perseverance, helped to transform London into the world's top swinging city during the early sixties and seventies, replacing it's hitherto dull and dreary image by introducing our cool colours, fashion, poetry and music with a rich mix of haunting rhythms that made you always want to dance. While the greatest gift of them all was the gift of carnival that we gave to the nation.

There are areas, too, where we have made a huge difference in strengthening the workforce in areas not too difficult to identify. These include the Health Service, London Transport Systems and the Post Office. And we continue to make an impact on changes in education, politics, civil society, the professions, sport and business.

On the subject of enterprise, first of all, I want to let you know that what I am about to share with you, has not been by way of being tutored at business schools but rather rooted in the 'can-do' school of lived personal experiences. I would also like to let you know that personally, I subscribe to the school of thought which believes that 'capitalism with a human face' despite its many short comings, represents the fairest of all economic systems—and a system that calls for the personal involvement of each of us.

It was this conviction, after being exposed to the huge potential of the market place in a large organisation for which I worked as their cash book reconciliation clerk that led me to switch from following a course of study in public administration to that of a business career.

My new boss at the Smart Weston group of companies, Finance Director Louis Segal, was a man with great presence bristling with immense energy and wearing a permanent smile of contentment with his life. He drove a Rolls Royce and shopped at Harrods, both symbols of taste befitting some one of his standing.

From the outset, Louis impressed on me the importance of my task, especially its demand for accuracy. He also pointed out that as far as he was concerned, the cash balances on the company's books were for him the most important tool in managing the whole organisation, from that moment on Louis became my inspiration and my mentor! The wisdom implicit in that statement remained fixed in my mind. I was later to appreciate fully the intricate implication of the cash book as a key tool in the science of management.

Under Louis Segal's tutoring, it soon became clear to me that I was destined to go into business on my own account. He fed my hunger and drove my ambition. It's the kind of effect a mentor can impart to his charge. The power and magic of mentoring cannot be underrated. It's a case where success breeds success and its application takes different ways in manifesting itself. At the launch of my book *The Adventures of an Economic Migrant* in London in October 2007, Joy Nicols was the keynote speaker. She was the owner and chief executive of Nicols Employment Agency, a £22 million company she built by herself. She flattered me by disclosing to the gathering that I was her inspiration and mentor. Perhaps another example of how success feeds on success.

My change in direction, as it happened, turned out to be a major turning point in my journey. It ushered in for me far reaching outcomes that I never could have dreamt about, not just for myself and my colleagues, but for the entire black community in Britain.

What followed may seem a little astonishing, but nevertheless, factual. My business partners and I were to become role models to the black business community. This was a period in the history of black business development in Britain that saw, as it were, a seismic shift in the black community becoming engaged in enterprise and the business of wealth creation.

For immigrants who arrived in Britain during the early fifties and sixties of the last century, conventional wisdom dictated two main considerations. One, that you pitch in with the working classes and did the jobs the white community were not keen on doing. If, on the other hand, you were lucky enough to belong to the student group, you did your level best to get good grades, head back home and try to find work in fields that you considered met with your desired life style. In the meantime, there were a small number of professional people, the movers and shakers from the private sector, who were still finding their feet. In this uncertain situation, there was no consideration about becoming employers or to join the self-employed classes.

The process of wealth creation was still out of reach for ambitious business minded black folks. My colleagues and I were to challenge what seemed the impossible—launching out in business. The business option was frowned upon by the banks and other financial institutions whose contention was that blacks were not bankable and all bad risks. I will show later how the community has, over time, turned this distorted perception on its head!

Fortunately, as it happened, a business founded in 1965 was to fire the first shots in this widely held belief by punching a not insignificant hole in that perception and was to become the first black multi-million pound company in the UK.

Financing: A Major Hurdle

Among the challenges, racism in particular, was the failure to get bank support for our ideas, but we stayed focussed on our objective, refused to let others put limitations on our ambitions, and pressed on with the development of our industry which at some point, was to touch the lives of the entire black community in the land.

Defying the financial barriers of exclusion from bank borrowing, a solution had to be found to fund the growth of our business. How we did it? This was always a curiosity question, in view of the prevailing lack of access to loans from the financial institutions. I knew there had to be a way around this funding blockade and here, my friends, is how it was done.

After researching a listing of the key manufacturers in the US where the market was already fully developed, I deliberately set out on a mission of building partnerships with the companies I was to visit.

An essential part of the make-up of every entrepreneur has to be passionately confident, be conviction driven and innovative. This was the pattern of my approach to each senior executive of all the companies I visited. My company's offer, I explained, would be to act as their unpaid sales force in Europe in building their stake in what was still virgin territory. All I asked was for decent lines of credit to do the job. It was an approach that paid off handsomely. My arguments were convincingly sold and, to my amazement, they all readily agreed to my proposals. I surprised myself. Next steps were to turn the stock into cash — and there you've guessed it — my funding problem was solved.

Entrepreneurial success, to begin with, requires in the first place sincerity of purpose, grit and the will to succeed, with Herculean efforts to push ahead with whatever your dreams are. As a pioneer initiating and driving the industry at the time, I can look back with a certain sense of pride and confidently tell you that this was a timely needed breakthrough and a major turning point that opened up new horizons to wealth creation activities not seen before in the community. It was the beginning of a movement of change.

An outline of the steps that blazed the trail might be helpful in painting a picture of what actually transpired. One retail outlet, in time, became seven to cater for the needs of a beauty products starved community. My dear sisters greeted the news of choice with great rejoicing and began to spread the word around. London is a big place and local distribution had to be quickly introduced to cover the city.

Nationwide distribution was to follow to service the towns outside the city. The logical next step was to move into exporting into some of the huge markets of Africa — Nigeria, Kenya, Ghana, Uganda, South Africa and others were to significantly account for the lion share of our business.

Manufacturing: An Obvious Choice

Underpinning the hive of activity, just mentioned, called for a policy of vertical integration. As pioneers of the industry we had carried the investment cost of its development. It was, therefore, quite understandable that our every move was closely watched and monitored by the competition. It became an absolute necessity to protect our backs, and to that end, we moved into the manufacturing of our own home grown brands.

How was this goal achieved? Vision, enterprise, partnerships and spotting the best talents I could lay my hands on. On the matter of spotting talent, my secretary, Mrs Joan Sam, walked into my office one day and advised me that she was quitting her employment. While she was happy in her work, she explained that her real goal in life was to become a hairdresser. I gracefully accepted her resignation, thanked her for her services, wished her well and explained that I would miss her and asked her to promise me that after her training she would come back to see me. She did. *'What is your next goal?'* I enquired. *'I would like to have a salon of my own, but have no money,'* she replied.

Without hesitation, I gave her the good news, *'Provided you are willing to have my colleagues and I as your partners, you can start looking for suitable premises to start your business'*. She was dumb struck by my answer. From that meeting, a new company known as Supreme Hair Design was founded with Joan as both director and company secretary. Two years later, the salon incubated a new entity—the Supreme School of Hairdressing.

Both the salon and the school prospered and became nationally and internationally famous. These two new entities became crucial in the development of the Dyke and Dryden brands. It was a vision waiting to manifest itself. The salon was crucial in our products testing programmes and gave us an edge in our marketing activities. Here ladies and gentlemen, is an example of how we can, through partnership, networking and vision, strengthen our position in the marketplace.

Manufacturing of our own brands, Super Curl and Natural Beauty products, was visionary and, in truth, one of the most strategic steps we took in moving our business forward. It gave us independence within the industry and eventually became the backbone of our business. In some markets our brands became best sellers—on the home front, in Holland and the markets of Africa.

Up to this point our growth was totally organic, and in June 1982 we rounded off our operations with yet another first—the founding of a subsidiary called Afro Hair and Beauty Limited, an exhibition outfit which became Dyke & Dryden's marketing arm, and used to promote and service our brands and the industry.

The exhibition is currently held annually in North London and has over the years become the premier event in the black hair care industry. 'Bringing beauty to the world of Colour' was a catch phrase that became a popular theme for the industry and provided for a great fun day out for the entire family. The event runs for two days and draws its support from all parts of the world, with London as a date in the calendars of manufacturers, hairdressers and businesses eager to share in what is still today a celebrated event in the black beauty and hair industry.

Partnerships in Community Building

I would now like to turn to partnerships. Partnerships for our purposes are essential building blocks in helping to create new businesses, strengthen existing ones, engage in knowledge sharing and know-how and, generally, by way of support in cash or kind.

My work in the hair care industry was to prepare me to take on senior leadership roles in helping to resolve some of the problems that were brewing during the early eighties and nineties Britain. The 'politics of neglect' induced a climate of hopelessness and despair across some sections of the black community. This prevailing climate triggered disorder that forced the government of the day to act. An enquiry was ordered and carried out by an eminent and well respected judge, Lord Scarman.

His recommendations known as the Scarman Report met with popular acceptance. At the time, I became a member of a working party and was subsequently invited by the government to become chairman of a body known as the North London Business Development Agency, one of the agencies to implement the report.

Building partnerships with the community was the key solution that worked for us, and as it happened it was enterprise driven. Well defined strategic partnerships within communities, nine times out ten always work. I would like to show in the following paragraph what actually took place by way of correcting the problems that existed through partnerships.

Policy initiated at central government level created task forces; these task forces developed partnerships. Partnerships forged ways that drove change. These changes, in turn, created opportunities which were the keys that brought about quantifiable outcomes. I will not dwell on the specifics of the various intervention packages, save to say that the Agency became a resource centre using the formula I have just mentioned. This is a model that worked, and one that I have no hesitation in recommending for situations we were experiencing.

The question you may well ask is what has been the outcome of the Agency's work? First of all, I can tell you that the Agency was instrumental in helping to fund over some 2,000 new businesses to bat for Britain. Two decades on and the latest ground-breaking research carried out by the London Development Agency, a government body, has shown that black-owned businesses are now a rising economic force in London. The research is supported by one of our largest financial institutions. Barclays Bank revealed that the majority of new businesses are now started by people from ethnic minority backgrounds—a large proportion of whom is black.

Black owned businesses now generate a combined annual sales turn over in excess of 10 billion pounds, and employ over 100,000 people, coupled with 4.5 billion pounds spending power. African and Caribbean people are now wielding increasing economic power.

There are now around 16,000 businesses owned by people of African and Caribbean decent in London—making up 4% of all businesses in the capital. A further 27,000 black Londoners are self-employed—up by 80% over the past decade. Black business women are an integral part of the black business story as they now own more businesses than any other female group. Government figures show that black women have the highest level of business ownership in London with 29% owning businesses, compared with 21% white and 15% Asian.' The above is one element of change that is making a positive difference in the lives of many within the black community.

In closing, if you were to take away one thought from anything I have had to say let it be your refusal to allow anyone to put limitations on your abilities and ambitions to reach your goals in life! Stay focused on your dreams, remembering always, that the world does not owe you a living, and *your every achievement, will be down to your own efforts!*

THE DEPARTMENT FOR INOVATION & BUSINESS SKILLS: THE DIVERSITY AGENDA
9 October 2010

Throughout my business career, diversity has been a core value for me. I will look briefly at how I believe we can all become active stakeholders in pursuing the Diversity Agenda of our country.

What is diversity? Diversity is a philosophy and a concept—a way of working and sharing across society that has for its subscribers and the workforce, mega potential for changing attitudes and improving national productivity.

Diversity in all areas of our human endeavour with shared opportunities for all holds the key to social advancement. Equal access to opportunity and the transparency it affords is a basic entitlement which removes doubt and creates a climate of fairness. Equal access to higher educational institutions, for example, offers youth opportunities for work experience and training, and for engaging in the social economy. These are just some of the current issues of concern that calls for our active attention.

In these competitive times, we need to show, by our actions, how diversity opens up opportunities which make us, as a society, collectively stronger in achieving our corporate goals. Diversity engenders the spirit of goodwill and promotes an awareness that sharing serves the mutual benefit of all concerned—individuals or corporations. Diversity helps to foster the organic growth of new businesses to ensure and expand the productive business base. In this connection, procurement opportunities for small businesses are critical for their survival and for the expansion of the economy as a whole.

Perhaps I may sound a little presumptuous and one may well wonder what my credentials are for speaking on the subject. Briefly, I do so as one of the pioneers of a segment of the black hair care industry which today employs thousands of people in Britain. It is an industry which officially remains one with a history of continuous growth and even in bad times the industry performs well. Considering the issues that gave rise to the founding of the industry, I can assure you that seeing diversity in action has played a significant role in getting the project off the ground and fills me with a certain sense of pride. The industry has made a huge difference to the lives of thousands of people in our country.

Quite apart from my experience in the industry, my involvement and leadership roles in a wide range of organisations have equipped me with considerable understanding of what is really at stake. Indeed, one should also consider my standing as a former member of the Captains of Industry Club, the Governing Council of Business in the Community and as a founding Director of North London Training and Enterprise Council the most successful of all the London Enterprise agencies. I have also been a director of New River Health Authority, as well as the founding chairman of the Stonebridge Housing Action Trust, regarded as one of the most successful inner-city regeneration stories in the whole country.

Additionally, as a former chairman of the UK Caribbean Chamber of Commerce and also the founding chairman of the North London Business Development Agency—the body created to implement Lord Scarman's recommendations after the Brixton Riots—these assignments all attest to my knowledge on the subject matter.

Throughout, I took a keen interest in promoting small business development, and it follows, therefore, that I have been exposed to the issues and concerns that affects us as a society. On the issue of diversity, in an open letter as early as July 1982, I made recommendations and put forward my ideas on how we could further improve our economic progress and advancement by way of procurement opportunities for small businesses.

If I may, let me quote from a Chamber statement of the time:

We have so far succeeded in arousing national awareness of the difficulties small businesses face in acquiring start-up or expansion capital and of the harm it does both by way of demoralising and rendering to waste, skills and human resources that should be gainfully employed.

Lack of capital not only denies the right of equal opportunity, but it also restricts the ethnic community to develop and make itself more self-supporting but will perpetuate poverty for generations to come. Access to capital by itself, I contended, was not enough; management skills to use funds that become available went hand in hand. In this connection, I invite the institutions of learning to contribute by preparing tailor-made programmes to assist young entrepreneurs to further their business ambitions.

I would also remind the leadership in industry and commerce that it is incumbent on them to carry out their moral duty to promote people who qualify for middle or senior management positions. This can only make for a society that is more productive and harmonious.

Diversity is, without a doubt, the quality that makes our country unique. Our diversity is a vital source of strength, derived from our different cultural backgrounds, found in our creative and innovative character which determines the people we are. We are a people with shared ambitions, a people with respect for human rights, whose beliefs are grounded in fairness and in the rule of law. These principles and personal attributes are the bedrock and foundation of an equitable society.

Britain is today a multicultural society and the most colourful and cosmopolitan nation in all Europe. Her history and traditions make her a magnate that has attracted a rich mix of cultures, which blend together into a remarkable melting pot and is the envy of the world. Although one would not have known this at the time, each wave of immigrants has enriched the cultural and social fabric of British society and represents building blocks of prosperity.

Leadership in diversity, it is pleasing to note, has now been taken forward by the highest office in the civil service. In a Cabinet Office release of 27 November 2007 Sir Gus O'Donnell, head of the service, notes:

> In order to meet the new and evolving challenges which society faces, it is essential that we have a workforce that is diverse in its make-up and capable of bringing a fresh perspective of how we deliver. The Summer Diversity Internship Programme is an excellent opportunity to gain a real insight into the challenging and exciting work on offer from the Civil Service and I would encourage you to get involved.

This forthright prescription for diversity is sound and well received and is the kind of message that is certain to unite and strengthen our society even further. Perhaps we might also look at what some world-class business leaders are saying and doing about diversity.

J.P. Morgan for example, is an equal opportunity employer and here is what they have to say about diversity:

At JP Morgan, we believe it is important to attract, retain and help to develop people, regardless of race, gender, sexuality or disability. The case for encouraging diversity within our firm is simple. It makes our company stronger and helps us to serve our clients better.'

'Rooted in the company's guiding principle is respect for the individual. The JP Morgan culture promotes inclusion, mutual respect and cooperation and stands for outstanding achievement among people from varying backgrounds.

Here is what someone speaking on behalf of Ernst & Young has to say about the strength of networking and sharing in diversity:

Networks can be enormously powerful. They harness the talent of individuals, making them collectively stronger. Our individual networks enable us to get things done. They introduce us to new people and experiences, support us, help us and give us the belief that we can achieve or do something different to make a change.

Our black network is one example. It has grown from strength to strength and provides our black professionals with opportunities to positively impact our business, engage with key stakeholders and progress within the firm. It has created excellent opportunities to engage with our firm's leadership team and introduce new ways of working.

Harish Bhayani of Diversity Services, on promoting and supporting the Diversity Agenda, underlines the importance of procurement responsibilities. No diversity, he asserts, means no sales and spells out the consequences of no supplier diversity. More and more organisations are now forcing the diversity agenda via their supply chains by setting very detailed and challenging diversity standards for suppliers. In many cases, failing to meet those standards will mean no chances even to bid for contracts. For example: Three Civil Service pilot schemes (Jobcentre Plus the identity & Passport Agency and the Department for Education & Skills) bidders for multi-million pound government contracts will be rejected if they do not meet diversity criteria.

Transport for London's (TfL) supply chain diversity requirements of bidders on high value contracts is compliant with the Diversity Agenda—potential bidders are rejected if they do not meet diversity criteria. Important tips are offered by Diversity Services. For example suppliers are to be regarded as an extension of your work force, which is what they really are; what should you be doing about them as well as your employees? Put yourself in your customers' shoes. What are their expectations in respect to diversity in their supply chain? If you don't know, you need to find out. Determine the benefits of supplier diversity to them and to you.

The point in pressing this message home is to show how compassionate and equitable ways of sharing in the work place can positively impact on community relations and our overall prosperity. The workforce is the nation's most valuable asset, progressive thinkers and successful business people all recognise this fact, that their workforce represents the true heroes of corporate success.

Reward sweetens labour, builds trust and is precisely one of the functions visionary leadership must always bear in mind if we are to continue to improve our stake and share in the global marketplace. While management will set policy, it is the workforce who will execute and deliver that policy.

I have to say that lagging behind in the enlightened world of 21st century Britain are the barons of the book industry. Available evidence suggests that countless numbers of black writers are failing to gain access to shelf space in their stores. This situation requires urgent attention at the highest level of the booksellers industry. This is an industry primarily in the business of education. What message are they sending out on diversity? Advice by Neill Denny, editor-in-chief of the *Book Seller*, in his article of May 2006 'Books For All' is spot on:

> The importance of ethnic inclusion ... with the emergence of Britain as a multicultural, multi-ethnic society clearly has implications for the nation's publishers and booksellers in terms of what they produce and how they sell it.

The major difficulty, however, seems to be with the big chains. My own experience with one of the big chains is not uncommon. In September 2004, I visited the Brixton branch of one of the largest chains of book shops in the business. I met with the manager, Aubrey David and presented him with a copy of my first book and enquired if he was being asked for the book. To his affirmative reply I said *'Why are you not carrying it?'* I learnt that his head office would not allow him to stock it. This was in Brixton, mind you, the capital of 'black London' where there were complaints and concerns from the buying public.

What is the industry's policy on selling books written by black writers, I wondered?

I want to inform the barons of the industry that while they continue to frustrate the ambitions of young, black, talented writers, they are letting the nation down. Their views are blinkered and they look at the short term only and will at the end of the day lose out on millions in sales. But the struggle will go on until black writers who qualify for space gain acceptance and become part and parcel of the industry.

Thirty years ago, I went down this same road in another struggle with chemists, drugstores and some retail establishments refusing to stock black hair and skincare products. I challenged this attitude and today we have a fast growing and inclusive industry, meeting and delivering community needs. In this connection, let the book industry be warned and take notice!

The struggle for equal opportunity is a strategic plank in the mission for diversity, and perhaps I might just recall what I once wrote on the subject. Much is made of the glossy phrase 'equal opportunity' but this is often overlooked by the subtle distinction between 'equal opportunity' and 'equal access'. It is the denial of equal access which makes the going so tough on sections of our society. I have to say, that I am personally encouraged, however, to note that change is emerging in some areas of society.

As someone who has been down this road before, I can confidently say to anyone out there with a dream to get in the book industry, don't be deflected from your objective. Refuse to accept labels or price tags on your God-given skills and ability, pursue your goals with determination and achieve the goals you've set yourself.

This now leads me on to what I see as a huge opportunity for diversity in action that will soon be upon us in 2012 — the London Olympics. We all must have in some way been held captive by the recent sporting diversity exhibited in Beijing, and no doubt some of us are still savouring the spectacle.

The nation has already started to contemplate what 2012 holds in store for us. The stakes could not be higher for business, in particular, small businesses.

I am delighted to glean from the *Small Business News* of 26 September 2009. According to ODA chairman, John Armitt:

> 68% of contracts advertised so far by the Olympic Delivery Authority have been won by small businesses — a whopping five billion pounds since January 2008. Businesses of all sizes and from every sector are working together to deliver the largest project this

nation has seen for generations and poised to reap the benefits of millions of pounds worth of work.

In conclusion, as a nation that make things happen, I believe we all have it in us to foster the spirit of change, simply by subscribing to the principles and concept of the Diversity Agenda for a fairer, and more equitable society here in Britain. The ODA is pointing us in the right direction. Let us all be part of the only thing that matters in the workplace—sharing!

ETHNIC MINORITY BUSINESS CONFERENCE
Queen Elizabeth Centre, London
26 November 1991

I would like very briefly to tell you a little about some of the things we are doing at North London Training & Enterprise Council (TEC) as it relates to the ethnic section of our community, and, of course, our whole approach to the work in hand in general. Before doing so, I would like to mention, in passing, my personal view of the TEC philosophy.

I believe that the basic essentials in attaining a local industrious culture, in the widest possible sense of the word, are education and training which create opportunities and generate ideas and which, eventually, lead to prosperity. My contention has always been that every local community, whatever its makeup, needs to be assertive and innovative, ensuring that its local talents and skills are put to the best possible use for the common good of the local community.

I like the TEC concept and agreed to become involved because of the policy that seeks to put local people in the driver's seat of the local community and its basic needs.

Chairman, on behalf of all those TECs with whom the team has worked I would like to offer sincere thanks for the contribution the team has made in helping us to develop our corporate plans, in helping us to as it were cross fertilize our ideas and our thinking in some specific ways. I enumerate a few:

- The Team's influence has helped to emphasize the TEC's unique position to help in maximizing the economic contribution of ethnic minorities by removing barriers to training and enterprise opportunities;
- Through the national conference at Warwick University earlier this year, and through the very informative news sheet 'into the mainstream', and indeed by
- the production of their paper on the opportunities and threats to potential ethnic minority entrepreneurs.

Ladies and gentlemen, I am sure you would agree with me that these accomplishments represent really excellent work. I want also to say thank you to our present Minister of State and her predecessors for their vision and policy direction, resulting in tangible and quantifiable benefits.

I will now turn to the North London TEC. For the benefit of those who do not know our area, we cover the boroughs of Barnet, an area of 49 square miles, Enfield 30 and Haringey 11.7 square miles and with a combined population of 762,000. In Haringey we share, to a large extent, many of the characteristics of the inner city, though with marked contrasts between our eastern and western parts of the borough.

The social composition in Haringey reflects a wide ethnic diversity, which includes many refugee groups. In fact, our ethnic minority community constitutes over a third of the total population of 63,000 out of 190,000, which leads me to tell you that the catchment area of Tottenham presents us with the most formidable challenge.

Perhaps, if I may, I will just put in perspective the scale of the challenge. Government figures show that Haringey ranks as the sixth most deprived authority in England, in the Department of the Environment's own index of urban deprivation. In a study undertaken by the Department of Education and Science, to measure educational needs, Haringey was also identified as within the cluster demonstrating the most socio-economic disadvantage and educational need. The question you may well ask is, *'How are we approaching this challenge?'* First, our mission statement is clear and positive. We aim *'To make North London a recognized area of opportunity for individual and corporate prosperity.'*

Under the distinguished leadership of our chairman Tony Felix, we sought to ensure the involvement of our whole community through people who have shown a commitment to take on board the challenge, people who see the potential, people who see the opportunity, and are willing to work for a solution. TEED figures show that we have the largest ethnic minority representation at Board level of any TEC in the country — four out of 16.

Among the specific things we have done thus far are:

- Our adult/youth training provision reflects the high priority we place on targeting our marketing and promotion activities, to ensure the take-up on training programmes, reflects the ethnic make-up of those within our three Boroughs.

- The latest national statistical returns show that the take up rate of training places by unemployed ethnic minorities average only 13% nationally. This compares with NLTEC's 55% of all trainees coming from ethnic minorities.

- Our enterprise provision to assist self-employment again shows a high percentage of ethnic minority take up. We have advertised our new Enterprise Allowance scheme via ethnic language press which includes Greek, Turkish, Gujarati, Hindu and Punjabi papers.

- There has been the formation of an Advisory group to monitor our strategic objectives of the needs of ethnic minorities, in the areas of training, enterprise and education — advisory group membership comprises educationalists, representation of voluntary and ethnic groups. This group will build on the earlier work undertaken by our TASK groups, which resulted in the production of a report which was used to write up our corporate plan.

- Our community action programme, shortly to be launched is being delivered via a network of voluntary organizations, many of whom are directly involved with minority groups. This will ensure that those close to ethnic groups are funded to provide training and assistance.

- Our TEC has positively reacted to the newly launched EMG and has worked in partnership with local authorities and representatives of voluntary groups to ensure that every possible assistance is given to develop proposals for submission. The TEC has submitted 145 such applications on behalf of Kurds, Somali, Eretrians, Tamils, Greek, Turks, Iranian and groups representing others from Central Africa.

- Our equal opportunities and special needs commitment is real, demonstrable to our community and measurable. Our special needs responsibilities are acknowledged as a vital ingredient of the work of our TEC and our commitment to our community.

Our corporate plan is clearly defined and has broadly based strategic objectives:

- To provide effective training and development for adults (18+) to enhance their employment prospects and to meet the needs of employers.
- To provide the motivation, qualifications and achievement of individuals and their participation in education and training by ensuring that provision is accessible, of high quality and responsive to the needs of employers and young people.
- To help establish an environment capable of supporting the creation of more viable new businesses and the expansion of existing firms.

On the question of training, we find that at a time of rapidly rising unemployment there are still identified skill shortages which must be addressed.

- In education, the various strands of educational indicatives are being given coherence under our TEC, linking the six further Education Colleges with each other and the Middlesex Polytechnic.
- On enterprise, our commitment is already expressed in our mission statement to enhance our areas' appeal through the process of wealth creation which underpins all our efforts.
- Networking with our three enterprise agencies Barfield, Enfield and NLBDA are firmly established.

In summary, chairman, in all that I have said it is our Board's intention to give ownership and enrichment to the lives of all the people of Barnet, Enfield and Haringey.

LONDON INTERNATIONAL NETWORKING SYMPOSIUM
City of London Business College
14 October 2002

Ladies and gentlemen, I would very much like to let you know just how delighted I am to be sharing with you in this historic gathering. My subject is, in the main, about influencing change—attitudinal change. There could not be a better moment than Black History month to take another look at ourselves, celebrate where we are today, review the terrain we have covered on our journey, revisit our hard-won achievements and restate our vision for the future.

First of all, let us take a moment to look at some of the things we have to celebrate:

- Carnival is, today, Europe's largest street festival—something ethnic peoples have given to the nation.
- Afro Hair & Beauty, founded 21 years ago by my colleagues and myself, is the country's largest seedbed for giving opportunity for the promotion of black businesses.
- Diedre Passcall is a second-generation accomplished musician and composer. Last week she celebrated the work of Samuel Coleridge Taylor, the black eighteenth century classical composer.
- Dr. Winston Martin 35, another black second-generation trailblazer, is one of Britain's leading specialist consultants in cardiology.
- Black churches and gospel choirs are in the forefront of spiritual growth.

These are only a few of the things we have to celebrate. Influencing change, I believe, is by far our number one consideration. I will try to enlarge on the how and why this is an absolute necessity. My own contribution in making change happen, could be found by reading my books.

I could not help looking back some 20 years when the first black international conference took place here in the UK, dealing in part with some of the same issues as we are today. I am delighted to see that we continue to exchange experiences with our American brothers and sisters who share our mutual interests, and who have helped to enrich our individual thinking and our lives.

Twenty years ago, the first conference brought together central government ministers, local government officials, representatives from all the major clearing banks and trade unions and succeeded in raising awareness of the difficulties black businesses face. Together, we looked at ways in which might remove some of the many barriers that prevent the black community from taking its rightful place in the economic life of the nation.

As I pass the baton to the next generation, I want to share with you some of my experiences in the private and public sectors, my community involvement and my vision for the future.

I hesitate to dwell on the past, but as we all know only too well, it is the past and present that we must use to measure potential failures or successes in the future. I have argued, time and time again, that it is the denial of equal opportunity that makes the going so tough on the black community.

Evidence of unequal opportunity stares us in the face, and our commitment to work hard to eliminate it remains a top priority. Here, in the UK, we probably have the largest numbers of university graduate mini car drivers, fast food servers, underground workers, and security guards all working well below their qualifications, unable to make it into positions matching their abilities.

Not only is this situation soul destroying, but let us for a moment consider the waste of expensively trained people unable make their contribution in keeping with their abilities? Many of the employers of poorly paid people will tell you that they are 'equal opportunity employers' but yet the doors to middle or senior management positions remain closed to black employees.

The all important element of 'equal access' is missing and this is what keeps many of these graduates at the bottom of the pile, a situation that exists in most fields of employment. In a statement I made as early as 1982, while being chairman of the Caribbean Chamber of Commerce, I pointed out that lack of access to capital where one qualifies, not only denies the right of equal opportunity but, by extension, denies the black community the opportunity to develop and make itself self-supportive. This is a situation which, if allowed to continue, will perpetuate poverty for generations to come for the whole black community.

Access to capital by itself, I stressed, was not enough. The skills to use any funds that becomes available go hand in hand, and in this connection I suggested that we look to the institutions of learning to assist in preparing tailor-made programmes for those who need them.

I also appealed to the leaders of commerce and industry to provide leadership in promoting people who qualify for managerial positions, the outcome of which I believe could make for a healthier and more harmonious society.

How much notice was taken of what I had to say then I will never know, but it was refreshing to hear Prime Minister Tony Blair saying lately exactly what I said 20 years ago. The Prime Minister has the means to see if his exhortation is being taken seriously and, if it is not, we must hold him to account and be ever vigilant to see that our interests are kept in the frame.

Why do we need to keep a watchful eye on our politicians? In 1977, the Government White Paper for the inner cities stated, 'Minority groups living in the inner urban areas need to be given full opportunity to play their part in the task of regeneration.' Six years later, in October 1983, the *Financial Guardian* investigated the outcome of the 1977 policy statement. Its headline read, 'Minorities Find the Climate Cold and Bleak'.

Peter Wilson of the London Business School carried out the research. His findings were as follows:

> Constraints on access to finance, including difficulties with banks, constraints in the physical environment, including access to premises together with disadvantages imposed by racial discrimination.

These factors all combine to hold back the black community.

Two years later, in 1985, the labour force survey published by the Department of Employment found that blacks faced twice the unemployment rate.

Ladies and gentlemen, on 26 September 2002 a *Financial Times* headline written by Jonathan Guthrie declared 'Banks Tougher on Black Start-ups'. Afro Caribbean entrepreneurs face greater problems than other ethnic groups in raising finance says the report, presumably because of racial discrimination.

This was a Department of Trade and Industry backed report by the British Bankers Association:

> Seventeen years on from the 1985 Labour Force Survey, we find that this grossly unfair treatment continues to block black progress.

It is in the light of these facts that I ask the question in my book — has anything changed during these past decades? Yes, without doubt, there has been a marginal change, but the pace of change against the problems is dismally slow. I fear that the politics of neglect gets in the way and is frustrating the rich cultural diversity of our society from unleashing its huge potential in the business of wealth creation.

Let us be clear, there has been a lot of talking and no doubt a lot of good intentions but the failure to deliver is costing the society dearly in lost production and economic advancement.

Our diversity, ladies and gentlemen, is a major strength, and it is within this rich cultural diversity that we can influence meaningful change by releasing its full potential to interact and relate with the rest of the world. My vision, great hope and optimism for this view is backed by recently released figures which shows that 20 per cent of all London businesses are ethnic owned although we represent a mere 5 per cent of the population. This is a magnificent performance and bodes well for the future.

Clearly the time is right for the unstinted support of our financial institutions to stand squarely behind this magnificent effort and give opportunity for others to do the same in other parts of our country.

London is a knowledge-based, world-class city, a financial and magnetic hub, attracting people with creative drive and energy and, as I just highlighted, among these players are ethnic people. Circumstances and need are often the drivers for people who opt for the entrepreneurial highway.

A question I am often asked is this: *'Are entrepreneurs different from people who go into employment?'* The answer is that there is no real difference, but research has found that what distinguishes entrepreneurs is referred to as being people who are 'action orientated' whereas others will continuously talk about their ideas, but do not act on them. Being 'action orientated' was exactly what led directly to pioneering the development of the ethnic hair care industry here in the UK which currently employs thousands of people.

Influencing change is a subject of major concern and requires us all, as a people, to give it the urgent attention it deserves by joining forces with people working for change.

How are we going to achieve this objective? By being proactive, innovative, assertive and above all being action orientated, by continuously cultivating the spirit of enterprise and keep before us the simple truth that the world does not owe us a living. Anything we achieve is down to our own efforts. Let us get in the ring and win!

THE SMALL BUSINESS ASSOCIATION OF JAMAICA AGM
Kingston Hilton Hotel
25 November 2006

Laughter, it is said, is the world's best medicine and perhaps I might begin by sharing with you a laugh or two.

A good friend of mine rang his doctor's surgery for an appointment. *'I'm sorry,'* said the receptionist, *'we can't fit you in for at least two weeks.'* *'But I could be dead by then,'* said my friend. *'Don't worry,'* said the receptionist, *'your wife only needs to let us know and we will just cancel your appointment.'*

A lady, on receiving her washing, angrily telephoned her laundry to complain that she found among her contents six pairs of men's socks— *'And I'm not even married!'* she declared. *'We are so sorry,'* answered the helpful assistant. *'We'll put matters right for you madam and send a man round straight away.'*

Coming from a business background as I do, I would like you to know that I feel very much at home in your company and subscribe to the school of thought that believes that the small business sector is for the nation, and for that matter any nation, the engine of its economy. It might be good to look for a moment at why the small business sector is so important. Small firms allow enterprising people who value their independence to contribute to the economy. Small firms are an important source of innovation. The small firm sector is the breeding ground for new industries. In some industries the optimum size of units for efficient operation is small.

Many small firms supply large firms with goods produced at a lower cost than the large firms could achieve. Small firms provide competition for ever-growing, multi-product firms and thus help the efficient working of the economy as a whole. New entrepreneurial talent enters business through small firms which provide a seedbed from which new large companies will grow to challenge and stimulate established large firms in the economy.

Before dealing with the theme for tonight, perhaps if I may, for a minute or two, fill you in on the route of my journey that led me to being your guest speaker tonight.

Forty-one years ago, Len Dyke, a son of Jamaica, had the idea of starting a small business in the UK importing pre-released records from Jamaica. His business attempt almost did not see the light of day, in that he had invited some of his friends to support his idea and some promised to do so. On their given assurances, Len proceeded with all the necessary arrangements for the enterprise, but only to find that on the day for cash to be put on the table, none his friends were anywhere to be seen.

Dudley Dryden, another son of Jamaica, heard of his predicament and came to the rescue. The coming together of the two resulted in a partnership that carried their names, Dyke & Dryden. Their enterprise made a name for itself with music from back home that cushioned some of the discomforts found in a strange land and helped to brighten up the dark dull days of winter. But, alas, others had the same idea and business took a sharp downturn.

It was at this point that I was invited to have a look at what they were doing. After a quick analysis I spotted what I considered to be the root cause of their problem and recommended a change of direction, from selling records to selling hair preparations and cosmetics. I acquired one third of the equity in the business, and my new colleagues suggested that we rename company Dyke & Dryden and Wade. I felt that was too long and cumbersome. Dyke & Dryden, I suggested, rolled off the tongue easily and had a nice ring to it.

This new beginning became a landmark, for as it happened we made it into the history books for pioneering the development of the ethnic hair care industry and eventually became part of the black social history of Britain. The industry today employs thousands people.

At this point, I will now turn to the theme for this evening, 'Fostering Entrepreneurship in Jamaica'. A fundamental question we must ask ourselves is this—How can we continue to inculcate the spirit of enterprise in our country? How can we make Jamaica a world-class nation? A goal that I believe is absolutely necessary and one we must all aspire to.

We must strive for excellence in everything we do as a people. Luckily for us, we don't have to re-invent the wheel – models of good practice already exist, and good examples to look at, are for example the tiger economies of South East Asia and ones that comes to mind are Singapore, Malaysia and Thailand. Getting there in my view is attainable, for we are a nation blessed with everything necessary for prosperity. We have at our disposal, what it takes.

Let us have a quick look at the principle of the three 'PPPs' people, place and our product. 'Jamaica land we love' encapsulates the mix and true spirit of enterprise among our people and if we were to live by that prayer in song, we could move mountains.

Our institutions of learning are continuously cultivating brilliant minds, some of whom hopefully will become world class entre-preneurs. This month alone, for example, we saw the University of Technology release 1,250 graduates, people educationally equipped to raise the levels of our productivity and of the product itself, the 'Brand Jamaica'. It is a question of seeing that there are no limitations placed on our position in the marketplace—the world must be our market!

'Fostering entrepreneurship in Jamaica' calls for, in the first place, robust visionary leadership, it calls for policies and partnership, together with projects that are capable of transforming and delivering certain predetermined goals and objectives. My working partnership experiences, tells me that leadership with well thought out policies with integrated partnerships across the board is the mix that delivers sustainable development.

Let me give you one or two specific examples of what I mean in terms of what worked for us in fostering entrepreneurship in the UK using our most precious resource—our human capital.

Change at the grass roots in my neck of the woods back in Britain came about via an organisation known as the North London Business Development Agency, (NLBDA) of which I was chairman.

Hopelessness and despair across sections of the black community in Britain triggered disorder and destruction that forced the authorities and the government of the day to act. An enquiry was ordered and carried out by an eminent judge, Lord Scarman. His report and recommendations known as the Scarman Report met with popular support and it was at this point that I came into the picture and was invited to implement his recommendations. I must state that I am not implying that disruption exists here of the kind we experienced in the 1980s, but what I do see are situations of unemployment capable of causing disruption.

In an effort to put you fully into the picture perhaps I might just quote a sentence or two from Lord Scarman's report:

> The encouragement of black people to secure a real stake in their own community, through business and the professions, is of great importance, if future social stability is to be secured—I do urge the necessity for speedy action if we are to avoid the perpetuation in this country of an economically disposed black population.

A question you may well ask is, *'what was it that worked for us in correcting the problems we faced at the time?'* Policy from the Home Office initiated task forces which developed partnerships which forged synergies that drove change. These steps, in turn, created opportunities which were the keys that brought about the beginnings of a more equitable society. I will expand on that statement later.

I will not dwell on the processes of the various intervention packages, save to say that NLBDA became a Resource Centre using the formula stated above that was urgently needed to kick start broadly based initiatives that started to build partnerships and a part ownership portfolio of UK Plc, as Lord Scarman recommended.

The initiatives, to begin with, were open to all and sundry who had business ideas and wanted to explore their feasibility. A team of professionals were put in place to deal with anything that was thrown at them. A further question you may ask is how was it funded?

It was funded through partnerships, in the widest possible meaning of the word. What is partnership? The *Concise Oxford Dictionary* gives the following meanings: *'a contractual relationship between two or more persons carrying on a joint venture'*, or *'the deeds for carrying out such a relationship'*. In our case initial core funding came in part from two sources, central and local government but mainly from the private sector, from national trusts and by way of the secondment of staff from professional bodies, legal establishments, and financial institutions etc. With that mix of integrated support, the Agency prospered and succeeded in founding some 2,217 new businesses to bat for Britain.

Mobilising Britain for the advent of globalisation followed the same formula through the National Training Council via local TECs, (Training and Enterprise Councils) on which I served as director for

12 years. Apart from the scale and co-ordination of that project, the process was the same—partnerships were put together to deliver a determined outcome and it worked, and I recommend using the same formula here in Jamaica.

I will in a moment turn to the theme of 'fostering the spirit of enterprise in Jamaica' but just before doing so, perhaps I might just put you in into the picture of the outcome after building partnerships at NLBDA. I quote from the 2005 latest report on black business performance in London 20 years on from the founding of NLBDA:

> Ground breaking research by the London Development Agency, a government body, has shown that black owned businesses are a rising economic force in London. The research is supported by Barclays Bank which reveals that the majority of new businesses are now started by people from ethnic minority backgrounds—a large proportion of whom are black.

There are now around 16,000 businesses owned by people of Caribbean descent in London, making up 4% of all businesses in the capital, and a further 27,000 black Londoners are self–employed up by 80% over the past decade. Black owned businesses now generate a combined, annual sales turnover of 10 billion and employ 100,000 people. Coupled with the 4.5 billion spending power, African and Caribbean people are wielding increasing economic power.

Black business women are an integral part of the black business story as they now own more businesses than any other female group. Recent government figures show that black women have the highest level of business ownership in London with 29% owning businesses, compared with 21% whites and 15% Asians.

In fostering entrepreneurship in Jamaica we can proudly claim examples of excellence and nowhere is this better expressed than at the Heart Training Academy at Runaway Bay. This institution must fill us with a certain pride and a deep sense of satisfaction. Here we have a world-class facility, turning out the best there is on offer in Jamaican cuisine and also filling the employment needs of our hotels and catering industry.

The Caribbean is now flying its kite as the relaxation capital of the world, and Jamaica plays no small part in this lucrative industry. We must grow our agriculture in tandem in order to supply much of the produce needed by the hotel industry.

The creativity of our music industry must not be underrated. Reggae has gone global, and now has universal ownership in places where it is hard to believe—in Japan, Algiers, Sweden, Germany and others, cutting across the boundaries of languages and has put the Jamaican stamp on her musical creativity. Our visual arts, too, given the marketing push it requires is also waiting to explode. Jerked meats and seasonings, like reggae, are creations we have given to the world, and one is left to wonder if our patents and intellectual property rights have been protected?

We have, too, companies that are world class. I think of Grace Kennedy, Lasco, the brand Red Stripe, National Commercial Bank and building societies such as Jamaica National and Victoria Mutual. The *Gleaner* and the *Observer* are world-class publications whose informative influence spreads across Europe and North America. These are all areas of reaching out in the global marketplace that we must be proud of and emulate.

Replicating the partnership success formulas referred to across other areas of our development, is critical for the continued success of moving Jamaica forward. The provision of workshops and show rooms to give visibility to many of our talented craftsmen in the furniture and upholstery industries, are in my view candidates ripe for the kind of partnership to drive business forward.

Red tape is often cited as a barrier to fostering entrepreneurship in Jamaica. a common complaint by many individuals wishing to contribute to the development of their homeland.

It has been the experience of, for example, Mr. Derrick Evans—better known by his stage name as Mr. Motivator—a returning Jamaican from Britain and the owner/manager of Heavens' Scent, an eco-tourism project located in the beautiful rural area of Freehills in St Ann. The project started one year ago in an area where there was little hope and where people walked the streets all day. The success of his enterprise has created employment for 18 persons and it is projected to increase that number by a further 10 in the New Year.

In my earlier remarks, I referred to your organization as the engine of the economy, the energizers, and visionaries that make change happen. In conclusion, I want to say to you that networking through our cultural links overseas is a sure foundation for engaging in the rich emerging markets of the world. How are we going to achieve this objective?

I believe by being proactive, innovative, assertive and above all, by being 'action orientated' and by continuously cultivating the spirit of enterprise and keeping before us a simple truth, that the world does not owe us a living, anything we achieve is down to our own efforts by Developing Small Businesses for Jamaica's greater good.

CELEBRATING THE YOUNG
ARTIST OF THE YEAR
Sand Castles Jamaica
28 Jan 2007

I am honoured to be the keynote speaker this evening in celebrating with you what is certainly a landmark in the life of our esteemed artist, Mr Neville Scarlet, who has distinguished himself in teaching art, first at Ocho Rios High School and currently at St Mary's High.

Neville is a young and talented gentleman at the tender age twenty. He was trained at the famous Edna Manley College of Visual and Performing Arts. He came away with a Diploma in Art Education and a major in graphic design. Much of his work is conceptual, which means he draws on his imagination, and is also strong on acrylic on canvass, also with pen and ink as part of his tool kit.

The influences on his decision to become an artist, he tells me, come from the study of great artists such as Picasso and Henri Matisse. I am confident that this young man will go places. You might well ask, *'What is it that makes you feel so confident?'* Well, there are several reasons! First, I observe from his work the blossoms of genius coming through. I can see the fulfilment of self-expression and creativity and get a feel for the competitive spirit that is driving him along.

The artistic gift with which he is blessed captures brilliantly the picturesque and scenic environment to which he is exposed. It is, therefore, simply a question of staying focused on his subjects and nothing I believe can stop him achieving that distinction for which he is destined.

As an artist, no one understands and captures as well as he does butterflies and birds in flight, the lush and haunting beauty of the landscape around him, the rugged honey-combed hills and mountains, with views from which you can conjure up and capture crimson sunsets, take in a deep breath of the sea, listen to the murmurings of rivers and streams, watch cascading water-falls endlessly heading for the sea, and you can as it were literally inhale the beauty of the surrounding environment and rejoice in the joys of living in a place like this.

Almost two years ago I was asked to address 'the young artists of the year' and was forced to educate myself a little about art.

The art world I soon discovered is a very broad church and I was compelled to ask myself the question, what is art? In the broadest sense of the word, art is skill in making or doing something physically. Some people, for example, are skilled in the art of, say, playing football, building fishing boats, some skilled in the art of tuning guitars and some skilled in the art of playing cricket. In these kinds of applications, there are many arts and many specialized activities that we engage in.

The word art is used in several other ways. The arts that produce beautiful objects for us to look at. The decorative arts that adorn our homes. Schools offer courses in the liberal arts in topics such as history and philosophy, applied courses such as architecture and mechanical drawing. Teachers use the term 'language arts' to mean the related skills of reading, writing, speaking and spelling, and there is graphic art—connected with printing and bookmaking—whereas painting a picture, writing a novel and composing certain types of classical music are often called fine art.

Now perhaps we could look at the reasons for art. Civilizations as far back as we care to look will show that we human beings are makers of many things and make them for many practical and social purposes. During the age of primitive man, some creations served for survival needs, tools to dig with, for cutting, for hunting and for killing and so on.

In all cultures and civilizations, people seem to have had two less obvious purposes for art. First they want to make things in a form that is satisfying in a special way for their direct experience, something that is worth looking at or worth hearing, and secondly people make objects that will remind other people of certain memorable occasions and events—referred to as formal and commemorative art.

This is so, because certain events and ideas take on the highest importance in for example religious worship, social and political life. From the earliest times, people have used some formal symbol or ceremony to mark the event or to preserve the idea. The ancient Greeks for example represented ideal human of courage, strength and beauty in their statues of gods and goddesses.

Today, we mark graduation from high school, college or university with speeches and in forms of dress that makes the occasion unique, memorable and heightens the sense of its importance. Works of art, as an aesthetic experience take place when the formal interest and the commemorative interest come together. They satisfy our desire for form, and at the same time, remind us of something we consider valuable.

At the same time, works of art differ in important ways. Some, such as an opera, can tell a story, Others like a still-life paintings or say chamber music cannot. Some art forms such as music or poetry take time to unfold. Still others like conceptual art that we have here today are presented all at once. Some works of art such as sculpture we know comes to us just as they left the hands of their creator— while others must be performed for us to follow—examples are orchestras playing music or a builder who puts an architect's plans into solid form for us to appreciate.

Scholars have classified arts in terms of the elements that make them up. Arts that use words differ from those that do not—hence we have groupings of arts—art with an aesthetic experience takes place when a formal interest and a commemorative interest come together.

Then there is a classification of beauty and significance. Scholars differ on this definition. On the one hand some identify the formal interest with the desire to make and enjoy beautiful things, whereas others claim that the formal satisfaction of sheer design and the intensity of the commemorative aspect both contribute to beauty.

Also there is the classification of Beauty and usefulness. Beauty, even in the broader sense of the word, is independent of usefulness, as certain kinds of works of art, such as paintings and music have no use apart from their value as works of art. The definitions quoted above merely serve to show the complexity of the subject.

And now just a little bit of what is being said about enjoying the arts. People who love music, as I know you do, can lose themselves in a musical piece, or who can spend hours painting a picture, know the deep satisfaction that can be found in art and for them, it is not easy to express this satisfaction in words. But, in some partly mysterious way, works of art are among the things of highest value in our lives. A fine piece of music, a master piece of a painting, or a first-rate play has the power to capture and hold our fullest and most concentrated attention.

We find ourselves getting completely wrapped up in it, and everything works out just right. The music comes to the right close at the right time and in the right way. The play ends not necessarily on a happy note, but in a way that seems inevitable and appropriate. As we grow more and more aware of a painting, its parts seem to belong together and to be made for each other. We perceive harmony within ourselves. When the aesthetic experience has ended, we often feel uplifted and refreshed. Our eyes and ears, or our insight into other persons, may be sharpened and refined. We may feel more at home with ourselves. Works of art have value for us in some such way.

In conclusion, I would like to quote from John Keats my favourite poet. What comes to mind is a line from 18th century English poet, John Keats: *'A thing of beauty is a joy forever.'* I am sure we can all agree that—Jamaica land we love is nature's gift to us—a paradise for us to cherish and enjoy!

OBSERVATIONS FROM FRIENDS
Heart Institute Runway Bay
4 January 2007

Managers all, my dear friends, I deem it a great honour in sharing with you in what is truly a remarkable landmark in the life of your organization—20 years in serving the public—and tonight, recognition and appreciation of all the people who have made HEART the trendsetter in the vital business of wealth creation, employment and changing attitudes in the work place. Throughout the six years that I have been a regular guest at HEART, I have had nothing but tremendous admiration for the Institute that I can proudly vouch for.

My admiration for your organization all began with a truly great house warming party which you organized for my wife and me, my family and friends in November 2000. The event was meticulously presented, well organized, the food was a gourmet's delight, and remains a talking point whenever I run into old friends who were present after all those years. Such was the professional skills you applied in the execution of the service that was provided—not to mention the quality of the food you provided.

The impact on all those present was only half the story, your artistry with ice, the food display and its preparation also created longings from palates in several American homes to come and sample what they had seen on the box. The whole event was filmed by an American company looking for marketing opportunities to introduce Americans to what a real Jamaican home party was all about and what fine Jamaican cuisine looked like, and inviting them to come visit. The strategy worked. Some folks came and I have all the evidence on CD.

You my friends, are the embodiment of this institution which is a wholesome model of success. Success breeds success, and the more we can talk about it and demonstrate success, it is the more you will consolidate your position in your industry and in the marketplace of the world.

Let us look at a few examples of some of the credits that you have to your name. Here we have in this our garden parish of St Ann, an organisation that has fostered organic growth that speaks to excellence. Your institution has been rated world class, recognized, endorsed and certified by the Green Globe Organization that sets world standards for your industry.

You represented your country in world culinary skills held in Helsinki and you walked away with the Caribbean regional prize for sustainability. In August 2005, in Washington DC, you hosted a banquet that left your guests lost for words at the standards displayed in your culinary arts presentation. In Brussels in 2006 you set diplomatic taste buds dripping by the quality of the food dished out to them.

These wonderful achievements, my friends, are due to the dedication, hard work and discipline which you bring to your various tasks. They make a formidable contribution to the brand we call 'Jamaica' and fill the nation with a deep sense of pride. You are positive in the marketing of your organization, and your country, and a catalyst for change.

Surely, it must warm your hearts to be the inspiration of pointing the way ahead, in putting our country to work, and to show to the world that we are as good as anyone else, and will not be written off.

Currently, your institution takes pride of place in focusing minds in the national debate taking place on television, in the press and on radio of how to put Jamaica to work across her many sectors. You have put into practice the modus operandi of how it is done by example. It is a powerful message, a message I would urge you to share with other sectors of industry of 'how to do it' and win as you have done!

In commending your organization, I want to be careful not to miss anyone out of the picture. And quite clearly everyone understands that the whole organization is equal to all its parts to succeed, that each is dependent on the other, and that equal opportunity across the board is a key success formula that drives progress and productivity.

The mechanism that drives and facilitates a horizontal movement across the organization, depends on aptitude and ability—from the floor to reception, from reception to management, from management to the chairman and the boardroom.

My remarks, my friends, come from my own personal experience, and I will tell you that my first substantive employment began working in a kitchen pushing dishes through dishwashing machines, moved to management, the board room and on to becoming the chairman of the board. From the kitchen to CEO's office could equally be your own route and destination to the top job by staying focused.

As you continue to develop your expertise, you are acquiring skills that carry premium tags on them, and quite apart from filling home demand for your services don't forget the bigger picture, that your skills are the passport that could take you to anywhere in the world to compete alongside the best in your field. In truth and fact, the world then becomes your oyster!

Finally I have publicly aired my own appreciation both in the press and on radio about the Heart Institute. But being an admirer goes beyond talking, it is demonstrated by example, by spreading the good news of what a great place this is, by bringing my special guests and friends to share my experience about this place and introducing them to the fine food and great hospitality that is to be found here.

In conclusion, of all the things I've said this evening, if you were to take away one message, let it be this, protect and build on the twin core values of your organization—quality and service—credentials that will keep you always as a place of excellence to be proud of and remaining part of.!

Once again, I want to say a big thank you, for allowing me to have a conversation with you!

STONEBRIDGE CELEBRATION PARTY
Wembley Stadium
26th July 2007

Madam Chair, Hat Officers, Council Officers, our project Partners, ladies and gentlemen, good evening. First of all, I want to thank Caroline and her staff for the opportunity given to me to say a big thank you to all the residents of Stonebridge for the privilege of being their chairman in taking forward the formidable challenge of the Stonebridge Hat Redevelopment Project.

With the confirmation of my appointment as chairman of the 6th Action Housing Trust in Britain, I thought the first thing I ought to do was visit Stonebridge, meet with some of the residents, and get a feel of the tempo of the place. I hopped into a regular black taxi cab and headed for the journey. The driver looked me over a little strangely, and his look naturally caused me to worry a little. I calmed myself and did not question him about the way he looked me over. On reflection it occurred to me that Stonebridge was under the microscope.

As we neared Stonebridge, he pulled up a little distance outside the place and declared, *'Here you are mate.'* I was a bit astonished and reminded him my destination was Stonebridge.

'Yes,' he said quite politely, *'but I have to tell you sir, that this is as far as I am prepared to take you.'*

'Did you have a bad experience at Stonebridge?' I enquired.

'No,' he said, *'but from what I've heard about the place, this is the nearest I want to get to it'.*

As you might guess, that story painted a graphic picture of what Stonebridge was like in those bad old days. He was dead serious. We both laughed. I paid him his fare and we went our separate ways. With that introduction from a stranger, I couldn't help wondering what on earth I was I letting myself in for at Stonebridge.

After that encounter, it was clear to me that the first matter to be addressed was the perception and image of Stonebridge painted abroad. This situation, I decided, had to change. I later communicated my thinking to the residents and insisted that whatever it took to change the perception of the place it had to be at the top of our agenda. The taxi driver's remarks stood out in my mind like a fixture. As we look around the place today in celebration, we can all be the judge and jury about the changes that have taken place. I, for my part, can now disclose that in my memoirs *The Adventures of an Economic Migrant* there is a chapter titled 'The Challenge of Stonebridge' and I hope you will all get a chance read the book.

Days after my informal visit, Lucy Robinson, my shadow chief executive, joined me and we arranged for a formal meeting with the Stonebridge Advancement Committee, better known as STAC.

We explained to them during our meeting that we were bearers of good news for all the people of Stonebridge with an initial budget of £200 million pounds to get cracking in dealing with some of the problems of the place. Right from the start, we laid our policy of plain speaking on the table and advised that transparency in every area of our work would be the order of the day. This manner of candid speaking earned us the trust and respect of the residents which enabled us to take the project forward in a business-like manner. That promise was carried out with solid commitment which I can tell you, was a major source of strength which helped to propel the project along.

However, we were soon to discover that the people of Stonebridge had a dream and a vision, which revealed itself in a special way. At one of our very first public meetings, I invited the residents to come up with a slogan that we could live with and work by, and asked all present to put their thoughts on paper in a single sentence, and drop them all in the hat. A small residents' committee was charged with selecting what they considered to be the most appropriate slogan that we might use.

I shared with the committee the thinking behind my idea of the slogan which they all readily agreed was a good one and accordingly they all filled in their slips of paper.

There was, however, one question they addressed to me *'Are you going to put a slogan into the hat yourself?'*

'Well, no,' I said *'I didn't really plan to do so.'* I wanted the people of the estate to own the slogan.

They promptly reminded me of the promise I made earlier, to be a part of Stonebridge. I had no choice but to place my slogan into the hat with the rest. And guess what, my slogan was the one chosen — 'Working Together for a Better Stonebridge'.

This slogan, I might tell you, was their dream and it worked its magic. It focussed minds and hearts. There were banners on the hoardings, in the offices and in every committee room. Those six words carried their message, encapsulated the vision the residents of Stonebridge wanted for their estate. The words represented their common objective and represented a call to action as well as a constant reminder of their mission. To this day, that slogan remains a bold and prominent display on their note paper and notice board and, needless to say, am gratified by it.

Finally, let us look at where Stonebridge came from. Before we arrived Stonebridge was one of the most under-developed parts of London. Where is Stonebridge today? It is rated as one of the most successful inner-city regeneration stories in the whole country. This must fill us all with a deep sense of pride and immense satisfaction. It has been for me, a truly fulfilling spell of service to the community.

On this note, as we look back and continue to celebrate, I would like to publicly acknowledge the efforts of Lucy Robinson and Sorrel Brookes who succeeded Lucy, Clive Lloyd my deputy chair, and the entire Board and everyone else who supported me during the tenure of my office. They were the true heroes in the first phase of the change that took place in Stonebridge. Today is a wonderful moment in the history of Stonebridge to be savoured by all the people who have helped to make it happen. My heartfelt thanks to everyone.

LOOKING FORWARD TO THE
2012 LONDON OLYMPICS
ABCN Conference, London
27 October 2006

Conference chairman, ACBN officers, ladies and gentlemen, first of all, I want to thank you for your kind invitation to address your conference. 'Working together and achieving together'. Your tag line sets the tone for what, in my view, constitutes the first step in commitment for partnership and in shaping the future of our people and our country. ACBN has set itself the goals of building a 'one nation society' and, in doing so, must aim to cut across political divide, avoid outdated rhetoric of tokenism, and concentrate on one word—winning—in the business of wealth creation.

I am personally delighted to see the creativity and entrepreneurial drive that we are bringing to the table, sweeping away old beliefs, old perceptions, and redundant thinking in the 21st century. Give yourselves a pat on the back. Show the world, as I have done, how it is possible to translate negatives into positives, remove gloom and despair and walk a path of self-assuredness and commitment in driving what at first may have seemed an impossible situation. Settle for nothing less than success!

I will give you two examples arising out of my own life experiences. I recall the hesitation of many a manufacturer refusing to work with my company without good reason. One company half-heartedly agreed to take a chance. After spending the first £250,000.00 with them, their attitude changed from cold reluctance to that of a warm embrace. My supplier was an ardent cricket lover and had as one of his most treasured trophies a vintage cricket bat that carried the signatures of the history making 1984 test series England versus the West Indies in which England got, in cricketing language, a black wash. This trophy was to him a collector's piece and it occupied a pride of place in his home. He showed off his precious trophy to me with a challenge: *'If in any one year,'* he said,

'you were to spend with me £500,000, that trophy could be yours.'
Not one for ducking a challenge, I took him on. The very next year,
I spent £800,000 and duly collected his prized trophy which today
takes pride of place in my home!

I say to you ladies and gentlemen, reject imposed limitations on
black entrepreneurship, break down the barriers that stand in your
way, refuse to accept price tags on your talents and your skills. Pursue
your purpose and your dreams. Stay focused on the possibilities and
make them happen!

The formulas for success vary and depend to a large extent on
keeping your head and on the all-important approach. I once heard
a tale two salesmen from two shoe manufacturing companies that
were sent to a remote country to promote business. The first
salesman, after his first day in the country made a telephone call
saying that he was returning home because *'Nobody here wears
shoes.'* The second salesman also called home, but he said, *'Send
everything you can lay your hands on, everybody here needs them!'*

Equally important, too, in wining are the challenges of keeping
your wits about you. In a debate in the House of Commons between
the late Sir Winston Churchill and an Honourable lady who accused
him of being drunk, Churchill agreed *'I am drunk'* he said *'and you
are ugly. In the morning I will be sober but you will still be ugly.'*
He won the debate hands down, simply by disarming his opponent!

Inherent in the theme of your conference, Contacts for Contracts,
capture for a minute in your mind's eye what the Olympics is all
about. It is all about challenges and more challenges and you my
friends through 'Contacts for Contracts' are at the starting line in
preparation for the races, races that will not be an easy walk over.
The course will be long and hard, rough and tough and there will be
times when you feel like giving up. But, never do that for it is in
moments like these that you must call on your inner reserves of
strength to take you through to the finish line.

I know, I have been there as another of my many experiences will
show. Some years ago, back in the '80s, I literally combed the country
in search of a company to produce an item for me, but they all refused
my business for no good reason. I was on the verge of giving up, but
kept on trying and at last found a taker almost on my doorstep, Atlas
Plastics in Wood Green about three miles from where I lived. Mr
Gooch, the manager, did not hesitate in taking on my contract, for the

manufacture of Afro combs. They produced hundreds of thousands of combs for my company and we cornered the market. The lesson of not giving up was worth its weight in gold and became for me a major turning point and a milestone in the history of my company.

The question you may well ask is: *'What was it that motivated me that drove me to press on even when the going was tough?'* It was nothing other than recognising the hard fact that the world does not owe me a living. That unless I carved out my patch in the world for myself, no one would do it for me.

Let me go back to the beginning, 'Contacts for Contracts'. ABCN2 must ensure that there is a level playing field, that there must, of necessity, be equal access and equal opportunity policies in force and that these are clear and transparent, with no lurking issues of lip service in any form or guise. The stakes for 2012 are high and require each of us to prepare ourselves in a professional manner that rules out question marks about unfairness whether from the companies awarding the contracts or those receiving them.

To the representatives of budding businesses attending this conference, I want to say this, building a business is in many respects like looking after a baby. It is a constant process of meeting needs, putting them first, enabling the baby to grow, and as it gets bigger, it becomes more expensive till it comes to a point, hopefully, that it can stand on its own feet.

In the process of doing this, you will encounter an unavoidable set of problems. How do I handle non-existent, but desperately needed capital? How can I hope to exercise the various management skills that come into play with which I am not equipped? In my case, the old adage held true: *necessity is the mother of invention* and if the need to succeed is strong enough, then the learning curve for a particular skill will shorten. This has been my experience.

In conclusion, Britain is today the most colourful and cosmopolitan nation in all Europe. Her history and traditions make her a magnet for the intake of a rich mixture of cultures which blend into a remarkable melting pot which is the envy of the world. Each wave of immigrants has enriched the cultural and social fabric of British society. Ladies and gentlemen, the conference has my very best wishes and it is my firm belief that 2012 will significantly add to the richness of our country. History will be our judge, as we continue to work together to build a new Great Britain!

BEING A BLACK MAN IN 21ST CENTURY LONDON
South Bank University
19 October 2012

Mr. President, distinguished guests, officers of the organisation, ladies and gentlemen. First of all, I want to let you know just how delighted I am to have the opportunity to join with you on this milestone event, in celebrating 10 remarkable years of solid work in laying the groundwork and foundation for the future of our community.

A good friend of mine on learning that I was going to speak at this event, reminded me of the golden rule about making a speech. *'Whatever you do,'* he said, *'follow the line of a lady's skirt; it should be long enough to cover the subject and at the same time, short enough to make it interesting.'*

The celebration of your first decade in the first decade of the 21st century is a great omen. An omen in that because it sends a message of endless possibilities for the '100 Black Men of London' in this century. It is, I believe, a moment in time that is filled with hope and fortified with optimism, for us as a people. This my friends, is a century in which we are better equipped to build on our successes, past and present, with conviction and a firm resolve, to face the future for a better tomorrow.

Before coming to the subject on which I was asked to speak, I would like to first congratulate the organisation on its vision and mission. The founding and leadership of your organisation fulfils a dream that people with the same mindset like myself were longing to see, a group like yours, serving and meeting the needs of others, and showing how being action-orientated can change and transform our destiny and our place in this society and indeed the world.

We live in difficult times and must be prepared to take on board whatever the challenges that may present themselves. I believe our first obligation is to maintain and safeguard our basic interests, by keeping our country safe and making it the greatest place in which to live and work.

I will now turn to the subject that I have been asked to address—'Being a Black Man in 21st Century London'. This is an experience that is truly illuminating, exciting and indeed challenging. Work and community involvement for me stretches back to the mid-1950s, when I teamed up with others who had similar ideals to do our bit to create a harmonious society and share our stake in our country through the West Indian Standing Conference founded over 50 years ago. It is, therefore, refreshing to see this bold new leadership being taken forward by the100 Black Men of London, supporting and encouraging our young people to urgently take their place in society. This course of action is worthy of the highest praise and all round support by the rest of us in the community.

As an old soldier, now passing on the baton, I am proud to tell you that the major part of my life has been engaged in service to the community and society as whole, in a number of truly absorbing areas of work.

Being a black man in 21st century London, calls for someone with guts, vision and a sense of purpose of what he wants out of life. Inherent in his makeup, must be the dream of achieving excellence in everything he does. He must be visibly active, a critical thinker and someone who leads by example both in his private and public life. He must be a loving husband, a caring father, and community builder. These are but few of attributes that qualifies a 21st century black man to squarely face up to the challenges of this century.

In my case, my business life was the most challenging, and also the most satisfying. With two colleagues, we pioneered the development of the black hair care industry in Britain. Our two companies, Dyke & Dryden Ltd and Afro Hair & Beauty Ltd employed thousands of people and have enjoyed significant growth year by year.

Our companies by their success was responsible for kindling the spirit of black enterprise in the community, and as such, has been role models that led by example in motivating many members of our community who supported us and wanted to follow in our footsteps. Correspondingly, the companies benefited from the tremendous community support they received during their three years history.

This is an appropriate moment to let you know that the Dyke & Dryden story is an episode in black history waiting to be told and is currently being discussed by two film companies, Green Acre and Bravura Films.

Recognition of the company's achievements was recognised by the highest office in the land when in 1987 Her Majesty the Queen conferred on me the honour of an MBE in the civil division with a citation for 'contribution to employment'. This was truly a humbling experience. Of equal importance too, was the granting of a Lifetime in Business Achievement Award, sponsored by *Smooth FM* in collaboration with the *Colourful Network* and others and presented at the Guildhall in 2005. Of significance, also, was a public celebration by the industry in the company's honour, at City Hall, on 19 January 2007.

Quite apart from my business life, there have been a number of senior positions held both in the public and private sector of service to the community and the nation. I mention these facts merely to show how coming from a humble background, one can create his or her own opportunity, through disciplined hard work.

I served for ten years, from 1985, as chairman of the North London Business Development Agency, being invited by the Home Office to implement Lord Scarman's recommendations on riots of the 1980s. My length of stay in this assignment was noteworthy. We founded some 2,212 new small businesses in the economy and we celebrated this milestone success at the London Hilton on Park Lane on 7 September 1996 with 800 invited guests from across the land for what was, in the view of all concerned, a remarkable piece of work.

Training and Enterprise Councils have been among the most successful management innovations of the last decade of the 20th century, and I have been privileged to be a part of this national movement as a Director for ten years from start to finish.

Directorship of a Heath Authority was by way as it being press-ganged into action. The recruitment task force for the Enfield and Haringey Health Authority aware of my public involvement short-listed me as one of the members for the Board. I declined the invitation, on the grounds that I could bring nothing to the institution as I knew little about health matters.

They promptly rejected my statement. What they wanted, I was told, was to have the benefit of my management experience as part of the strategic changes taking place across the health authority. Reluctantly, I joined the Board and was assigned to work with the Resources Director in helping to solve a low morale problem they were having right across the Authority.

As a first step, I asked for permission to interview a cross section of the staff right across the organisation. After two weeks, I spotted the problem, prepared a report and recommendation for the Board which was accepted and implemented. It not only solved the problem, but introduced the investors in people charter which had a profound effect on the working of the organisation. Demand for my services was to follow in quick succession.

The re-development of Stonebridge in July 30 1993 marked the beginning of yet another challenging assignment. On that day a letter arrived from the Department of the Environment to confirm my meeting with officials to talk about the Shadow Chair appointment for the proposed Brent Housing Action Trust. That meeting took place on the 9th of August, and a further meeting with Sir George Young, the Housing Minister, on the 15th of September which confirmed my appointment for the post.

This was a huge project, with an initial budget of one hundred million pounds to rebuild 1,750 new homes and re house 5,000 residents. The brief was to carry out a major programme of renovation in consultation with residents; bring empty properties back into use, improve the way in which estates are looked after; and generally help to improve the economic, environmental and social condition of the area. This project has been regarded as one of the most successful inner city development projects in the whole country.

It would be true to acknowledge and point out that during the 20th century, despite the hardships of the time, black men and women have paved the way while getting on with their lives with remarkable resilience, in all areas of the workplace and especially the professions and small businesses. I am delighted to see the new thrust we are making in the entrepreneurial field. This new dimension is of paramount importance and cannot be taken lightly. I will take a few minutes to look at why small businesses are so important.

The small business sector is the engine and backbone of every economy, in developing nations or developed nations. They have traditionally been the breeding ground for new industries. They are an important source of innovation. In some industries the optimum size of units for efficient operations are small. Small firms bring into play the division of labour, splitting processes which they are better at handling. Small firms provide competition for ever growing multi-product firms and thus help the efficient working of the economy as a whole. I say hats off to all our small businesses that are making their valuable contribution to the economy.

Black History month, that we now celebrate, is just one good example of where we can see some of our products and services on show. This display must fill us all with a deep sense of pride, discovering who we are, from where we have come and making our contribution to society.

Another important breakthrough is the release of *The Oxford Companion to Black British History*. I quote from the text:

> For decades, black parents are at the forefront of efforts to support their children within an education system that undervalued their educational ability, have mobilized within and outside formal educational systems to support the teaching of black history to their children.

It is a great credit to David Dabdydeen, John Gilmore, and Cecily Jones, who with the support of others edited the *Oxford Companion of Black History*. With the concern of the Qualifications and Curriculum Authority over the teaching of black history and the endorsement by the Department of Education, the black presence in Britain is now finally recognised. That this recognition has taken place in the first decade of the 21st century after 2,000 years is another landmark fact for us to digest and celebrate, especially in Black History month.

Today, ladies and gentlemen, we have a new generation of highly qualified and ably equipped leaders, who in 10 short years have strenuously laid the groundwork and foundation for others who think like they do- people who are prepared to make the 21st century our century by signalling and placing on it their stamp of responsibility and actively engage in matters of interest, both at the local and national level.

In doing so, we will be playing our part in making our country a more equitable and a more caring society for all members. Can we make it happen? I will give you my own views, but just before doing so it might be helpful to mention in passing, my personal beliefs in this connection. I believe that the basic essentials in attaining ownership of an industrious and caring society, in the widest possible sense of the word, is by way of education and training, which creates opportunities, that generates ideas, and leads to prosperity. T. Harv Eker sets out in his book, *The Secrets of the Millionaire Mind*, a formula for success. *'Thoughts,'* he declares, *'lead to feelings. Feelings lead to action. Actions lead to results.'* These simple steps, my friends, are a corollary of what exactly create a winning path!

Now, let us look briefly at ways in which this may be done! Creating a more equitable society begins by making sure that our civic rights and responsibilities are at all times exercised by cultivating a keen sense of awareness and involvement in community affairs. At election times, we must make our local councillors and members of Parliament answerable to us for the promises they make. Holding the threat of de-selection over their heads is one way of getting things done, if they value their jobs.

By attending important council meetings and becoming familiar with the issues of the day that affect the lives of people in the community; by becoming school governors and members of other relevant bodies. In that way, we make our voices heard and our presence felt. All of this helps to make for a more cohesive and healthy society.

This short summary, ladies and gentlemen, describes my views and attitude to life in Britain, a place I love and where I have lived for over 50 years. In this context, I can readily agree with Dr. Samuel Johnson, the 18th century essayist, when he said, *'When a man is tired of London, he is tired of life.'*

In conclusion, let us remind ourselves that London is a world-class city of which we are a part and we must all work hard to improve it and enjoy it.

EPILOGUE
The Spirit of the Company Lives on in Word and Films

The pages in this book will have served to summarise the efforts of the company, by way of its contribution in shaping the philosophy of the Diversity Agenda and its belief that equal opportunity remains the true force for good in a free society.

As a nation, our strengths are enormous and I will restate views I previously expressed in an earlier title, *Black Enterprise in Britain*. Britain is today a multicultural society, the most colourful and cosmopolitan nation in all Europe. Her history and traditions make her a magnet for the intake of a rich mixture of cultures which have blended into a remarkable melting pot which is the envy of the world. Each wave of emigrants has enriched the cultural and social fabric of British society and represents building blocks of prosperity.

I am indebted to Dr. Victor Thompson of The Right Business Network and Michael Williams of Bis Publications, for organising the following venues for a number of speaking engagements where I have had the opportunity of meeting many of my fans and to pay tribute and due respect to them all. The following dates show some of the many places where I have had the privilege and pleasure to speak.

2011

11 October (6:30 - 9pm)
Westminster City Hall.

22 October (6pm - 9pm)
Waterstones Bookshop, Islington Green, N1 2XH.

27 October
Tony Wade was honoured with the Akoben Award at Harrow Black History Month at the Harrow Civic centre, he also featured in a book on UK Role Models and in a New Rap CD.

December
BBI (Black British Initiative Awards Ceremony).
100BMOL (Keynote Speech along with Trevor Philips) South Bank University.
The Windrush Festival (Stratford Circus).

2010

17 October
BBC Northampton (Broadcast) (BBC Interview).

19 October (12-2pm)
The Department for Business, Innovation & Skills 1 Victoria Street, London, SW1H 0ET.

22 October (6.30pm -9.00pm)
Waterstones 11 Islington Green, Islington, London, N1 2XH.

December
BBI (Black British Initiative).

2009

23 May (6:30-9:30pm)
Centerprise 136 Kingsland, High Street, London R8 2NS.

28 May (6pm - 8:30pm)
Westminster City Hall, 64 Victoria Street, London SWIE 6QP

16 October (2pm - 4pm)
University of East London (SU), North Building, Docklands Campus, University Way, London E16 2RD.

18 October
Fitzrovia Hotel, 20/28 Bolover St, London W1W.
Organized by Lorlett Hudson of One Hand Can't Clap.

October
Black History Month Celebration—BWUSG–Black Workers Support Group presentation at their main BHM event. Clarendon Hall, York House, 44 York St, Twickenham, TW1 3BZ

21October (12pm - 2pm)
Black History Month Celebration—BWUSG—Black Workers Support Group, Clarendon Hall, York House, 44 York St, Twickenham, TW1 3BZ.

22 October (6pm - 8pm)
South Bank University. Thomas Doyle Street, London SE1 6OG.
Omega Radio, West London (to promote the Stone Bridge event).

23 October (6.30-8pm)
Westminster City Hall, 64 Victoria Street, London SW1E 6QP.

28 October (7pm – 10pm)
The Pavilion Stonebridge, Recreation Ground, London NW10 8LW.

4 November (6:30pm - 8:30pm)
Bucks New University Owen Harris Building, Queen Alexander Road, High Wycombe Campus, Buckinghamshire HP11 2JZ.

23 November (6pm - 8:30pm)
Westminster City Hall, 64 Victoria Street, London SWIE 6QP.

'Behind the strivings of Black Power, 1970's style, lies the work of Marcus Garvey. Attacked by the black intelligentsia of his time and ridiculed by the white press, this immigrant Jamaican, in four years, built the largest and most powerful all-black organization the nation had ever seen. Garvey sowed the seeds, a half-century ago, of a new black pride and determination which is now coming to fruition. To understand the Black Revolution of the 1970's, an understanding of Marcus Garvey is essential.'

Dyke & Dryden

1965-2015
50TH ANNIVERSARY SERVICE OF THANKSGIVING

'The Cosmetics Kings'

Len Dyke, Dudley Dryden and Tony Wade

Saturday June 20th 2015 at 3PM
The Bourne Methodist Church
Bourneside, Southgate N21 6RS, London

Moderator: Rev. Vernon Thomas

Welcome Address | Rudi Page

Hymn | Praise My Soul the King of Heaven

Praise, my soul, the King of Heaven;
To His feet thy tribute bring.
Ransomed, healed, restored, forgiven,
Who like thee His praise should sing:
Praise Him, praise Him,
Praise the everlasting King.

Praise Him for His grace and favour
To our fathers in distress;
Praise Him still the same as ever,
Slow to chide, and swift to bless.
Praise Him, praise Him!
Glorious in His faithfulness.

Father like He tends and spares us,
Well our feeble frame He knows;
In His hands He gently bears us,
Rescues us from all our foes.
Praise Him, praise Him!
Widely as His mercy flows.

Angels, help us to adore Him,
Ye behold Him face to face;
Sun and moon, bow down before Him;
Dwellers all in time and space,
Praise Him, praise Him!
Praise with us the God of grace.

Henry Francis Lyle, 1793-1847

Prayers – Rev Dr Baroness Kathleen Richardson

Selections | London All-Male Voice Choir

Lessons | Sharon Dyke

Tributes | Rudi Page, Joan Sam, Norma Ellis, Karen
Hamilton-Bannis, Clayton Goodwin and JD Douglas on
behalf of absent friends

Keynote Address | Dr Keith Davidson

Sermon | Rev Dr Baroness Kathleen Richardson

Hymn | Now Thank We All Our Lord

Now thank we all our God,
With heart and hands and voices,
Who wondrous things hath done,
In whom this world rejoices;
Who from our mothers' arms
Has blessed us on our way
With countless gifts of love,
And still is ours today.

O may this bounteous God
Through all our life be near us,
With ever joyful hearts
And blessed peace to cheer us;
And keep us still in grace,
And guide us when perplexed;
And free us from all ills,
In this world and the next.

All praise and thanks to God
The Father now be given;
The Son, and him who reigns
With them in highest heaven;
The one, eternal God,
Whom earth and heaven adore;
For thus it was, is now,
And shall be evermore.

Martin Rinkart, 1556-1649

Blessings

MESSAGE FROM TONY WADE

The Voice Interview

Working man's hero

he second edition of **How They Made a Million** has en called for by kind folk who wanted to learn more out my thoughts and vision for black enterprise in e 21st century. In responding to the call for my oughts, I am humbly gratified that people should re enough about my views on enterprise and agreed rise to the challenge.

ne thing for sure is clearly a must, our educational nbitions, out of necessity, must keep pace with the st-moving technological changes taking place ound us. This approach, I believe, together with stering an increased effort in promoting the iversity Agenda, will help to keep us as a mmunity firmly on the frontiers of science and at e cutting edge of the changes taking place in ciety.

As forward looking citizens, our major aims should always be to become visibly active and striving to become fully engaged stakeholders in all aspects of local and national life. In this connection, I suggest aiming to share meaningfully thus becoming part of the fabric of society, politically, economically, socially and that we direct our aspirations to make an input into the policy formations that shape our lives and our destiny.

Interestingly, the calls for jotting down my thoughts came from a broad-based group of individuals of inner-city reformers, social scientists and a host of others, including budding young business persons looking at ways in which they may improve their opportunities. Some of the questions to me were quite personal, down to earth and reasonable. It would have been great, some folks suggested, to see some of the trophies and awards collected over the years. These are telling and carry the same message.

Management Today, one of Britain's leading business magazines, in its 1987 issue dubbed my colleagues and me "the invisible men" with a caption that read, "at long last Britain is beginning to produce home-grown entrepreneurs.

My colleagues, Len Dyke and Dudley Dryden, were men of immense vision, lending their names to a partnership, which in June 1968 became a limited liability when I acquired one third of the equity. They were equally magnanimous in their call to rename the business Dyke, Dryden & Wade, which I decided was unnecessary.

As a team, our skills were complementary. We shared a common philosophy- that of putting the needs of building the business above everything else. Without their vision, hard work and drive, there would be no story to tell.

WE AT DYKE & DRYDEN ARE HONOURED TO BE AMONG THE TRAILBLAZERS!

TRIBUTE FROM

RUDI PAGE

Len Dyke, Dudley Dryden and Tony Wade, as the leaders of Dyke & Dryden Ltd, were men of vision, steel and action. They were "Caribbean Titans" of the 20th century who challenged socio-economic stereotyping and overcame the challenges of discrimination, yet still stayed true to the Caribbean communities aspirations to make progress, despite the unrelenting obstacles of the time. They were social entrepreneurs long before it became a popular term within the UK and were particularly dedicated to the social needs of the Caribbean community. Dyke & Dryden Ltd was the largest provider of trade credit to black business sector, which included salons, retailers, wholesalers, beauticians and self-employed stylists.

I joined Dyke & Dryden Ltd, Tottenham, as their first sales representative during June 1981. I had met Tony Wade a year earlier when I was working for an advertising company. I visited salons, retail outlets and exhibited the leading products such as, Sta-sof-fro,

Carefree Curl, TCB, Hairlox, Johnson, Natural Beauty and Super Curl, all over the UK. I was with Tony Wade when Boots decided to stock black hair products for the first time and I visited the stores and met the managers and staff.

During July 1982, I was promoted to sales and marketing manager and as part of a delegation of 40 Hairdresser's and retailers arranged by Dyke & Dryden Ltd, I visited the world-famous Bronner Bros, Exhibition & Showcase, Atlanta, USA, at the time the largest black hair and beauty showcase in the world. It was for this reason, I obtained my first passport and have worked in 21 countries since that time.

I was tasked to coordinate Dyke & Dryden's first exhibition which I titled, "Afro Hair & Beauty 198. The showcase was opened by Lady Pitt, who said, "Black is beautiful and we must never be tired of saying so or showing how true that is." All the objectives set by the company were achieved; to promote black hairdressing and hair-care products, help educate and motivate others into an awareness dignity and self-respect. Also to ensure that black hair-care and beauty business owners should receiv the serious attention of the people who should know and care.

The excellent student styling competition, organise by Caribbean and Afro Society of Hairdressers, wa won by Ashia School of hairdressing, Electric Avenue, Brixton. It underlines those sentiments. Jo Sam of Supreme School of Hair Design, Turnpike Lane, N8 and Supreme Super curl technical consultant, expert demonstrations on BBC TV "Breakfast Time" and "Pebble Mill at One" have contributed to the total awareness as we were are al striving to be accepted as professionals in the industry.

Len Dyke, Dudley Dryden and Tony Wade handed me the baton and over the last 30 years, I have done my best to continue their legacy of self-reliance, determination and the willingness to make a significant contribution to the advancement of our community through community development, healt management and international development.

MEMORIES FROM
SHARON DYKE-MILLS

Some of my earliest memories of Dyke & Dryden Ltd were at 43 West Green Rd, Tottenham, during the 1970s. It was a 4 storey building: the first floor was the wig and cosmetic shop, travel agency, later moved to 93 West Green Rd. This was run by Mr Dyke; second floor was Mr Wade's and the third floor was let to tenants.

Before 43 West Green Rd became a wig cosmetic shop, Mr Dyke and Mr Dryden sold vinyl records as Double D Records. The music was primarily reggae imported from Jamaica and the USA. There was a small selection of products including cosmetics such as lipsticks, powders and Dax pomade. Mr Dryden acquired a market stall selling cosmetics and wigs at Ridley Road Market, Dalston.

Dyke & Dryden expanded and moved to 126a West Green, managed by the late Mrs Elsa Robinson, who was extremely meticulous when styling and combing the wigs, assisted by Mrs Myrna Thompson. There was also a small selection of natural foods and herbal remedies.

During school holidays, the stock room was a mini factory. My brother, Lenny and I painstakingly filled bottles of castor oil as well as other oils, labeled the bottles and packed them for distribution.

TRIBUTE FROM
MRS JOAN SAM

Anthony Edward Samuel Wade is a man deserving of his full title whenever he is addressed. He has been instrumental in the early development of my hairdressing career, which was encouraged by the three directors of Dyke & Dryden when I started working for them in the early sixties in West Green Road, Tottenham, North London.

During my employment there, I expressed my wish to qualify as a hairdresser and then open a hairdressing salon and school. I was encouraged to take the first step towards that dream and I enrolled in the well-respected Morris Masterclass in London's West End.

After graduating with honours, Mr Morris asked me to become a tutor, which I readily accepted, as that experience was invaluable to achieve my ultimate aim to go into the beauty business. I enjoyed the job immensely, but eventually I knew I had to return to fulfilling my goals.

I was always in touch with Dyke & Dryden and especially with Mr Wade as I had recognised a special like-mindedness between us. We had the same positive approach to business development ideas and there were lots of things I could learn from him and maybe vice versa. My huge problem at that time, however, was lack of enough finance. Tony and the other directors decided to become my partner and Supreme Hair Salon and School of Hairdressing was born.

The business flourished, gaining recognition from local government offices, enabling us to win contracts to train unemployed young people and adults. Apart from locally, we were getting applications from abroad and had a healthy influx of overseas students.

With that going well, Tony and I started to work on product development ideas with our chemist, which resulted in us travelling to The Bronner Brother Hair Show in Atlanta, Georgia, USA, and visiting the home of the founder of the M&M International Hair Co., and meeting a few celebrities on the way.

Tony and I were invited to Nigeria to participate the first Oyo State Hair Exhibition. There, w successfully demonstrated our own product calle Super Curl, which ultimately became one of the mo popular curl-creating exports from the UK.

There is so much more to my business experienc with Tony Wade and his positive influences on m first, as my boss, then business partner and no friends for always. He is a man with a vision whic develops into a mission, a man with integrity and strong sense of fair play. I have been a better pers for knowing him and honoured to be called his frien – December 29, 2013

TRIBUTE FROM
MRS PEARL GOODRIDGE

Anthony Wade was my boss for 10 years, when worked as his personal assistant/human resourc manager. He was an excellent example of a goo leader, a visionary, in his choice of business. He wa never afraid to break new ground, at the same tim encouraging others to venture into their ow businesses.

He was never too busy to become involved. He is th epitome of one who serves his fellowmen ar country. For me, he was my mentor, my inspiratio one who saw possibilities and made them a reality.

On my return to Barbados in 1988, I worked as human resources manager for American Airlines ar in my interaction with the staff, became aware of th need for a nursery facility near the workplace in th city. After some research (a practice of Tony Wade), opened a day care centre, which caters to childr between ages three month to five years. He was m inspiration.

cember 7, 2013.

RIBUTE FROM
LAIRE JACKSON

ire Jackson, Afro Hair & Beauty events manager for 10 years, who has been a central pillar in the organization, s, "I look back on my years as events director of Afro Hair & Beauty Exhibition as a period of great joy and llenge."

er address in Afro Hair & Beauty '97 magazine, Jackson wrote, inter alia, "Afro Hair & Beauty has always been ud of its commitment to the progression and development of the community and make a point of giving ething back. To that end, we are pleased to benefit The African Caribbean Mental Health Association, the ican Caribbean Leukemia Trust and UNICEF. The behind-the-scenes team has also expanded. We are delighted welcome Brownstone Communications, the New Nation production team, as well as firm regulars, Key mmunications. But all of this is irrelevant without the support of our exhibitors and visitors. We extend our rmest and most sincere thanks to you all."

RIBUTE FROM
ARGARET ALEXANDER

2004, quite by chance, I borrowed a copy of **How They Made a Million.** I found it compelling reading and shed within a few days. After decades of not knowing, I had within a few days, been greatly enlightened on the iggles and triumphs of three men, Dudley Dryden, Len dyke and Tony Wade, who together made their North ndon-based hair care and beauty business, Dyke & Dryden, hugely successful.

as subsequently privileged to be able to spend quality time speaking with Tony Wade and listening to his detailed ount of his business years. There were truly eye-opening discussions as I was one of many customers who ularly purchased Dyke & Dryden products, one of their popular navy blue hair picks combs was always in my metics bags.

ile listening one day to Smooth Radio FM, I heard that in collaboration with Colourful Network and others, they re sponsoring the first Black Achievement Awards. Nominations were invited. After hearing of the various egories, I took down the details. Around this time, Len Dryden was terminally ill in hospital. I had visited him h my mother who told me how kind and helpful he had been on a particular occasion when she needed assistance h officialdom as a trainee teacher.

recognition of what I regarded as ground-breaking achievements by Tony Wade and his business partners, I eided to make a nomination for the lifetime achievement award. My nomination had to be made online, in no re than 100 words, and read as follows:

ke & Dryden Limited, one of Britain's largest black enterprises during the last century, pioneered the UK's black 'r-care industry. Serving D&D as chief executive and chairman, Tony Wade's business experience spanned 31 irs, covering every sector of the industry. D&D's subsidiary. Afro Hair & Beauty, was founded in 1982 to mote the Afro Hair and Beauty Show at London's Alexander Palace. Now an institutionalized event, this annual -day exhibition attracts international participation and is included in the Tourist Board's events calendar. The ge employment generated by D&D was recognised with Tony Wade's MBE honour in 1987.

There were many impressive nominees who went through an interview process, followed by shortlisting. '
presentation took place at the London Guildhall, a wonderful event showcasing the best of British black busin
My anxiety must have been palpable as the nominations were read out. Then came the winning announcement,
nominee, Tony Wade.

Life Time Achievement in Business Award 2005
to Dyke and Dryden Limited
Sponsored by the Colourful Network

Tony Wade MBE
Len Dyke
Dudley Dryden MBE